4281

330 Milner, Brian.
.971 The hidden establishment : the inside story of
Mil Canada's international business elite / Brian Milner. --
Toronto : Viking, 1991.
 xviii, 270 p.

04769031 ISBN:0670827681

1. Businessmen - Canada. 2. Immigrants - Canada -
Economic conditions. 3. Canada - Economic conditions
- 1971- 4. Canada - Emigration and immigration -
Economic aspects. I. Title

671 92FEB24   06/he 1-00553863

THE HIDDEN ESTABLISHMENT

THE INSIDE STORY OF CANADA'S INTERNATIONAL BUSINESS ELITE

BRIAN MILNER

VIKING

VIKING
Published by the Penguin Group
Penguin Books Canada Ltd, 10 Alcorn Avenue, Toronto, Ontario,
Canada M4V 1E4
Penguin Books Ltd, 27 Wrights Lane, London W8 5TZ, England
Viking Penguin, a division of Penguin Books USA Inc., 375 Hudson
Street, New York, New York 10014, USA
Penguin Books Australia Ltd, Ringwood, Victoria, Australia
Penguin Books (NZ) Ltd, 182-190 Wairau Road, Auckland 10, New
Zealand

Penguin Books Ltd, Registered Offices: Harmondsworth, Middlesex,
England

First published 1991

10 9 8 7 6 5 4 3 2 1

Copyright © Brian Milner, 1991

Queries regarding radio broadcasting, motion picture, video cassette,
television and translation rights should be directed to the Author's
representative: Peter Livingston Associates, Inc., 92 King Street East,
Suite 311, Toronto, Ontario M5C 4K2.

Printed and bound in the United States of America on acid free paper ∞

Canadian Cataloguing in Publication Data

Milner, Brian
  The hidden establishment

ISBN 0-670-82768-1

1. Businessmen—Canada. 2. Immigrants—Canada—Economic
conditions. 3. Canada—Economic conditions—1971– .* 4.
Canada—Emigration and immigration—Economic aspects. I. Title.

HC115.M54 1991   330.971   C90-095705-0

To Sylvie, who taught me to see my own country, and much else, through different eyes.

ACKNOWLEDGEMENTS

I OWE A great debt to all of the people who gave so generously of their time and knowledge, and who worked so hard to guide me down useful paths in the preparation of this book. Some of them are named in these pages, but many, at their own request, are not identified. Still others had remarkable stories to tell, but I could not include all of them. They have my thanks and my assurance that their efforts were vital to my understanding of the subject.

I am extremely grateful to the people whose behind-the-scenes efforts helped make this book possible: Iris Skeoch at Penguin, who decided I could do it, and then persuaded me that I could; David Johnston, who brought us together; and my editor, David Kilgour, whose talent, commitment and sage advice enabled me to say what I wanted to and not what I didn't (and who laughed at my more outrageous asides—before removing them so that no one else would).

I am particularly indebted to my wife, Sylvie Voiseux, who provided valuable background material and a one-person cheering section whenever the going got tough; my assistant, Catherine Dowling, whose dogged determination to get things right is a wonderful obsession; and Deborra Schug, Jerry Collins and Carolyn Adolph, whose tireless efforts on my behalf will always be remembered. Keiko Saunders, a generous friend, helped steer me through the world of the Japanese. Peter Cook, my editor at *The Globe and Mail*, never wavered in his support, but probably hopes that I never do this again. Ian Brown lent me his advice and his files and then left the country.

My parents, Nat and Ruth Milner, and other relatives and friends, especially Michael Hirsh and Elaine Waisglass, were gracious in accepting my long absences from their midst. I also wish to thank Sandra Bucovaz, Nobuo Iromoto, Lee Leng Lee, Jacquie McNish, Mehran Omidvar, Margaret Piton, Nancy Sandrin, Bob Scott, Elizabeth Wilton and all the immigrants, rich and poor alike, whose own courage and determination provided all the inspiration any writer would ever need.

Brian Milner
Toronto
November 1990

THE HIDDEN ESTABLISHMENT

CONTENTS

INTRODUCTION

PICTURE CANADA AS a giant field waiting to be sown. Not very exciting, perhaps, not mysterious or exotic; but rock-solid, safe and accessible, far from the world's earthquake zones and as close to the American behemoth as any sane person would ever want to get.

You're now standing in the shoes of the well-heeled foreigners who've been silently plowing billions of dollars, marks, pounds, francs, lire and, more recently, a ton of yen, won and more dollars into fertile Canadian ground, all in search of security in an uncertain world. Only a portion of that capital is sighted and tagged by the federal statisticians. Most of it is hidden by design, barely visible—until recently, that is, when it finally became too obvious to ignore.

From 1986 to 1990 alone, some 17,000 business immigrants entered Canada with assets of more than $13-billion,* according to federal figures. But if this country were merely a silo for the excess cash spilling out of the pockets of the world's wealthy, it would hardly be remarkable. What makes the new money intriguing is that it's

---

* All dollar amounts are Canadian, unless otherwise specified.

moving into new fields, sowing thousands of jobs in industries that Canadian financiers considered poor risks, all of which will have a strong impact on our economy, society, politics and ultimately the way we see ourselves and the rest of the world.

As I began tracking the still largely hidden establishment, I realized quickly that merely producing a starched laundry list of acquisitors and their acquisitions would leave the most essential questions—about the people behind the money—unanswered.

Looking only at property purchases—which have sparked national speculation and pockets of paranoia—would reveal little about the true intentions of the new money in this country. Like anybody else who can afford it, rich newcomers have jumped into real estate. It's something they understand and trust, a safety net for their corporate trapeze acts elsewhere in the world.

But buying a safety net is a bland pursuit, merely a sideline for the dreamers of big dreams. And those are the people I set out to find. If they're in property (and many are), they're out to make something of it, to leave their mark for future generations, not to flip for a quick buck—unless, of course, there's a great deal of money to be made by flipping it.

Learning that wealthy Japanese or Chinese or Iranians or East Asians or Europeans have snapped up this or that hotel or mall or wilderness resort or city block might show us where some of the money has been going—but not the road it will ultimately be taking; or what brings it here in the first place.

What lures people who seemingly have it all to a strange, parochial land so far from their known universe of money and privilege? What are their hopes and dreams for themselves and their families? What do they think about Canada and its future? What, if anything, separates them from the earlier waves of immigrants, the kind with whom we're so much more familiar and comfortable—the ones who knew their place in the Canadian pecking order, working their way from the ground up, instead of coming in at the top, already owning the ground?

To find out, I went looking for the human side, for the motives and feelings behind the numbers and numbered companies. And I was determined to wade into more than the flood of "visible" new money from the Orient, which has deservedly attracted so much attention in the past couple of years (some of it from me as a reporter with a daily newspaper).

The wealthy refugees of Hong Kong have been moving dollars and family here in unprecedented numbers over the past few years (more than 20,000 people and close to $4-billion annually), joined by like-minded people from Singapore, Japan and, more recently, Taiwan and Korea. But there's other foreign money here that is also worth exploring. What, after all, do we really know about the tax-revolted Europeans who have been tiptoeing into this country for years, largely concealed behind equally reticent immigrant middlemen? Or the rich driven from their more exotic homes like East Africa or the Middle East?

I set out with no preconceived notions of what or whom I'd find, just a need to dig some answers out of the blizzard of statistics and dollar signs. The first stumbling block I encountered was the fact that people who have deliberately kept out of the spotlight throughout their lives aren't sitting on the edge of their Louis-something chairs waiting to be discovered by someone armed with a notebook.

This made the task more daunting than I'd thought it would be. Once in a while, it became downright threatening. "Do you know your curiosity can get you in trouble?" a contact helpfully inquired when I began snooping around the affairs of a fun-loving Japanese couple with an unusual past. "There's a danger factor here that you should be aware of," someone else said of my efforts to develop a meaningful relationship with a wealthy Vietnamese, *any* wealthy Vietnamese.

An Iranian builder slammed down the phone; a Lebanese wheeler-dealer didn't bother picking it up; an Israeli with his fingers in several pies didn't want me looking in any of them; a host of Chinese told me to get lost in a thousand polite ways. I got stood up, down and occasionally sideways. One well-connected lawyer who made some inquiries for me among wealthy Europeans came back with a familiar response: "Sorry, they have no interest in telling their story to the world."

"But it's for a book," I protested, "not a mass-circulation newspaper."

"That's even worse. It's there forever," he replied before ringing off forever.

A Canadian lawyer who operates in Hong Kong out of the splendidly named Splendid Way, and who represents some of the colony's high and mighty, says his clients would never understand if he publicly discussed his activities. There isn't even a name on his office door, and he's far more interested in how I found him than in what my questions might be. Talk about a low profile!

A Hong Kong native puts it a little more colourfully: "People are afraid to be famous, like a pig is afraid to become too fat. He knows he is ready to be killed. They fear attracting unwanted attention."

But as any dogged politician or journalist will confirm, persistence does pay off. Some people did set aside their natural fears, inhibitions and cultural differences to give me far more time out of their hectic schedules than I had any right to expect, although a few changed their minds afterward. Most were extremely gracious and generous once they decided to open up. Sometimes it took a few phone calls to persuade them, or in one case, so many messages left on an answering machine that I'm sure I got the interview just so they'd have room on their tape for important calls. Others scarcely asked what I was working on before agreeing to speak with me. One person was halfway through a lengthy discussion of his family history before he thought to ask what I might be up to.

Some asked that their names be changed, and this I did

for refugees who feared for the safety and bank balances of family members still in the old country. Others only agreed to talk about their communities to help me understand the people better.

The vast majority of the new immigrants and their money are settling in the major urban centres, primarily Toronto and, to a lesser extent, Vancouver, though others have been a bit more adventurous, scattering across the country. There is so much new money that it would be impossible to deal with more than a fraction of the people who have brought it with them or are making it here. I didn't set out to write a definitive book on immigration or even wealthy newcomers, so you won't find every Ho, Ko, Lo and Cloppenburg in these pages. What you will find are people who dream their dreams in wide-screen technicolour, regardless of whether they arrived through careful planning, by sheer accident or because there was no other place for them to go.

Some of them move with eggshell caution, fearful of making unnecessary waves, but they each have an enormous capacity to shape a different future not only for themselves, which they're clearly doing, but the rest of us as well. These are people who bring not just huge piles of cash but remarkable energy, drive and indispensible international connections to the Canadian table.

Few of those profiled here are ever in the public eye, even in their native countries. We all know of a handful of tried and true immigrant legends, but it was not my intention to add to the fat biographies of people like the Reichmanns, the Ghermezians or Tom Bata. You will meet some extremely well-known Europeans, but their Canadian activities are almost completely hidden from our view.

A handful of others, like Hong Kong tycoon Li Ka-shing, are legends wherever their billions go, too influential to ignore. Apart from a couple of cameos, though, Li appears here mainly in the company of his two sons, both Canadians. Like other rich kids—many of them in exclusive private schools, mingling with the scions of old money—they're the ones who will some day be making the decisions on where the family money will go in this country.

The new money moves with much greater rapidity than the old. Many of us today know of Li, better known as "Superman" in the Chinese press back home, as a man with large Canadian oil and property interests and a growing influence in finance (some wags suggest that if he said jump, the Canadian Imperial Bank of Commerce, which has joined him in several ventures and in which he has a stake, wouldn't even stop to ask how high).

Yet just sixteen years ago, when Peter Newman completed *The Canadian Establishment*, his ground-breaking study of the rich who run this country, Li was just an ambitious plastics manufacturer and property speculator little known outside his British colonial base—though he'd already started investing in Canadian real estate some six years earlier. (For that matter, the influential Reichmanns, considered part of the old guard today, regulars on everybody's list of the ten richest business families in the world, merited only a footnote, for their clever development of a tower in downtown Toronto with irregular sides, to provide more corner offices.)

It's a sign of just how much Canada and the world have changed since then that so many newcomers are crowding the old establishment; that an Eaton would think it valuable to belong to the Mandarin Club, a gathering spot for young Chinese entrepreneurs and professionals in Toronto; that the establishment schools would be filled with as much new money has old. This doesn't mean the old monied families have been displaced. Not yet. Not by a long shot. They continue to wield the serious power in the boardrooms, backrooms and clubs across this nation. But the hidden establishment is growing steadily and vigorously; and before long their children, Canadian-born and -bred, will be considerably less hidden and a lot more established.

CHAPTER 1

The Man from Shanghai

JAMES TING IS engaged in one of his many frustrating efforts to enlist the Bay Street crowd in his ambitious scheme to turn International Semi-Tech Microelectronics, the mouthful of a company he started in 1981, into a member of the exclusive league of global trading and consumer products giants. His information-cum-free-booze session is at the National Club, a bastion of old money in the heart of Toronto's financial district. For some reason, these overstuffed old boys' clubs also attract some of the newer money. The parvenus have their own networks and favourite restaurants, even their exclusive, pricey clubs; but if they want to catch the attention of the clannish Canadian financial establishment, they still have to come calling at their heavy oak doors.

One elderly Japanese consultant, Shinichi Funasaka, proudly takes guests to lunch at the club—not, presumably, because of the roast beef that has aged as badly as some of its members, or the overcooked green beans or the mushy rice pudding. No. Funasaka, once head of the Canadian arm of the mighty Mitsui trading company

1

and still well-connected in Asian business circles, wants to show that he fits right in with the old Canadian guard as well, that he's as comfortable in their surroundings as they presumably are, even if his is the only Oriental face in the place. And that desire for establishment acceptance, at least in a corporate sense, is why the shy, diminutive Ting is sitting here, albeit as unobtrusively as possible near the back of the room, late one rainy November afternoon.

At the front, Ting's smooth-talking vice-president and chief pitchman, Michael List, is gliding effortlessly through the charts and graphs plotting the company's various incarnations and future plans. Click go the slides; clink go the ice cubes. Certain that a refill for their empty glasses is close at hand, the Bay Street denizens don't mind putting up with List as he drones through a lengthy presentation he has made dozens of times before. As the thinning-blond, athletic-looking executive rhymes off the impressive numbers with practised ease—30,000 employees worldwide; 78th in revenue and 109th in assets among all Canadian companies—the remarkable native of Shanghai, now almost 40, who has built it all leans back in one of the padded red leather seats, his slight, unathletic frame dwarfed by the heavy furniture.

Ting, whose 32 percent controlling chunk of Semi-Tech puts his worth somewhere in the neighbourhood of $40-million, is fidgety. He slumps lower in search of a more comfortable posture in this alien environment. Perhaps he's thinking of taking one of the patented naps that enable him to work crushingly long hours even after jetting in from his hectic and frequent jaunts to the Far East. But despite his near-reclining position, Ting is awake, on auto-pilot, his hands crossed behind his head, probably wondering why he's not out doing something more enjoyable.

The man who started Semi-Tech on a shoestring and a dream and rapidly turned it into a multinational corporation with sales well over $1-billion a year is outwardly impassive as his Bermuda-born deputy, List, sketches the company's bold strategy for its latest and biggest baby, the giant Singer sewing machine company. The Singer purchase had instantly put Ting and Semi-Tech on the world map.

Singer has a fabled history dating back to its founding as the high-tech company of the day in 1851, List reminds the bored brokers. It's the most recognizable brand name in the world after Coca-Cola, he adds hopefully, but that only reminds them of their thirst. List wraps up his warm-up routine. It's time for Ting to have a swing at this old-guard clergy of capitalism, who have defended their temples so zealously against upstarts like him. He might as well be dropping leaflets to the illiterate—and he knows it.

Ting talks softly, still uncomfortable in public—particularly this public. His accent clipping the ends off some of his words, his low-key speech littered with little jokes that die a lonely death in the arid club atmosphere—he could easily pass for a nervous college kid shivering in front of a bunch of uninterested professors.

The skilled deal-maker has been building, right under the turned-up noses of the local establishment, a Canadian conglomerate with tentacles stretching around the world. The trouble is that his naturally diffident manner isn't ideally suited to persuading the skeptics that it's all for real. He hasn't got an ounce of razzle or a trace of dazzle in his bones. And he doesn't have much of a corporate record that would inspire the ever-cautious Canadian investment types. But he does have a plan, rooted in the practical ground of his engineer's mind and welded to his immigrant experience, that has attracted some remarkable foreign backers.

Ting has no trouble selling himself or his clever strategy in tough towns like Hong Kong or London or Tokyo. Powerful Asian interests have moved in to back his play; wily British and German investors seem delighted with what he's doing. So why does he come on like the Rodney

Dangerfield of Canadian business, still trying to get some respect in his home town from a crowd already made largely irrelevant by the dizzying shifts in the international financial marketplace? The audience he's working so hard to impress is filled with fringe members of a cozy little anglophone investment club that's staring extinction in the face at least partly because globally connected entrepreneurs like Ting have other places to go when the doors close on them here.

He tells the blue-suited dinosaurs as much. "All in all, people in Hong Kong realize what we've done. We've successfully acquired a company of international stature." If it's ever to compete, he warns, Canada needs his kind of company, one capable of going toe-to-toe with the world's electronics and trading giants. That's his goal, and those who know him well believe that if anyone can do it in this forbidding climate, he can. But the street whose cold shoulder sent him into the welcoming arms of foreign money in the first place remains a hard sell.

The story of new money in this country is embodied in James Ting. He arrived with nothing, an immigrant in the classic Canadian mould, working his way up through sheer grit and hard work, taking huge risks, betting everything on himself. But when the big dollars here weren't prepared to back what seemed to them a hopelessly deluded wager, the entrepreneur was able to take his gamble to the receptive offices of the super-rich back home, names that open doors throughout Asia. Even ten years ago, such international bridges would have been exceedingly difficult—if not impossible—to build. Yet in Canada, the old guard was paying no heed to the persistent banging on the establishment gates from someone who still carried the label of an outsider in their midst after almost twenty years.

"Everybody is trying to do things in a global sense," Ting says between flights one day. "We don't have a company that's major in manufacturing or trading here.* As a nation, in terms of population, we're very small. We've got to have a global mind, like how the British were in the nineteenth century. They had this venturesome attitude, and Canada needs that, not to conquer people but to conduct business elsewhere, make money and use the great resources we have here. One day when we finish cutting the trees and we can't cut it any more, we have got to do something else."

Such "un-Canadian" behaviour, such hubris, must inevitably lead down the road to disaster, as far as the ice-agers of Bay Street are concerned. The lack of enthusiasm for this pasty-faced, bespectacled Chinese immigrant who didn't go to their schools and would never belong to their clubs has less to do with racism than with the defining *isms* of Canadian business: parochialism and conservatism. These are the continuing hallmarks of a banking and investment community that has yet to come to grips with the new money once it turns aggressive and starts moving out of nice, safe term deposits, bonds and real estate into the heady, sometimes dangerous world of the deal-makers and the dream-weavers.

Ting is in the vanguard of what may turn into an army of such people from Asia, determined entrepreneurs hooking up with family money back home or other foreign funds to fulfil truly globe-girdling aspirations. He and others like him with strong ties abroad and international skills that are in short supply here may well represent Canada's last best chance to stand clear of the towering American shadow and find its own spot on the changing world business stage. For the first time in our history, we are looking at a wave of immigrants whose importance to this country lies not in their traditional

---

* Ting is speaking here of giant multinationals like the Japanese Mitsubishi, the Korean Samsung or the Dutch Philips. He is well aware that a handful of Canadian companies such as Northern Telecom have carved an impressive international niche for themselves.

role as a handy source of labour, skilled or otherwise, but in their access to risk capital and entrepreneurial spirit sorely lacking among the natives.

Many of these fervent newcomers have an extraordinary commitment to Canada's future, and ambitions to match the size of their newfound home. Lacking the baggage of inferiority lugged around by too many Canadians, Ting and others like him aren't prepared to accept that this country must always remain an industrial backwater in a sea of giant trading blocs. And their patient foreign backers seem content to let them plow their gains back into their dreams, rather than shipping sacks of money out of the country to ungrateful head offices, as so many Canadian companies do.

When Ting started Semi-Tech, along with his then-wife Lisa Williams, and Frank Holmes, one of his engineering professors at the University of Toronto, he had little idea where it would be heading. His sights were always set on distant horizons; but as recently as 1986, he was running a struggling computer maker with second-rate technology. It appeared doomed to follow the paths of most other pioneering Canadian high-tech ventures—down the nearest drain or into cash-laden foreign hands. But Ting wouldn't let his dream die so easily.

He turned to Hong Kong money early in the game to stay alive, and he didn't hesitate to go looking for more to pay for his increasingly ambitious deals after Bay Street slammed the iron gates in his face. "I found that Hong Kong is much easier. The people are more venturesome. They are more receptive to new ideas and more risk-oriented." He added the "International" to Semi-Tech's already awkward moniker in 1987, just in case anyone had any doubt about his intentions, and set off in pursuit of other companies that fit into his quickly evolving global design.

The low foreheads in the investment community have had trouble drawing a bead on Semi-Tech and its enigmatic president ever since. They were never comfortable with Ting's close business connections with China, even though

it was those connections that saved his company from almost certain death when the North American computer
market collapsed in the mid-1980s. "Bay Street couldn't
understand it. They suspected that it wasn't real," says
John Thompson, a politically plugged-in merchant banker
who engineered the reverse takeover that put Semi-Tech
on the Toronto stock market* and who remains a big Ting
booster, investor and member of his board. "They were
scared that the China thing was just going to evaporate,
that it was here today and gone tomorrow."

Then the unknown computer tinkerer really mystified
them when his Hong Kong subsidiary picked up the
money-losing Consumers Distributing catalogue chain in
the United States in 1988. The price for a bunch of stores
nobody else seemed to want was about $100-million (US),
more than five times what his own company was bringing
in annually. And what the devil could he have been planning to do with the two large Canadian computer service
outfits he snapped up later that same year? Then, to top
it all off, in 1989 he jumped in over his head against a
couple of international sharks and walked away with his
limbs intact and the giant Singer company tucked safely in
the inside pocket of his conservative grey business suit.

It was all part of an elaborate strategy for the cheap
production of name-brand goods in the Far East and the
distribution of those products around the world, with
everything controlled through sophisticated computer
networks run out of Ting's Canadian headquarters. But
only a few astute international investors, like Macau
gambling and property magnate Stanley Ho, were quick

---

* This is typically done through a shell company — in Semi-Tech's case,
Shawnee Petroleums — whose only value is its stock market listing.
Thompson and his cronies bought Shawnee, put enough money in
to make it solvent and then arranged the reverse takeover, whereby
the moribund company technically bought Semi-Tech. It's one way
of getting a stock listing when you don't have enough shareholders
to qualify on your own, or when you're looking for a tax break. Ting
admits that he misinterpreted the value of going public in helping him
gain the respect he craves.

to latch on to the possibilities. "I like the company," says Andy Sarlos, a well-connected Bay Street money manager and himself an immigrant, from Hungary. "Nobody else does. They don't understand it. The product is complicated, the connections are complicated, the sponsorships are complicated."

To James Ting, it all seems perfectly simple. He had long wondered why this country couldn't produce its own Mitsubishi or Philips, companies he greatly admires. "What we want to do—global trading, global manufacturing, global distribution—is seen by Bay Street as far-fetched. They think that it's only people like the Japanese or the Americans who can do this kind of thing," he says with a shrug of his slouched shoulders. There is anger simmering beneath the placid surface as he touches on what irritates him most about Canadians, this inherent lack of faith that one of their own could belong in such exalted circles. But he rarely lets such emotions cloud his enthusiasm for his adopted land. "Let me tell you, for a management holding company, Canada is still better than any country I can think of, because it's so stable. If you start something here, it's always going to be here."

A Hong Kong banker who has watched Ting's meteoric rise says, "If he wasn't in business, he'd do well in politics. He has vision and the determination to achieve it. But people with vision need very strong support to succeed. From a banker's point of view, I worry that he doesn't have the support systems to cope with it." The vision is that of the born deal-maker who has thrown all his considerable energy into building something few Canadians would even dare to try. The obstacles in his path—including the closed financial minds and his own lack of experience, which has even admirers wondering when he's going to bite off more than he can chew—are merely puzzles for the engineer in him to work out.

"If I set my eyes on something, I have to do it," Ting says, not long before his performing seal act at the National Club. "I'm not a detail person, but I look after the big picture much better."

He is sitting in a simple, sunny conference room near his large corner office on the second floor of Semi-Tech's modern headquarters in Markham, Ontario. Designed with more flair than the usual monotonous low-rise buildings that dot the industrial landscape just north of Toronto, it exudes quiet elegance and the smell of money, from the pink marble that greets the visitor in the lobby to the decorator furniture, tasteful lighting and corporate art placed everywhere with professional skill. Pottery and sculpture that Ting has picked up for a song on his trips inside China offer stylish signposts of the company's bridge to the Orient.

The neighbouring Canadian offices of Toshiba, the Japanese electronics and computer giant, and Samsung, the Korean trading and manufacturing colossus, both emblematic of the kind of international powerhouse Ting seeks to emulate, look plain and lumpy by comparison. Could there be any truth to the rumours that there's more style than substance to this player with dreams of entering the land of the giants?

The man with the answers freely concedes that in the early days he deliberately sought to make Semi-Tech appear a lot grander than it really was to impress visiting Chinese dignitaries. A man who eschews the normal trappings of wealth himself, he even took to driving a company-owned Mercedes (*sans* chauffeur) because it was expected by the Chinese, who were once so essential to his company's survival, and whose support later enabled him to lure the big bucks from Hong Kong. A huge Chinese state corporation owns a small piece of Semi-Tech's Far East subsidiary and a seat on the board; the Chinese sent over technicians to Markham for training in computers; and Ting agreed to set up a global distribution channel to handle their goods—the basis for his move into Hong Kong trading and his jump into retailing through, first, the Consumers stores, and then Singer, with its outlets and dealerships in more than a hundred countries.

He makes it seem just a lucky break that he was able to hook big Hong Kong fish when he went trolling for dollars in the British colony's golden waters in late 1987. But it was no accident that the moneyed crowd, in the persons of Stanley Ho and an even wealthier tycoon, Cheng Yu-tung, opened their hearts and wallets to one of their own. Ting has told friends how he carefully zeroed in on the increasingly nervous elite in the colony, playing on his close business relationship with the Chinese government, his Canadian identity and his strategy of going global, at a time when the rich and famous were looking for just such a situation with which to cushion their fortunes from the possible shocks of 1997, when the colony will revert to Chinese rule.

"People who have bags of money and cannot be perceived to be leaving Hong Kong saw him as a vehicle for diversifying their interests," says a close ally. "It's perceived by China to be a good investment. Hence, the interest of Stanley Ho and Cheng. These are the people who own the power utilities, the gambling casinos, the transportation networks that are most vulnerable [to nationalization or breakup] after 1997. It's a brilliant strategy. The assets of the Hong Kong families go into the makings of a multinational Chinese company, but one based in Canada."

Ting and others say that Hong Kong's main hope of survival as a capitalist enclave lies in its ability to generate vital hard currency for the Chinese. "It can only be useful to China in one area," says Ting. "That's money. My strategy was to build Hong Kong a very worldwide distribution network, so that after 1997 it can be a centre for export for the country. I think that's why they liked my idea."

The youngest of four children, Ting Wei was born in Shanghai in 1951, at about the time the Communists were consolidating their control over the city. His father, in Hong Kong at the time, simply stayed there. Young James, as he came to be called, was seven by the time his mother obtained permission to take the rest of the family to the British colony. And he was only thirteen when his father, who had a small garment business, fell ill and died. With little family money and no well-heeled relatives to look after him, Ting left Hong Kong right after high school without looking back. "In Hong Kong, if your uncle is someone well-known, you can get someplace very easily. But if you're a quasi-refugee, as I was, there's nothing for you there."

After three years at an Australian technical school, where he met his future wife, he went to work in a Magnavox speaker factory to raise money for the family. While he liked Aussies enough to marry one of them, he knew he could never give his heart to the land down under, with its policies favouring white immigration. "It really hurt me to know that they were importing Italians and Greeks and paying them to immigrate, and here I was working my guts out for two or three shifts every day and I was paying them [for a yearly work permit]. I didn't get respect. Australia is going to miss me."

Arriving in Canada (where his sister had already moved) in 1973, with the proverbial $200 in his pocket and a burning desire to accomplish something on his own, he enrolled in the engineering school at the University of Toronto. Unlike some Hong Kong students here on daddy's dough, he had to muck his way through several menial jobs to pay for his schooling. "The first year was tough. I was cleaning office buildings. I don't think I need to clean any more washrooms in my life."

Ting was actually fired from his first Canadian job, as foreman of a small, family-owned appliance factory. Told to keep a closer eye on the women who were always leaving the assembly line to go to the washroom, he instead complained about the shoddy engineering that caused them to constantly cut their fingers on sharp metal. The plant engineer, who also happened to be the boss's son, didn't appreciate his unsolicited advice on how to improve the parts to protect the workers' hands. It wasn't Ting's last brush with bullheaded executives who don't like getting their hands dirty on the factory floor, and helps to explain why he normally boots the top echelon of management out the door almost as soon as he takes over a company.

A later employer was much more appreciative of his efforts. After spending a summer cleaning in a synagogue, he found himself embraced by the deliriously happy rabbi.

Ting was an eager second-year student in electrical engineering when he first appeared on the doorstep of K. C. Smith, then head of the department. Ting had come looking for work—Smith only found out later that he was already holding down two other jobs—and went on to epitomize everything the veteran prof had been trying to instil in his students for years.

A remarkable engineer-philosopher with a deep conviction that Canadians have been for too long the unconscious victims of the myth of American superiority, Smith set about trying to persuade his students that they could create businesses based on their own original ideas. Unlike many in his class, Ting believed him.

"The notion in the young people I was seeing was that products came from God or the United States," says the very professorial-looking, grey-bearded Smith. "Our conservatism tends to make things look impossible. They were leaning to engineering as a service job. They were discussing pension plans. They had already retired in their minds."

Immigrants like Ting don't carry such notions around in their suitcases. "They know what hardship really is, and they have a real insight into technology and its impact on their survival."

Ting says the last thing on his mind was spending his working life in the employ of a big, faceless corporation. "It doesn't make sense, after all those studies, to work for an IBM for twenty years." With his rare blend of entrepreneurial instinct and engineering ability that went beyond the dry-as-dust textbooks, he's become a role model for Smith's other students, many of whom are also Asian in heritage.

The professor's influence on the impressionable young immigrant shines through today in their shared distaste for American management methods, and the bean counters, lawyers and investment types who spend all their time shuffling society's existing wealth, instead of creating more. Listen to Ting dump all over the brokers and corporate lawyers who complicate his life to no end, and you start hearing echoes of his old teacher, who believes such people have helped turn this country into a "goddamn mess." Ting leaves all the legal work to partner Frank Holmes, and goes out of his way to avoid dealing with the legal beagles in negotiations. It's a lot easier to do in Asia, where lawyers rank somewhere near office cleaners and most deals are done on the basis of personal trust.

Ting was a graduate student when he teamed up with Holmes, then a young assistant professor who had been approached to design a telephone accessory. He asked Ting and another student if they wanted to build the prototype, and a lasting partnership was launched.

"I didn't have an early sense of what he would become, but he was always driven," Holmes says. "He would come in evenings and weekends, even though he wasn't paid for it. He never really lived a normal life, going out and enjoying himself like other students."

Ting and Holmes ended up forming a consulting business off-campus, with help from Smith and some graduate students. People would come to them to have their visions turned into reality. Nobody took any salary or expenses, says Holmes, who was still teaching full time. Any extra money went into their dream of building their own microcomputer.

An Ottawa group bought the business, turning it into the engineering arm of a new computer company called Nabu. Ting ran the division—the one and only time he has worked for someone else since leaving school, an experience he vows never to repeat. Under the terms of their deal, Ting had to work two years for the fledgling high-tech firm, which had grandiose plans but was never able to live up to them.

"There was too much politics," he says, shuddering at the memory of the backstabbings he witnessed at the now defunct company. "Nabu hired too many senior people from the U.S. Everyone had their own idea. I got people like the president coming to me and saying, 'Hey, let's gang up, and during the board meeting I will motion to fire the chairman.' I said, 'Oh no, I don't want to be associated with that.' "

Ting, who soaks up experience like an oversized sponge, has been careful to avoid the mistakes he witnessed firsthand. He's fought his way out of the single-product syndrome that plagues most high-tech innovators, and that brought his own company to the brink of disaster. And his senior executives and friends say he genuinely despises the Machiavellian office types who are always off scheming in the corners, instead of working with others to make their company prosper. Some chief executives like to keep their managers in a constant state of fear and doubt. But Ting strives for the Oriental ideals of harmony and consensus, while staying firmly in the driver's seat. He even makes a point of staying on good terms with the predators he has dealt with in the business world, including Paul Bilzerian, the U.S. corporate buccaneer who was jailed for securities fraud soon after selling Ting his controlling stake in Singer.

Ting had earned his master's degree and was on his way to a Ph.D. when the business bug bit. He never did write his thesis. But with a bit of effort from his friends, he'll soon have one of those honorary doctorates carried so proudly by Stanley "call me Dr." Ho, Cheng Yu-tung and the rest of the Hong Kong upper crust. It's the next best thing to a knighthood for the men who have everything money can buy. (Ho does have a knighthood—the Order of St. Gregory—awarded by the Vatican in 1989. His associates said the tycoon, a Buddhist, attempted to run his gambling empire in Catholic Macau in a way that "does not offend the Church." Nor, apparently, was the

Pope put off by the decision of one of Ho's companies to provide risqué videos on its ferry running between Taiwan and Macau. The service proved unpopular and was dropped.)

When he was setting up Semi-Tech, Ting took a majority of the shares. But he made his wife, Lisa Williams, the president "to please her." Holmes and a few "techie" friends who came over from Nabu each took minor slices of the pie in exchange for tossing in a few thousand dollars. Of the original group, only faithful sidekick Holmes remains.

Williams's term as president ended abruptly when Ting's first Hong Kong backers, the Chiaphua group, objected that they were investing in him, not his wife. The others who started off with Ting walked away with fat wallets after the company went public. All held between 1 and 2 percent of the stock, giving each of them a windfall of as much as $2-million.

"They saw James, who seemed to be just like them, becoming very successful and they thought there was no reason that they couldn't do it too," Holmes recalls. "None of them had a clue as to financing or the hard work that went into James's success." Holmes, who has kept his own small holding of less than 2 percent, had no intention of trying his luck on his own. "I recognize my limitations. I knew I couldn't do the things that he was doing. I saw all the problems he had to overcome. But I was closer to him than the others."

The company's name stands for Semi-conductor Technology, to describe the integrated circuits (the brain of a computer) that Ting wanted to—but never did—manufacture. Exciting names have not been this bunch's strong point. They were never thrilled with it, but couldn't come up with anything better. This was but the first of the identity problems that would plague the company, including the one caused by the unfortunate choice of a corporate trademark.

"We realized about six months after we started that we were getting strange comments about our original logo,"

Holmes laughs, a shy, nervous giggle that bubbles to the surface often. "The logo looked like an open toilet seat. And this was what everybody assumed it was. It was actually supposed to be a semi-conductor wafer with a whole bunch of integrated circuits on it."

Six months later, the name might as well have been flushed down with the misunderstood design. The 1983 federal budget made it too taxing for a small company like Semi-Tech to get into something as costly as building integrated circuits. "We looked at what else we could do, and the only thing we could fall back on was the microcomputer area, where we knew what we were doing," Holmes says.

That's when Ting lined up his first vital financing from Hong Kong. The wealthy Chiaphua group, controlled by Y. C. Cheng and his family (not to be confused with Cheng Yu-tung), liked Ting's ideas and took to him personally, the key to all the Asian money he's added up over the years. If they don't like and trust the person in charge, the most brilliant business plan in the world won't pry a dime out of Oriental pockets.

"We invested because the fundamental idea was sound," says an ebullient member of the Cheng family, who manages its Canadian investments and lives year-round in Toronto. He has reluctantly granted an interview in his suburban office, but won't allow his full name to be used. "It was a very workable plan. And James appeared to us to be a man of high integrity. He was needing financial assistance, so we said, 'Okay, fine.' We put in two-and-a-half million bucks just like that. The decision was taken by the family in less than two days. We had a meeting and said, 'Let's take a chance on this guy.' "

Chiaphua was just getting into computers in Hong Kong and the Chengs thought they could do Ting's manufacturing as part of their contribution, but he preferred to set up his own factory. That didn't seem to bother a family that practically revels in its low profile. The private Hong Kong group, with a wide range of manufacturing interests—from aluminum pots and pans to brass and paperboard—and a family worth well into the nine figures, controlled just over 20 percent of the stock when Semi-Tech went public, making it the second-biggest shareholder after Ting himself. But in typical fashion, the shares were divided among different family members and investor friends, including Charles Sun, who is related by marriage to one of the Chengs and played a key role in building Ting's bridge to China. As a result, there has been no public disclosure of the group's involvement, even though its members have always spoken with a single voice. With more shares issued since they came into the picture, the Chiaphua stake today is somewhere between 10 and 15 percent.

Their Semi-Tech role is typical of the family's Canadian strategy. After a false start in the property game during the recession of 1981-82, the family money has been moving into fledgling companies, such as a Wasp franchisor of Chinese fast food, that it could take over and operate if necessary. But as long as the original entrepreneurs do the job, the family says it will stay well clear of the spotlight. "We're very passive investors. We don't take a seat on the board and we only ask questions once in a while," the head of the family's Canadian branch says.

Others, though, have described how much Ting disliked having to appear before the family inquisitors to answer those questions. "James hated to have to go back and explain how the company was doing, what products were coming out, what went wrong with some idea," an associate says. "He had to go back and basically face the music."

Ting himself says the investment put tremendous pressure on him. "I was actually under a lot of stress. You feel morally obligated when the investment is in you as a person."

When the North American computer market crashed at the end of 1985, the family, still ruled with an iron hand by seventy-five-year-old patriarch Y. C. Cheng, actually was prepared to kiss its investment goodbye. But Ting refused to give up. "I was quite hurt by their decision.

In 1987, when this thing revived, they were surprised." They were also enriched. One insider estimates the Cheng family has made something like eight to ten times its initial investment. And some shareholders are irritated that the Chengs have been selling off stock to cash in.

Ting saved his company by turning far eastward. He sold his Pied Piper* personal computers in Malaysia and China, at a time when there were no other takers. He also sold production lines and know-how to the Chinese, helping them get into computer manufacturing. "We got some money and we survived that way. Ever since then, we've been in business doing technology transfers."

The Cheng family says that without its contacts, Ting might never have forged the links that set his company on the road to its current status. "We stepped in and took a very active role in getting him introduced to China. The company's present standing really arose from that connection," the Chengs' Toronto member says. "The credit has to be given to James, but we were instrumental in making the contact and cultivating the relationship." Although Ting didn't know it at the time he went looking eastwards, the elements of his grand strategy were falling into place, cemented by his budding relationships with powerful men like Cheng Yu-tung and Stanley Ho.

Of all the Hong Kong aristocrats, none is more visible or flamboyant than sixty-nine-year-old Stanley Ho Hung-sun, who appears in the colony's "best-dressed" lists, is still known for his ballroom dancing and is often

---

* Ting and the gang had constant trouble coming up with names for anything. Every time they thought they had a winner for their new computer, somebody else—usually one of the car makers—had beaten them to it. Pied Piper was proposed as a name that would suggest even a child could use the machine. But marketing tests showed half the people thought it was a toy. "We gave up looking for names after that," Holmes says. "We call them by their model numbers. Our laptop computer we call Laptop, like everybody else."

described as "charming" by the adoring local press. Fluent in Cantonese, English, Portuguese and Japanese, he's also the only known Chinese member of an exclusive French gourmet club, *La Confrérie de la chaîne de rôtisseurs.*

Few believe Ho's worth less than $1.2-billion. But so much Hong Kong money is hidden from view—and with local real estate and stock values soaring and dipping with the changing moods of a jittery population—accurate assessments are virtually impossible. His vast holdings include transportation, property, shipping and finance companies.

He's also one of the more prominent Hong Kong investors in Canada, with land (appropriately, at the entrance to Stanley Park) and two formerly Canadian-owned hotels in Vancouver (Le Meridien, purchased for $47.7-million cash in 1988 and neighbouring La Grande Residence, a $22-million bauble), investments in fashion and restaurants, about $20-million worth of Semi-Tech and a luxurious $5.5-million, twenty-five-room mansion in the money-littered Bridle Path neighbourhood of north Toronto, where one of his two wives (perfectly legal where he comes from) is ensconced.

But it's his hotels and gambling operations in Macau, a quaint, if somewhat seedy, relic of Portuguese colonialism that reverts to Chinese rule in 1999, that provide him with his greatest income and notoriety.* The Chinese are among the world's most serious gamblers, but only horse-racing is legal in Hong Kong. If they want to play the tables, they have to head eighty kilometres by sea to Ho's roost, usually on one of his company's thirteen high-speed jetfoils or two

---

* When then Ontario Premier David Peterson visited Hong Kong, he was warned by advisers not to appear too buddy-buddy with Ho, who is disdained by some of the old colonial money for the way he's made his fortune and for his bloodlines. Peterson ignored the advice. And Ting certainly hasn't been hurt by his close links to a man whose rise to financial power has sparked gossip for years. Like Ting, Ho started low down the ladder, but only because his once-wealthy Hong Kong family lost everything in a disastrous stock-market gamble when he was still in his teens. Two uncles committed suicide and his father fled to Saigon.

conventional ferries. There, they drop millions in his five crowded casinos or at the jai alai matches or greyhound races. Ho's gambling consortium nets about $600-million (HK) a year, and a similar amount fills the colony's tax coffers. But the licence to print money runs out in 2001, two years after the benevolent Portuguese leave, and it's hard to picture the sanctimonious old men who run the show in Beijing renewing it.

Perhaps looking to that future, Ho threw his considerable weight behind Ting's strategy, opening important doors and bringing in investment pals like the sixty-five-year-old Cheng Yu-tung, who's also in the hotel and property game in Vancouver and Toronto through his company, New World Development. Cheng is often a quiet but crucial player in Ho's ventures, most notably his gambling empire, and in the enterprises of other members of the colony's billionaires' club. He has as big a stake in Semi-Tech as Ho, but prefers staying in the background. New World, one of the top four property companies in Hong Kong, where real estate is king and outsiders rarely get to play, also has interests in construction, engineering, freight and television.

Cheng (pronounced *jen*) got his start in the jewelry business as a teenager, and today remains the largest diamond dealer in Hong Kong. (Ho's family is into jewelry too. His twenty-nine-year-old daughter, Pansy, a Canadian, runs a large store in Hong Kong owned by her mother, who prefers life in that Toronto mansion with a couple of other members of the family. Pansy Ho is also Semi-Tech's Hong Kong director of corporate development and public relations. But she's easier to find at the jewelry counter.)

Cheng has been cautiously raising his profile here since his first investment in 1985, a choice commercial office block in downtown Toronto. The place didn't impress him when he first saw it more than twenty years ago. "The whole city was very quiet. Also, it was in winter and very cold and snowing," he says through his interpreter, a secretary with movie-star looks named Joyce.

His slightly cluttered office is on the thirty-first floor of the New World Tower on Hong Kong's bustling Queen's Road. The address is prestigious, but his aerie, decorated with a few photos and his prized golfing trophies behind glass, would be rejected by any self-respecting Canadian executive on the fast track. Breaking into his own English, Cheng says that with the dramatic growth of the Chinese business community in Toronto, he finds it a more hospitable place these days — though he usually makes his visits in the summer.

He added the New World Harbourside (formerly the Holiday Inn Harbourside) in central Vancouver, where he naturally prefers the weather, for a mere $27.75-million in 1987, and sank millions more into renovations. He also took a piece of golfing chum Li Ka-shing's controversial Expo lands development in the same city and is involved in a venture to build townhouses near Toronto's Pearson International Airport. His two sons, Henry, a University of Western Ontario grad, and Peter, are increasingly calling the shots within the family empire as it spreads out of its cosy Hong Kong base, taking control of the huge Ramada hotel chain and about 2,000 parking lots in the United States. The elder Cheng apparently prefers spending most of his time these days on the golf course.

If Canadians had more knowledge of the way business works in the Far East, they would have realized what a coup Ting had scored with Ho and Cheng. It was, he would recall later, as if the Reichmanns — easily the rich Canadians Ting and other Asians admire most, because they made it big as immigrants, but with an appealing low-key style and strong sense of family — had given their blessing to the owner of a small local business, told all their friends to invest and encouraged the use of their name whenever it might be useful.

Ho even agreed to become Semi-Tech's chairman. "In Hong Kong, to be a chairman has a different meaning than in Canada," Ting confides. "He is personally responsible for anything the company does. If we should ever go into bankruptcy, he probably has to come up with the money to pay all this, because it is his credibility on the line." Any failure by Semi-Tech would be a terrible loss of face to peacock-proud Ho who, even more than most Chinese, doesn't treat such things lightly.

When it looked as if Vincent Tan, a wealthy Malaysian Chinese with his own powerful, silent backer, might win the contest for Singer, Ho warned that this would be terribly embarrassing in status-conscious Hong Kong. "James, we can't let this Singer thing go," he told Ting in the midst of the heated bidding war. "It's my personal reputation at stake. If I lose to this Malaysian guy. . ." He didn't have to finish the thought. Ting managed to buy the sewing machine company for $266-million (US), $56-million more than his initial offer, but well below what Ho would have authorized in the name of honour.

North American investors simply didn't realize what was on the line in the battle for the venerable Connecticut company with the household name. The big-money players who regularly make killings during such takeover wars stayed on the sidelines, because they had no idea who Ting or his Malaysian competitor were, or where their money was coming from.

In a characteristic move, Ting quickly brought Tan on board as yet another well-heeled participant in his grand strategy. The deal-maker never lets an opportunity to forge another alliance go by, and his powers of persuasion — everywhere else but on Bay Street — are considerable. Soon afterward, he quietly sat down with Tan's powerful backer, Yap Lem Sing, in Bali. The tête-à-tête with the head of a family he lauds as the Reichmanns of the East lasted six hours, as they explored potential joint ventures and other business deals. It seems Yap, a huge land developer in Singapore, Kuala Lumpur and Sydney, Australia, had been looking for an entrée into North America, but struck out in a bid for the real estate holdings of one major Canadian company. He quickly became yet another powerful Ting ally.

Ironically, all the Asian money that has flowed toward Ting partly as a gesture of support for China, from investors who see Semi-Tech's strategy as furthering Beijing's commercial interests, has enabled him to reduce his exposure to Chinese political winds — a necessity after the brutal student massacre of June 1989. A few days after Chinese tanks had rumbled over the students encamped in Beijing's Tiananmen Square, Ho said he would be maintaining his investments in Hong Kong and Macau without fear of the Chinese takeover.

"My business will be here and so will Stanley Ho," he told a magazine interviewer. "I will not leave. I expect I will be buried here." A month later, the man often called "Mr. Macau" was proposing that the United Nations lease both colonies for a hundred years, move its headquarters to Hong Kong and turn the territories into an Asian "Switzerland" to restore the residents' shaken confidence in their future. The idea, he said, came in a dream after he had fallen asleep to the strains of a *fantaisie* by Schumann.

Ting makes a point of stressing that, despite all the foreign cash pumped into Semi-Tech, his creation is still as Canadian as a beaver with a maple leaf tattooed on its tail. The company's aggressive strategy has been masterminded not from Hong Kong or Beijing but from that corner office in Markham, or one of the trans-Pacific jumbo jets on which Ting spends a good deal of his thinking and snoozing time.

Semi-Tech is particularly sensitive about its ties to the powerful money-spinners of the Orient. "We are not a foreign company," insists company executive Mike List. "You will hear constant references to us being owned by Chinese interests. We're spending a lot of time trying to undo that image. James Ting is a Canadian. Frank Holmes is a Canadian. Stanley Ho is a British subject who owns 3 percent in the parent company and 8 percent of Semi-Tech (Far East)," the first Canadian-owned company to be listed on the Hong Kong Stock Exchange and the subsidiary* through which Ting has engineered his fanciest deals.

"We're 90 percent Canadian-owned," List says almost by rote. This, it turns out, is a slight exaggeration, unless the $25-billion British Merchant Navy Officers Pension Fund, the second-largest single shareholder after Ting, has secretly moved its headquarters to Halifax harbour.

But there are good reasons for the display of ultra-nationalism. Quite apart from their efforts to woo the Canadian investment community, which wouldn't care if the company were secretly owned by Mao's second cousin as long as it didn't depend on China for too much of its business, Ting and his staff have had a problem with snoops of the Ottawa variety, who care a great deal about who calls the shots. Semi-Tech acquired classified computer work for the defence department when it purchased Datacrown, a large Canadian data processing company, in 1988. The thought that the Chinese government might actually be pulling Ting's strings was enough to send our spy masters into a tizzy. It didn't help that a former business associate of Stanley Ho's was once linked to the leak of atomic secrets to China.

"CSIS [the Canadian Security Intelligence Service] has been up in arms about us being Chinese-owned because we do so much business with Ottawa," List says, a frown creasing his suntanned features. "We inherited sensitive contracts with 'secret parts' of the government. We were fingerprinted and checked by the RCMP several times." His voice grows louder and he speaks slowly. "For the benefit of our friends up in Ottawa, this is a Canadian company." (Does he think the place is bugged?)

Asked what he'll do when CSIS staff show up in Markham to check out the company's ownership for themselves, List replies, "I'm just going to take them in and show them the share registrations, all of them."

If vital Canadian secrets should happen to fall into

---

* In typical Ting style, he later chose a more expansive name — Semi-Tech (Global).

enemy hands, it won't be because CSIS isn't on the job. Ting makes sure the ever-vigilant spy service knows in advance each time he's heading into China and what he's going to be doing there. "I'm not interested in politics," says Ting, who hasn't been asked to check in with CSIS and has never knowingly met any of its agents. "I'm just trying to be a good citizen."

It isn't only CSIS that's wondered if there were secret hands at work in Semi-Tech's overnight rise from obscurity. More than one observer who has watched the company grow far too rapidly for conservative Canadian tastes thinks that Ting must be a front man for his powerful backers in Hong Kong — or for other unnamed interests.

"Semi-Tech started out as this rinky-dink company that was going to make a portable computer called the Pied Piper," says a financial journalist who tracked the company in its early days. "I just regarded Ting as a two-bit player. I didn't get the impression he was the one pulling the strings." A Hong Kong immigrant who's been painstakingly building his own international company without Ting's access to deep pockets regards Semi-Tech with an increasing mixture of envy and resentment. "They have had overnight growth because of other people's money. You cannot do it that way on your own. It's easy to build a company his way."

It takes only a brief conversation, though, to affirm that Ting, a driven workaholic and loner who thinks nothing of working through the night* and who used to schedule meetings for Sunday mornings until his married staff rebelled, runs his own show. Dressed as usual in a conservative suit, white shirt and bright silk tie that stands out beneath his pallid features, he answers financial questions with ease, while artfully dodging efforts to dissect

---

* Ting loves taking advantage of his deceptively frail appearance by staging all-night negotiating sessions, as he did in the Singer deal. Usually, his overly confident opponents collapse in a heap long before he does.

his personal life. Asked about Semi-Tech's numbers, he lights up, turning over the back of a business card to do a few hurried calculations with a felt-tipped pen. There are no flunkies or a handy computer to feed him the answers. He doesn't need them. The dreams are all his own.

The wall of shyness goes back up when the questions turn to himself or his family. "It's not that I don't like to talk about personal things, it's just that there's not much to tell." He does say he's from a "middle-class" family. He mentions an older brother, Paul, a linguist who used to work for Lufthansa but is now in charge of Semi-Tech's computer division, and a sister, Maria, who also lives in Toronto with her husband and two daughters. Both are Canadian citizens. Another brother stayed in Australia. No social life, little private life, no hobbies. Home's a small condo on Bay Street, almost within shouting distance of those stubborn stock market analysts Ting's been trying so hard to woo.

Months of prodding later, he's picking without much enthusiasm at a late-night meal of fish and chips in a midtown luxury hotel. A nighthawk who's either a lot more relaxed here in a favourite haunt or who's just trying to be rid of a pesky reporter, he grows expansive. He talks about his father's early death; about his struggles to get where he is today, and why he has so little interest in money or the other obvious material benefits of running a prosperous company. He's even willing to discuss his rarely mentioned ex-wife, Lisa Williams, an industrial engineer every bit as ambitious as her shorter, slighter husband.

Their five-year marriage ended in 1982, a victim of Ting's murderous work schedule and, perhaps, of the inevitable clash of cultures and personalities as both adjusted to life in a strange land. "He had the opinion that marriage didn't make any difference. That it was just an extra person to work with you," a confidant says. "He didn't appreciate that wives like to do something else besides electronics all the time." Williams ended up running Semi-Tech's California marketing office until Ting closed it to trim costs in the crunch of 1985. She now runs a business in San Francisco importing Asian antiques.

The two remain friends, a good thing since she retains the right to half his share of the company, while he has all the votes and no intention of selling. "As far as James was concerned, the important thing was who had control," a friend says. "He didn't care about the economic benefit to himself. There's nothing in writing. It could be very messy if he ever remarries." Ting does talk about marrying again some day and perhaps having children, a fervent prayer of his hard-pressed executives, who think it might force him to keep more regular hours but know in their hearts that it probably wouldn't.

Ting hasn't changed much from his first years in business. Still driven, he's made few concessions to success. "I keep on telling all my friends that I am actually a very poor man," he says with almost irritating but obviously genuine modesty. "On paper I'm very rich. But because of the commitment to the company, because of the way I want to drive it, I can't see myself selling the stock." He has no other investments or business interests. "After a certain point, money is not important. If money and success can change my character, then it was not very well-formed. The important thing is to develop a certain philosophy of life. The saddest thing is successful people who have no other purpose than to make more money."

The tall, angular Frank Holmes, who perpetually wears sun-sensitive glasses, expensive suits and a "How did I get here, anyway?" look, laughs when he describes his friend's Spartan lifestyle. "James used to move every year or two. He used to joke about what incentives the landlord would give him to move in, and as soon as the incentives would expire, he'd move to another apartment. It would drive me crazy to up and move everything. But not James. He'd say, 'Well, all I've got is a bed, so it's no big deal.' And literally, that would be it. Even now, his furniture is two phones and a fax machine."

Ting did buy a stereo a while back, which he plunked down in his living room. "That was just on a whim," says a bemused Holmes. "Whenever James shops, he's really looking at what new technology is around, what new ideas he can generate. He's not shopping because he wants to buy something, but because it intrigues him. It's a new kind of gadget for him to try to figure out how it works and to see if he can improve on it."

Ting's an engineer, entrepreneur and small boy all rolled into one. He picks up a mini-tape recorder in mid-interview, turns it over in his hand and launches into an animated description of the latest version he's seen on the market. "James is an engineer," K. C. Smith, Ting's old professor and long-time mentor, says proudly. "Engineers have a curiosity about the world. These are the kids who always tore their toys apart. They rarely put them back together."

But Ting is also a compulsive wheeler-dealer whose mind is fixed on some distant point, his ambition always stretching his company's financial resources just beyond the limit. After each new venture, he vows to slow down and concentrate on what he's already built; but his associates long ago learned to take such pronouncements with large doses of salt. Even on his infrequent vacations, he grows bored and restive after a few days.

Last year, he piloted Semi-Tech through more acquisitions and joint ventures and was talking about turning its large computer services arm into a public company, so it could raise money to go into the satellite transmission business. One day, he might also like to get into merchant banking. And he would take the Singer company public too. In the meantime, he had bought up the European distributor of Singer products and was off looking for other deals in Eastern Europe and the Far East.

In a reflective moment, Ting talks not of further expanding Semi-Tech but perhaps of walking away from it, leaving its managers to manage on their own. . . . Starting something else . . . keeping the juices flowing. "I am forty now. You cannot take any of it with you. I don't have any great aspirations. I don't want to change history. Maybe I will settle down."

Could someone please pass the salt?

CHAPTER 2

The Chinese and the Land

ALEX CHAN SLOWLY steers his sleek grey Mercedes through the heavy afternoon traffic and the stoplight-oblivious crowds, past the bilingual signs, the Taiwanese tea shop, the barbecued ducks and the best egg-custard tarts in town. His destination: an overflowing neon-lit corner of downtown Toronto where have-it-all newcomers from the Orient mingle with the have-nots—or at least the have-a-lot-less—who've always made up the majority of Chinese immigrants to this country. With their millions, the new arrivals have been settling into fancy midtown penthouses and suburban palaces far from civilization as they know it, without even such basics of everyday life as their chauffeurs. When they want to do some business or a bit of shopping for the herbs, cures and delicacies they just can't find at their overpriced local boutiques, they drive themselves down here, to the ghetto comforts of Dundas and Spadina at the heart of "New Chinatown," a sprawling, up-market version of the "Old Chinatown" a few blocks to the east.

Spadina Avenue has long been the wide street of dreams for the poor, often desperate people who've scratched and scraped their way to the safety of these shores. Jewish immigrants once gave the core of the old garment district its distinctive ethnic character; but rice noodles, Oriental traders and real estate buyers with deeper pockets than any Spadina tailor ever sewed have pretty much driven the cheese blintzes, potato latkes and rack jobbers out. Now, it's the place where the poorer, less secure world of the traditional Chinese and, more recently, the Vietnamese immigrant meets the new Asian money of high-priced restaurants, handsomely appointed law, real estate and accounting offices and more bank branches than would seem possible on a couple of short city blocks.

Alex Chan manages to straddle both worlds quite nicely. He's got all the earmarks of the new money—the custom-built house on a moneyed suburban street, a condo in a building he's putting up downtown, a $180,000 ebony Rolls-Royce with metallic gold trim, the Mercedes for everyday use, two children in private school and millions of dollars to play with. He's a charter member of the Mandarin Club, an elegant paean to the new money on the southwest corner of Spadina and Dundas, where walking success stories sit down to golden plates of Chinese food at caviar prices (soup here runs nine dollars; but if that matters, you should be three floors below or up the street, where full-course meals cost less).

On rare occasions, Chan can actually be found lunching on mild Cantonese at his club, among all the rising young Chinese power brokers and the anglos lusting after their confidence and their favours. But he's more likely to be in the less affluent Chinatown just across the street, where he keeps his utilitarian office and where a tuna sandwich subs for lobster in garlic sauce. That's if he can manage even a brief respite from ministering to the medical needs of a long line-up of less than loaded Chinese patients, many of them elderly. To them, he's trusty, caring Dr. Chan, who speaks their language softly and still keeps office hours on Sundays, so they don't have to troop off to strange and frightening hospital emergency wards when the winter ills hit.

He's rushing back to them this very minute, looking for a gap among the shoppers, then wheeling his Mercedes smartly into the parking garage beneath his office. The garage could easily pass for an underground German luxury car dealership.

Careful not to mix his two worlds, Chan keeps his Rolls—a sure sign you've made it in Hong Kong or here—locked safely away in his suburban garage most of the time, rarely venturing out in it except after dark when the neighbours aren't looking. The Mercedes, chariot of choice among any Chinese who can afford one, is apparently more socially acceptable. And his business hat stays firmly in the closet when he's making like a Chinese Dr. Kildare. Even his super-rich Hong Kong mentor, Kenneth Lo, would never think of interrupting him there (although a portable phone is always at hand for those non-medical emergencies). Chan knows full well that his patients would faint if they ever found out their short, stocky doctor with the friendly, boyish smile and the soothing bedside style was leading a double life.

A couple of blocks south of Alex Chan's simple, white waiting room sits Polygrand Developments, the low-key nerve centre of his other world, the one in which he's rapidly become a millionaire real estate player with major-league ambitions and the Hong Kong backing to achieve them. Polygrand. The name sounds as if it was designed by a committee of Toronto politicians. Airily overblown, thoroughly innocuous, painstakingly non-ethnic, it's a bit like the homes some Asian immigrants like to build—large and plain, even ugly, on the outside, oozing money on the inside. Chan's long-time patients would need oxygen if they ever got a glimpse of the place where their humble physician parks his stethoscope in his spare time.

Polygrand's reception area is painted white, apart from one wall done in an eye-catching burgundy. A love-seat and two armchairs in matching upholstery — cream-coloured with a pink-hued print—are flanked by two costly silk flower arrangements. Across the room, to the left of the brass-and-wood reception desk, a six-panelled screen depicts armed horsemen ready for trouble. Copies of business and travel magazines and a wine publication aptly named *Decanter* are laid out on a marble end-table in a precise fan, exactly an inch apart. As far from a harried doctor's office as anyone could imagine, the place blends well into determinedly trendy Queen Street, with its pseudo-old-fashioned brick fronts above turquoise- and peach-hued cafes, au-so-courant clothing boutiques and computer stores lining what has become yet another high-rent Toronto gawking strip.

The thirty-six-year-old Chan started in real estate with a half million dollars of family money in 1984. With shrewd joint ventures, and a large injection of Hong Kong capital, he's built his company's assets to about $100-million. But as recently as 1986, tearing down the Hungarian church that stood on the site of his Polygrand headquarters and replacing it with $3-million worth of stores and offices was a big deal, a step up from merely planting the family money in existing suburban shopping strips, small buildings and townhouses—the preferred route of investors who don't yet know the ropes in their adopted home.

These $1.5- to $3-million "Hong Kong starter kits," as the real estate cynics have dubbed the purchases of homes and investment properties, are mainly passive, requiring neither entrepreneurial effort nor much precious time, which is still devoted to the money-churning businesses back in the Far East. Critics charge that they do little for the community, apart from enriching the sellers and a few savvy agents.

"This is unlike any money that we've ever seen in our society before," says a Vancouver lawyer who worries about the impact of the new money. "It is entirely discretionary. It owes no direction to shareholders or to lenders or to anybody else. It's just one guy who has $30- to $40-million. If he wants to buy a couple of shopping centres, he does it. These people seem to be able to spend fantastic amounts of money."

One real estate pro says it's time to cash in the chips whenever the Chinese money comes to the poker table. "Their ambition to win is the size of a farmhouse. And while they all want double security, they also have a bit of gambling lust. They have been educated to think that if the property is good, in twenty years it will have quadrupled in value. They have seen it in Hong Kong. That's why they will get into a project that has returns only half of what someone else would consider acceptable. So if they want something, there's no sense bidding against them."

But unless they're ready for retirement (as some undoubtedly are), the very nature that took them to the top of their dog-eat-dog world makes the newcomers far too restless to be satisfied with merely shuffling around pieces of property for speculative gains. Sooner or later, they, or their children, will move into endeavours that do more than fatten the wallets of aggressive land flippers.

Listen to an accountant describing the behaviour of wealthy migrants in a society he knows well. "They spoke a different dialect which was not popular. And they were not familiar with the local business environment, so they took a very low profile, until a few years down the road when they got comfortable with the way business was done. Then they started using their capital and expertise, and that contributed a great deal to the growth of the city." It's not Toronto or Vancouver he's talking about—at least not yet—but Hong Kong, transformed from a relative backwater into an Asian boomtown by the energy, skills and money of the refugees who flooded the British colony (much to the dismay of many long-time residents) in the wake of the postwar turmoil in mainland China and the subsequent Communist victory in 1949.

"We have similar elements here in Canada," adds the Hong Kong-born tax specialist. "Most of those people who can afford to come over are in their early forties. They may be financially capable of retiring, but they are not going to do so. They are entrepreneurs. They will start looking for business to do. That is their nature."

Most will stick close to the ground at first, as the British, Germans, Italians and others have done before them . . . and as Alex Chan's doing now.

For a people desperately seeking security, property takes on an almost mystical aura, seems proof somehow that they belong, that their new life won't be easily yanked out from under them. It's where most of them put their first dollars in this country, apart from straight bank deposits, and where some of the truly magnificent immigrant fortunes begin. "It's human nature," says Hong Kong native Connie Mak, a Toronto partner with a major accounting firm. "I compare it to the early fifties, when a lot of Europeans and Jewish people came over here, and the thing they invested in was real estate. It's their only form of security."

It is, affirms a Canadian banker who deals extensively with the new money, their "first comfort, regardless of where they are. In Canada, they are still unfamiliar with the customs and regulations and trade practices. Real estate is something they do know, or if not, something they can find out with some patience."

Andrea Eng says it shouldn't surprise anyone that the Chinese, of all people, turn to property for safety, security and, where possible, big profits. It's no accident that most of the great Hong Kong fortunes are rooted in the colony's fragile soil, where scarcity has combined with huge demand to drive prices into the stratosphere. The Canadian-born Eng once finished second in the Miss Canada beauty pageant, but she's since built a far more formidable and lucrative reputation selling millions of dollars worth of Vancouver real estate to Hong Kong and Taiwanese investors. "Culturally, there were two ways in old China to get ahead. One was through education, and that's why students study as hard as they do. And the second was through land, because this way you had food for your family for generations. So this is not something that's new."

Eng and a handful of other talented property pushers, like Singapore immigrant K. See in Toronto,* have spent years cultivating the new Asian investors with as much loving care as if they were tomatoes in Yellowknife. "These people are a unique sort of group who need very special attention and can't be pushed," says Eng. "We do all our homework and babysit and nurse each step along the way. A lot of it is patience and credibility."

K. See (his real name's Koh, but nobody, including him, ever uses it) started his company above a grocery store in Old Chinatown fifteen years ago and now employs some eighty people in two offices. See, who doesn't like seeing his name in print, is close-mouthed about anything to do with his booming business. But this former manager of a Singapore plastics factory is known to have been a consultant back in the early 1970s to the Yeung family, the first major Hong Kong investors to buy a serious piece of Toronto.

Hong Kong sources say the family, whose hotel (Miramar) and property fortune ranks it in the low thirties on the

---

* Despite the way it sometimes seems, the Chinese haven't limited themselves solely to the pricey Toronto and Vancouver markets, although these remain by far the favourite destinations for both the money and the people. Hong Kong and Singapore money has trickled into houses, hotels, apartment buildings and plazas in Montreal, but almost never condos. Calgary and Edmonton, both bigger markets than Montreal for Asian investments (mostly in retail and offices), are growing in popularity as the new money hunts down bargains. Winnipeg has attracted entrepreneurs like garment makers Henry and Manning Tang of Prosperity Knitwear Ltd., who were looking for lower factory and housing costs. "Winnipeg has the London, Ontario, syndrome," says one real estate specialist who markets to Asian investors. "Solid and stable, but just so boring." New money has gone into property in other Canadian cities as well, including industrial buildings in Saskatoon, a plaza in St. Catharines, a motel in Corner Brook—usually as part of increasingly controversial immigration funds that enable investors to take up residence here.

colony's chart of its fifty most wealthy, wasn't overly thrilled with its early experiences here. But you wouldn't guess that from the expansionist tendencies of Yeung Chi Shing Estates (Canada). Family loyalist Jeffrey Lau masterminded YCS's push into suburban development from the remarkably Spartan office (reachable only by private elevator) on the top floor of its flagship building at 80 Bloor St. West—a good midtown address with the lucky (if you're Cantonese or selling to them) number eight in it. Lau has since left to work for a smaller housing development company. YCS does massive projects that can take ten years or more just in the planning stages, Lau says in explaining his departure. "A lot of work without concrete results."*

Lau and other Chinese developers resent any inference that Asians are buying up all the choice property in places like Toronto and Vancouver, and pushing up prices in the bargain. Maybe they would, if they could get their hands on it. But the big insurance companies and other conservative financial powerhouses, European investors and a few mighty domestic real estate companies have a lock on most of the prime buildings in every major Canadian city. And they simply aren't selling—as the Japanese institutional giants have discovered.

When prized land, such as Vancouver's Expo site, does become available, the Asians are in there pitching with the best of them. But their ready cash and ability to make swift decisions still is no guarantee of success. An ultra-rich family made a serious run at one major West Coast developer, but was told the deal was as good as inked with a Canadian player. A Hong Kong syndicate thought it had the winning bid on a choice Campeau property in Toronto, only to find a Dutch pension fund mysteriously topping its offer at the eleventh hour.

---

* Hong Kongers have little use for all the paperwork, politics and hearings that accompany major land deals in Canada. "In Hong Kong, they only need to fill out two things: when they are going to close and how much they are paying," says a developer from the colony.

Most Chinese can't afford to play in this kind of league, cavorting with the likes of the Yeungs or the even wealthier families slipping their millions into the country. The smaller fry have been starting off slowly and cautiously, like someone groping for a light switch in the dark. But while he may have stepped warily at first, Alex Chan hasn't taken long to gather the nerve, experience and money to go for the brass ring. The painful, passive, learning phase is definitely at an end.

To hear Chan tell it, he's clawed his way up through the school of hard knocks, except that in his case, it's more akin to a private school, where the kids collect generous allowances and a leg up from the family if they happen to trip on the ladder of success. And always there, a hand on his well-tailored shoulder, is his quiet Rolls-Royce of a backer, Kenneth Lo, a Hong Kong textile tycoon and Canadian citizen. "He may not be as experienced in real estate development, but quite often he can tell me from experience what can be done," says an obviously grateful Chan. "He's gone through our size before and he knows the frustrations, the good and bad sides of things. Without him, I would probably be staying a small developer. I would be too chicken to look ahead. His is a mega-vision. And mine is becoming slowly like that. Now, quite often, we're looking at the same thing."

Today, the MD (as in Multiple-dwelling Developer?) plots massive schemes mixing offices, hotels, apartments, stores and cinemas. But as he nervously watches over the preparations for a lavish Chinese New Year's party that coincides with both the annual inspection visit of Lo and the other Hong Kong directors and the rebirth of his historic Essex Park Hotel on Jarvis (a street where the ghosts of mighty fortune builders have been rubbing elbows with the down-and-out for years), he has to pinch himself from time to time to make sure it's all for real. "Something in life that I treasure is that I don't take things for granted. When you look at it, I could have been a little peasant boy born in Szechuan province. You go to the farm. No matter your dream or what you want to do, you're still a peasant. I was born in Hong Kong and then sent over by my family and had this opportunity to meet the right people. It is up to me to do something."

Sitting at the marble-topped table in Polygrand's conference room, Chan talks about what drives him, and it isn't money. "It is this desire to be successful, to achieve something. We are the first generation. We need to establish a foothold here. Our partners are here. We live here, invest here. We've created close to 100 permanent jobs for Canadians. We donate to charities. We participate in the political system. Our future is here." He motions to the wide world beyond his office. Outside, the streetcars rumble quietly past, but even if a flood of noise were to penetrate these walls, it wouldn't drown out his fierce passion.

He leans forward to make a favourite point about the rootless Chinese refugees living in the diaspora; it reveals a sentiment that runs deep and goes a long way toward explaining their constant craving for material success and acceptance—and their obsession with security. "Over the last hundred years, Chinese people have been running around unsettled. We need to settle. That's the driving force behind all this. That's why we work hard, and in other people's eyes, we work extra hard. Because we're the new generation here. We do have a lot of expectations."

The benchmarks of the doctor's rapid rise up through the hard-nosed, red-tape-ridden, you-scratch-my-back world of the land developer line one wall of his conference room. Each scale model depicts something grander than the one before it. From the $3-million Polygrand building; to the $4-million medical centre (dear to the hearts of all doctor-developers); the $40-million Essex Park hotel-condo complex; $60-million worth of townhouse condos on a suburban street where Chan has managed to buy up an entire row of houses. Everything has been done with a touch of class; no Harbourfront eyesores for this immigrant developer. Then, his biggest deal yet: a one-third stake in a massive $300-million commercial redevelopment of the former G. W. Wood ("Sanitation for the nation") industrial property in the west end of Toronto. His partners are two old-line companies, one run by first-generation Britons and the other by second-generation Germans—a fitting troika for a Canadian real estate venture these days.

Behind Chan, the bold, gold Polygrand logo looks like five loops of fancy ribbon. They're actually Ps, shaped to resemble a five-petalled Chinese flower revolving around a circle, which stand for movement and growth. The gold's for prosperity, the blue background for solidity, says Chan, delighting in the Oriental subtlety and elegance of it all. From a distance, the whole thing looks like the Chinese symbol for big, though this was noticed only after the fact by Yvonne Lo, the sharp-witted wife of Chan's intensely private and immensely wealthy patron. It's obvious that despite the white-bread name, Chan's company has a solid Oriental pedigree.

The office is just four doors east of Spadina, the magnet that draws rich and poor Chinese alike from across the city—and yet it might as well be 1,000 miles away, for all Polygrand's links to the local community. Some Chinese entrepreneurs would rather stay in their familiar ethnic confines, feeding off each other; but not Chan. He consciously avoids setting up shops in any of the city's burgeoning Chinaworlds; once he'd branched out from his electrocardiograms, Dundas and Spadina were just too small to hold the bespectacled little man with the big vision. Soon he'll have to leave his patients behind as well.

Chan knows the time is coming to abandon his other life, but it's awfully hard to pull the plug. He's taken on an assistant for the medical work and no longer sees 300 patients a week, but he's still Hippocratical to the core. "People keep asking why I don't sell the practice. They think I must be crazy. It's not the money, it's not anything else. It's just that I've seen these people over the years. To say goodbye, some of them would be just devastated. I can't abandon them just because suddenly I am making all this money." After putting off a second interview for weeks, he confides that he's had nightmares about reading a headline that goes something like this: "MD Forsakes Medicine for Life of Property Magnate." "My patients would never understand. Never."

During a break in one of his feverish, fourteen-hour workdays that wind up late in the evening back at the Polygrand office after a full dose of flu, strep throat and the usual assortment of aches and pains, some of them his own, the doctor admits it's getting harder and harder to wear two hats. Behind his fashionable rectangular frames, his dark eyes shout fatigue; his quiet voice is bathed in weariness. The doctor looks as if he should be prescribing himself a long rest. He agrees with the diagnosis, but has no time to take the cure. "It's taking a toll on my health. Physically, you can only do so much. I'm tired. I wish I could do more."

Chan still loves that other world. Ask him to describe his approach to real estate and he draws a parallel between running a sound business and spooning out good medicine. Not many developers would even think of comparing the need for a fast decision on a mega-deal to the surgeon's axiom that the sun should never set on a bowel obstruction. Nor would they treat new ventures as if they were untested drugs, requiring extensive research and human trials before getting the seal of approval.*

"I don't think the training is a handicap in business," Chan says flatly. The problem with most doctors, or any other fat-cat professionals with spare change to toss around, is that they can't take the losses that inevitably

---

* Chan practises what he preaches. Before buying the Essex Park from a group of local investors, he researched the location in surprising detail. Yes, he says, he knew the area has been a prostitutes' hangout and that Allan Gardens right across the street is a place where drunks like to bed down. He even knows that at the turn of the century, it was Toronto's millionaires' row, that the mansions were converted to look after the wounded during the First World War and that the drunk-littered park was originally built so the nannies would have a place to stroll with their charges. He's also aware that it's being gussied up as a tourist attraction. There was, he says confidently, no other available hotel property downtown that looked out on such a pleasant prospect.

come with the ups and downs of the marketplace. "That's understandable, because how can you lose money being a doctor?" he asks of people used to relatively high income with no risk year-in and year-out. It's obvious he considers the ability to walk away from a bad deal the most important instrument in his entrepreneur's black bag. "I made up my mind that there would be good times and bad times. In business, sometimes you have to cut your losses and get out. You win some, you lose some." They learn that in the medical business too.

Chan is not the first dedicated medicine man to carve a name for himself in buildings. Dr. Charles Allard, the Alberta surgeon-turned-conglomerate-builder, readily comes to mind when Chan starts spinning his larger-than-life dreams. Another in his line of work is one of his own professors at the University of Toronto, Dr. George Woo, a prominent Shanghai-born gynecologist and pioneer in Canadian test-tube fertilization research, who develops medically related projects—including a $100-million condo community for the elderly in Scarborough, Ontario, complete with medical day care, and an $80-million private hospital in Hong Kong—with partner Dr. Paul Tam, a kidney specialist. But whereas Woo (who numbers among his patients Chan's wife, Marina) has no plans to give up medicine or his renowned work in *in vitro* fertilization, Chan has little choice but to walk away from his practice. Running a mega-bucks company isn't exactly something that can be done between hospital rounds, no matter how competent the hired hands. And it's in property development that the good doctor, like so many immigrants before him, intends to plant lasting roots for himself and his family.*

Chan arrived in Toronto in 1972, a fuzzy-cheeked

---

* Toronto dentist Jack Tse, who came from Hong Kong by way of Harvard and MIT, and can be seen around projects in a bomber jacket and work boots, is equally ambitious. The syndicator and investor picks up downtown buildings for fellow Hong Kong immigrants and himself. "He pulls teeth as a hobby," a business associate says.

nineteen-year-old out to fulfill his father's dream of being able to point to "my son, the doctor." The tidal wave
of big money from Hong Kong wouldn't start breaking
over Canadian shores for more than a decade; but the
dollars and sons were already flowing in from the more
astute and nervous of the colony's families. Chan's older
brother, John had come in 1967 to study accounting at
McGill, after Communist-instigated riots brought blood
to Hong Kong's streets during the worst excesses of the
Cultural Revolution.

The violence was a bad sign for a people still steeped
in their refugee mentality, and it started them hurriedly
looking for safer places to park their families and part of
their hard-earned fortunes. Chan's father, an entrepreneur
who'd fled Canton ahead of the Communist takeover,
wasn't about to let his children suffer through the same
nightmare. John, the oldest, returned to Hong Kong at the
end of the seventies to help his father in business while
building a career as a municipal politician. But the other
three brothers and their sister stayed here. All became
Canadian citizens. They expect to be joined by their aging
parents, who were finally persuaded by the Tiananmen
Square massacre of June 4, 1989, that it was time, even
in their seventies, to pack up and move on yet again.

Shortly after arriving, Alex married Marina, his Hong
Kong sweetheart, and the two of them huddled alone
in the vast coldness of downtown Toronto. "We were
by ourselves. As students, we really had nothing. Going
through medical school, she was working (as a nurse's
aide), helping me to pay the bills. There was nothing."
Actually, Chan's father picked up the tuition tab and
provided some pocket money, which came in handy later
when the young couple found themselves trying to raise
an infant on a doctor-in-training's meagre pay.

Chan remembers school as a rough time, not because
of his courses or lack of a fat allowance but because of
something many immigrants hate talking about openly.
"Sometimes I felt left out," Chan says of his school-days.
"I wouldn't say it's strict racism, but it's just that you feel

uncomfortable. Sometimes there were questions I could not help asking myself. Why would some people get grade A, and others would get grade B? At that time, there was already an outcry that there were too many Chinese-origin medical students. So we did everything very carefully to avoid offending anyone. We never talked in our mother language. We spoke to each other in English. I still heard some of my [Chinese] colleagues commenting on racism and events happening. But because of the sensitivity of the issue, I'm not too sure that they [his professors] may not have done extra to protect me."

Marina Chan, somewhat insulated from all this, only recalls the long hours she spent as a single mother while her husband was enduring his mandatory intern's torture, home perhaps every second or third day after putting in gruelling hospital shifts. To her, his most frenetic business day seems almost tranquil by comparison. Friendly, outgoing, a warm smile playing on her lips, Marina understands why her workaholic husband is shooting for the stars; though she prefers life in the quiet lane of suburbia, and wishes he would be home more often to help with their three kids. (He does feel guilty about that and has started phoning them, just so they don't forget him.) She doesn't seem the type who could ever get worked up about a custom-built house (by Iranian Shane Baghai, who's found the builder's version of nirvana in the new Chinese money) or a Rolls-Royce in the garage.

As in any typical Chinese family, it was the iron-willed patriarch of the Chan clan who set his son's course in life, first to medical school, then into the true family vocation. There was never a doubt the Chans would set up some sort of business here, just as there was no question of Alex being only a doctor, or his brother merely an accountant or a third brother solely a civil engineer. "I wouldn't say that's because it's a Chinese tradition. He was very happy when I became a doctor. Then he found nobody looking after business here and he said: 'I don't care. I want my son to be a businessman.' At that time, we were starting to have a little bit of real estate, buying plazas here, small buildings there. In his mind, you have to own a business to be successful. I have had that pressure from day one." (The decision to ban extra-billing by doctors also made the choice easier. Chan never did charge his patients more than the Ontario-approved rate; but along with most of the medical establishment, the Hong Kong free enterpriser in him couldn't stand the interference.)

Chan makes it sound as if his "middle-class" father was fortunate to put rice on the table. "Believe it or not, we were not rich," he says in the near-whisper that sometimes seems a national characteristic. "We didn't even own a car or any items you can brag about." But in Hong Kong, "middle class" is the tag attached to any common garden variety multimillionaire. When pressed, Chan agrees that his semi-retired father does indeed have the odd million or two put away for typhoon season. "We're not a very rich family, I have to re-emphasize. We own a restaurant. We own our own apartment. Yes, he's a millionaire in a sense, but there are so many millionaires in Hong Kong."

Dad always wanted the boys to work together, says Chan, offering a glimpse of the way Chinese families typically operate, and hinting at the friction that can occur when a Western-educated son—and the youngest, to boot—brings home some new-fangled, though scarcely radical, ideas. "We are a close family. But I have to say that sometimes I'm a little bit at odds with my father. You can't do it all in the family any more. We're a corporation now. We are hiring people who are not related. It's easier for me to handle the situation. It's just D.C. [his civil engineer brother, a bridge and tunnel expert who isn't building any while assisting his brother in the running of Polygrand] and me. It works out better."

Chan insists he's still close to his older brothers, but the road hasn't always been smooth since the family departed from the natural order of things, in which the younger siblings defer to age and experience. He's acutely aware of his important role in laying the family's Canadian foundation. "There's a lot of pressure on me. And if you have other people who are supposed to be senior in terms of

the family tree, it's difficult." Chan, who's also the youngest of all the investors in Polygrand, slumps slightly in
his chair, as if suddenly weighed down by the burden
of it all.

His father isn't involved in any of the Canadian corporate decisions today. "It's a slow, evolutionary process.
Ten years ago, he had absolute control over everything we
did. He was strict, authoritarian. Every time I went back
to Hong Kong, my father would say, 'What are you doing?
Why are you growing so big?' He started with nothing. He
did everything single-handed. And then all of a sudden
the next generation is talking about joint financings and
ventures with people he doesn't even know. It's difficult
for him to accept that. When you try to compare with the
multinationals, a person's or a family's wealth is nothing.
You need people working together."

That's how Polygrand evolved—with a giant push from
its chairman and biggest shareholder, Kenneth Lo, scion
of a mighty textile fortune. The Canadian company is
actually a complex fifty-fifty joint venture between two
holding companies, Varallo and Conwell International.
Varallo is part of Lo's Hong Kong-based global empire.
Conwell is a combination of the Chan family money,
which controls close to half its shares, and a group of
Hong Kong investor pals who own the rest. They all get
together in Toronto on the Chinese New Year, a holiday
in work-crazed Hong Kong, to see what Chan's been up
to in the past year and to approve his ambitious plans for
the next.

It's the only regular visit here by the elusive, reclusive
Lo, the Greta Garbo of Hong Kong zillionaires. As
Polygrand's chairman, he's the reluctant host of what
amounts to his protégé's corporate coming-out party at
the refurbished 109-room Essex Park Hotel, or at least
the parts of it that are finished. That the renovations are
incomplete conveniently keeps the guests from straying
too far when the usually trite and true speeches are served
up to commemorate the occasion.

On this slushy February evening, brushing away beads

of sweat that dot his forehead beneath a thick thatch of carefully coiffed hair, his nerves almost under control, Chan greets the well-heeled and their professional hangers-on. In his fashionable light grey suit, with the favoured long jacket that seems to end somewhere around the knees, he melts into the crowd of friends and high-powered supporters, then disappears completely amid a sea of taller blue and charcoal pinstripes, the uniforms of the bankers, lawyers, accountants, consultants and architects who have been cleaning up from their links with the new Asian money. Marina, making one of her rare corporate appearances, sends someone to fish him out of the crowd and coax him into posing for a photo with her. An outfit called China Syndrome Productions is weaving among the hors d'oeuvres trays, shooting everything for posterity.

Lo and his wife, Yvonne, stand quietly apart from the bustling shrimp-and-champagne set, where they're being accosted by an eager-beaver banker seeking a meeting. The bespectacled Mrs. Lo is a rarity among Asian wives, as knowledgeable and interested in the family business as her husband. Decked out in a black velvet suit and white silk blouse embroidered with tiny, exquisite pearls, she's no shrinking violet. It's Yvonne Lo herself who says she knows as much about the business as anyone because she's right in the middle of it: "We are the family business, the two of us." And they want to stay private "because there are too many restrictions on public companies. We don't like that." Beside the slightly built, shy man in the ubiquitous horn rims, conservative suit and short haircut that looks as if he ran into a nearsighted student barber, she positively radiates authority.

Kenneth Lo never has to worry about being picked out as the billionaire in the crowd. And that's just the way he likes it. He addresses the troops and assembled luminaries in a firm tone that suggests he's used to being in command; but the speech is brief, and he fades back into the shadows at the first opportunity. Chan says Lo is "a very shy, quiet person, and he doesn't like publicity too much." It's the understatement of the year. He's so eager to avoid the public eye that his palace guard at Crystal Knitting, his Hong Kong garment empire, won't even admit to a non-Chinese stranger that he exists.

Wealthy Asians like Lo "haven't fallen prey to that North American disease of having to tell the world about their accomplishments," says a veteran journalist, whose Chinese-language skills haven't been much help in getting through their gold-plated doors. "Here in Canada, what people know about you is considered an advantage. There, what you don't know about them is an asset for them."

Lo proves the point. "I'm not a wealthy man, I'm just okay," the forty-eight-year-old magnate says with a shrug when he's finally cornered. Just okay, that is, for a guy who employs about 10,000 workers in six countries sewing clothes for some of the top retail chains in the world: The Limited and a sister company, The Gap, as well as big department stores like Sears and J. C. Penney, put their private labels on his products. He's just okay for someone who's built a spectacular $24-million (HK) home overlooking Repulse Bay in Hong Kong, where the neighbours include the cream of the colony, and who can afford to keep an empty mansion on the Bridle Path, the most exclusive street in Toronto, until his wife decides what to do with it.

Not surprisingly, estimates of Lo's fortune vary widely. With his holdings completely screened from public view, he doesn't even show up on published lists of the colony's elite. "I'm very private. I never put my name in the magazines." Chan calls him a billionaire; others say he's probably worth less, but not a lot less. "Everything he has is private," a business associate says, his hand cupped over his mouth, lest other guests should accidently overhear him giving away state secrets. "He may not be in the top ten in Hong Kong, but the top twenty, easy."

His large family, led by his father, Law Ting Pong (who uses a different English spelling of the family name), came down from Canton in the early 1950s. They control a big chunk of the textile quota allotted to the colony by the United States. "They never have to do anything," a Hong Kong executive says. "They would be rich from selling their quota rights to other manufacturers. They never have to make any clothes." Law, the eighty-ish patriarch, whose private empire is separate from his son's, once paid $5-million (HK) at a charity auction just for a licence plate reading 8, a lucky number in Cantonese, because the word for eight sounds like the word for prosperity. (By contrast, you couldn't pay someone to drive around with licence plate 4—which, when pronounced, sounds like death.)

Lo and his wife finally agree to an appointment with that unctuous, smiling banker—they show up in tandem for business meetings—before heading off to Jamaica, next stop on the inspection tour of their widespread holdings. (Asked if she's looking forward to her sojourn in the Caribbean, Yvonne Lo shoots back: "Not really. I go from the hotel to the factory and back to the hotel again. It's all work.")

"The pace here is much quicker now than when I first came to Toronto [in the 1970s]," Kenneth Lo says in an accented voice so quiet it makes Alex Chan sound as if he uses a boom mike. "The bankers are much more eager to do business," he remarks. "Fifteen years ago, when I came, the Canadian banks were more like governments, big bureaucracies. Now, their attitude has changed. They're much more aggressive. The business people are all more aggressive."

That doesn't mean he's about to set up here. Just thinking about the high costs of making anything in this country is enough to give people like Lo a case of hives.* But he

---

* There are exceptions, but more typical is the case of one Chinese shoe and handbag manufacturer from the Caribbean, who says he'd love to start a factory here if the costs could be shaved by about 25 percent, or if the feds would give him a high tariff wall to keep out his own cheap products. Instead, he's looking into the fast-food business, apartments and shopping centres.

doesn't rule out moving his headquarters to Canada if things go completely sour after 1997, when Hong Kong reverts to Chinese rule. With modern technology, Lo could easily run his far-flung empire from anywhere in the world. "I don't think there will be operating companies here. There will be more corporate offices, with the operations in other [low-cost] countries." Even Hong Kong's become little more than a computer and design base for Lo. Most of his production's in more exotic locales like Jamaica, Malaysia, mainland China and Mauritius in the Indian Ocean, where the workers come dirt cheap and there are fewer hassles on exports to Western countries.

Like other Chinese, traditionalist Lo avoids the company—and companies—of strangers whenever possible. His business ties with Chan stem from a close personal bond that goes back years. The two first met in 1977 through Chan's brother-in-law, who used to work for the tycoon. Chan, then still a medical student, ended up as guardian for the Lo children when their parents headed back to Asia to mind their booming clothing business, after staying long enough to pick up the Canadian passports that would ensure their future safety.

"I never thought that this would become a business relationship, because for me he was always at the top of the world," Chan says, still amazed by the turn of events. "Why would he do anything with me? It is a surprise, in the sense that he's so big, and we were still struggling as a small developer. Why would he be interested? I said, as sort of a joke, 'Would you really trust me with all that money?' And then Ken said, 'I've seen you grow up. How wrong can you go? How bad can you be?' It is a trust that words cannot explain."

Maybe not, but it goes to the very heart of Asian dealings. It's why Chan's other investors are all friends, and shows that for all his efforts to build a thoroughly modern corporation, when it comes to business he hasn't really ventured far from his roots. It's why he can say with all seriousness that overseeing his company "is like running a big family"—and why he's not quite ready to admit outsiders into the closed circle.

Lo didn't put any capital into Chan's dream until 1987. He figured there was no point in sinking money into this country until his children were old enough to watch over it, another essential ingredient of Chinese family planning. But he was prescient enough to pick up the aforementioned Canadian citizenship for himself and every member of his family almost a decade earlier, when most of his wealthy compatriots were still wrapping themselves in the tattered Union Jack. He had considered Australia, but "Chinese people have to go where there are enough friends, where the community is large enough." Canada also offered more business opportunities, says the man who did nothing here with his mega-bucks until the Polygrand investment, apart from acquiring some houses he doesn't live in and some land north of Toronto. He's told friends he regrets not buying more real estate at the time.

The Los' vacant mansion sits on two of the most expensive residential acres in Toronto, where the Bridle Path meets Post Road—two streets favoured by new and old money alike. His wife, wondering what to do with the property, leans toward building a copy of a hotel she adores in Monte Carlo. Asked what she's thinking of spending, a prominent Toronto architect who's discussed the project with her says, "There is no limit. The sky's the limit. Money is not a factor."

They also have condos here and there, including the penthouse in a Polygrand building right beside, and linked to, the Essex Park—so its well-to-do denizens can order room service whenever they aren't in the mood to brave the supposedly safer neighbourhood. Chan also has a place there, as do several buddies: What are friends for if not to help keep property values high?

When the Los come to town, they stay at another of their homes, on the northern fringe of Toronto, where two sons and a daughter also live while attending university. Another son, their oldest, is already back in Hong

Kong learning the family trade. He's the only one slated for that apprenticeship. The others will make their lives here; and possibly the parents as well, after 1997. "Everybody is worried," Lo says of the mood back home. "Our family, we don't worry that much. We can still make a good living out of Hong Kong. We don't put all our assets there. Another five, six years, the picture will be clearer."

A couple of years before Lo decided he wanted to do some serious business here after all, Chan had started on a smaller scale with his brother, a couple of employees and the family money. They called themselves Flyton Developments. In Chinese, Flyton means "reaching out for the top." In English, it sounds a bit like a company that doesn't plan to stick around long. An image consultant suggested some names that would fit better locally, and Chan settled on Polygrand: *Poly,* because of the diverse backgrounds of the investors he was bringing together; *grand* because, Chan decided, it would be just that for them to team up.

Choosing a suitable English name can be a real headache. Multigrand was one choice rejected by the Chan gang. And they didn't even consider such sure winners as Polywonderful or Multimarvelous. Kenneth Lo says Varallo, which holds his Polygrand shares, has no meaning whatsoever. "We are very bad with names," he laughs. Toronto realtor and developer Frank Chau says the younger generation shies away from ethnically identifiable tags. "I use Goldyear. It sounds Jewish. Gold, you know." He says he really wanted to call his company Goodyear, but it seems this tire company got there first.

A lot of investors don't bother trying to find names to camouflage their activities or identities. They just hide happily behind bankers, lawyers and numbered companies, hoping never to be probed by nosy reporters, tax auditors or competitors. One consultant says that all the rich families have diversified—the code word for "getting the cash out of Hong Kong." This is just good business sense, even if there's no trouble with China. At least half of the fifty richest Hong Kong families (fourteen of them in the top twenty) are known to have investments here. That's remarkable, given Canada's relative unimportance in global finance circles, and shows why political stability has become this country's most important export. "I don't think anybody in town can give you an accurate number on how much has come into Canada," says the consultant, himself from a wealthy Hong Kong family.

The powerful Kwok family (ranked by published Hong Kong sources as no lower than third among the colony's super-rich) operates here under the thoroughly bland moniker of Ontario Land. When contacted in Hong Kong, the Kwoks say they couldn't possibly be of any interest to Canadians because their giant public company, Sun Hung Kai Properties, has no interests outside the colony, where it's easily the most cautious and conservative of the giant developers. "It has not invested overseas and is not likely to do so in the immediate future," a spokeswoman says flatly.

Ever sensitive to the stock market dangers, should already nervous investors in the colony think their captains of industry are abandoning ship, the Kwoks and other towers of power with hundreds of millions tied up in public companies usually do their foreign dealings as privately as possible. The Kwoks,* who've been involved in billion-dollar-plus projects at home (Sun Hung Kai's

---

* Not to be confused with the Kuoks or the Kweks, two powerful Singapore families. The Kuoks have poured some of their sugar-based fortune into Vancouver property, but decided a few years ago that the Toronto market wouldn't support one of their Shangri-La luxury hotels. Proof, says a Chinese real estate veteran, that even the best make mistakes.

The Kweks, who've made their billions in banking, trading, property and high-tech, sought to buy an existing West Coast developer as their splashy entry into Canada, but the deal fell through. Since then, "they are look-see, look-see," a Chinese source says.

generally listed no worse than second* among developers, behind only Li Ka-shing's mighty Cheung Kong flagship), have quietly moved into California, where they've
snapped up about $150-million (US) worth of property,
including a twenty-storey office tower in San Francisco;
or into Canada, where they've built a $130-million retail-
commercial complex in Scarborough, a favourite Toronto
area stamping ground of the new Chinese;† or that they
came close to sinking another $70-million or so into a
venture in Calgary, before deciding it didn't suit their
purposes.

Another of the land giants, Henderson Land Development, also mainly sticks to its steel knitting in Hong
Kong. Proprietor Lee Shau-kee does admit to personally
holding about $300-million worth of property here, half
in the huge Vancouver Expo lands with fellow magnates
Li Ka-shing, Cheng Yu-tung of New World Development
and smaller investors; and a large portion of the rest in a
180-acre residential development in Brampton, Ontario,
bought on an admitted whim, again with golfing buddy
Cheng. He's also picked up some real estate for a small
housing project near Point Roberts, Washington, at the
end of the spit of Canadian land that juts below the forty-
ninth parallel; but he struck out in a 1988 bid to buy the

---

* Sun Hung Kai also owns a securities firm, and has interests in cable
TV, hotels, buses, cinemas, construction, insurance and clothing. The
family patriarch, Kwok Tak-seng who died in late 1990, started by
importing Japanese zippers. *Forbes* estimates the family fortune to be
at least $1.4-billion (US). And the business magazine can only guess
at the hidden assets of people renowned for their skill at avoiding the
taxman and other unwanted snoops.

† Many Chinese immigrants and investors have settled on Scarborough,
in the eastern part of Metro Toronto, because they consider it luckier to
live toward the east, and they have taken the CN Tower as the city's
centre, insists Paul Cheung, a Chinese-born real estate deal maker. He'd
accumulated very little property in the area because he was "thinking too
Canadian" and focusing on the central part of town. Asked to explain
the sizeable Chinese community in Mississauga to the west, Cheung
says with a grin that these misguided types must have taken Hamilton
as the centre.

gas distribution business of B.C. Hydro because, reports say, the provincial government was still reeling from the backlash over the Expo lands deal.

The Expo '86 site was sold to Li Ka-shing in 1988 for a down payment of $50-million, with the rest of the $320-million—for 204.5 acres of central Vancouver—due in stages stretching into the next century. One local developer estimated that at current inflation levels, the property would cost Li about $120-million in 1988 dollars. The B.C. government was also planning to pick up the tab for cleaning up toxic waste on the site, which could run to $50-million. The development will have cost $2- to $2.5-billion when it's all done. What it will be worth will depend on the market, but vociferous critics both inside and outside the land business are convinced the deal was a great bargain for Li and the friends he took in later, led by Cheng and Lee.

Among the tycoons, only Li, king of the Hong Kong roost with a fortune most commonly tabbed at $2-billion (US) (though impossible to determine—estimates have ranged as high as a ridiculous $14-billion), has publicly stated his plan to invest at least 20 percent of his money—possibly double that—abroad. But then, he did get an early jump on the rest of the elite, buying property in North America when it wasn't yet the thing to do, and occasionally getting burned for his trouble.* His first Canadian investment dates back to 1969, when he acquired a shopping centre in British Columbia, long before his much more publicized oil and property purchases of the 1980s.

---

* Li made a disastrous foray into Texas real estate in the late 1970s, the kind of costly blunder avoided by the late Kwok Tak-seng whose caution and conservatism kept him on his own turf. Li was also reputed to have been angered over the terms of the purchase of the large Harbour Castle Hilton in Toronto—his first major Canadian acquisition—from Robert Campeau. But after keeping it on the selling block for years at what the industry considered an inflated price, Li finally unloaded it to the Japanese-owned Westin chain for a tidy profit.

Sydney Leong, lawyer, banker, property investor, director of the Hong Kong Futures Exchange, isn't one of the old colonial handful, like the Kwoks or Li or Cheng, of whom it's been said in all seriousness: "Every time they move, the earth shakes." But he's been amassing a considerable real estate portfolio in Western Canada and the United States over the past twenty years, run by two of his sons from Vancouver.

He oversees his quiet little empire from the conservative-looking offices of his private company, Henry G. Leong Estates, in New Henry House, a prestigious Hong Kong address just a block from Li Ka-shing's China Building. A secretary eyes visitors through a window at the main door. If you don't belong, you can't get in.

"We like Canada," Leong says, the candor spilling out like gold coins from a tightwad's purse. "It's a big country with good resources. There are good opportunities, good future. We have many relatives in Canada, on my wife's side. The people there are nice." Pressed for more details, a polite but anxious Leong says, "I don't think people who are new to a country should have a high profile." He'd be perfectly content if no one ever knew that he'd sunk some $400- to $500-million into North American property. By comparison, Kenneth Lo sounds positively effusive.

"Mr. Leong, what kind of investments have you made in Canada?"

"It's all on the public record."

"Can I get any information from your office?"

"No."

A journalist in Hong Kong explains that the colony's "a wonderfully simple place. Your status is determined by how much money you make. To these people, everything boils down to 'Am I going to make any more if I talk with this guy?' The usual answer's no, and this has and will cause problems for them in Canada. Canadians expect answers from everyone."

Alex Chan says his generation has no such problems. "I'm proud of what I've done. Why should I be afraid to

CHAPTER 3

The Defiant Ones

ALEX CHAN'S PASSION for privacy is understandable. By staying mum about themselves and their dreams, though, the Asian members of the hidden establishment have been inadvertently contributing to the gulf between themselves and the other residents of the communities in which they've been clustering.

The Vancouver cab driver, a typical example of the fearfully uninformed, breakfasts on weak coffee and strong cigarettes as she hacks her way downtown through increasingly heavy early morning traffic. The city's nowhere near the fume-choked chaos of a Rome or an Athens or even a Toronto, but it's a lot busier than it used to be. And with all the obvious signs of new money on the streets, one can only surmise that the grey market in Mercedes and BMWs is booming.

"The Hong Kong people, eh? They sure are everywhere. They own everything. They've really changed this city, I can tell you." She then launches into a guided tour designed to persuade her captive audience that the Chinese really do rule Vancouver.

"That hotel"—she points to the Meridien—"that's

Chinese, you know."

"Yes, but it used to be run by the French. And it was sold because it was losing money. And all the jobs were protected."

"This here's Robson. It's a tourist trap anyways, but the stores that charge the most—furs, jewelry, leather coats—they're owned by the Chinese. They always charge way more than white stores." The banal travelogue of off-handed prejudice continues, mercifully epithet-free.

She nods in the direction of Canada Place, with its striking white sails, constructed in time for Expo, and the definitive statement of bounding optimism for the city's shiny, cosmopolitan future. "That one, that's Chinese too."

"Japanese. It was built by Tokyu, a big Japanese hotel chain. The federal government wanted international participation in Expo."

"So what's the difference? I mean, I know there's a difference, but to me they're all money, lots of it. This city's changed because of them. It's not the place I grew up in, that's for sure. Not with the Asians coming."

For someone in her mid-twenties, the cabbie is remarkably nostalgic for the days when the order of things seemed clearer (and whiter); the pace of life more manageable; the future less threatening and uncertain. But most of the new Oriental faces she sees aren't fabulously rich. They haven't affected the property market nearly as much as some people like to believe.* And they share the same dream—her dream, except that she's never had to sit down and define it—of carving a place for themselves and their families out of good, solid Canadian bedrock.

---

* The Vancouver *Province* confirmed in a survey in June 1990 what Asian-born property masters have been saying all along: The city's "golden triangle," like most of downtown Canada, is dominated by the powerful domestic financial institutions, pension funds, big real estate firms and a handful of American and offshore investors able to tap into large pools of capital. Few of the "trophy" buildings, as the Japanese call the most prized office towers, ever go on the block. In about 1986, "we came up with a figure of about 5 percent of downtown Vancouver owned by Asians, including Chinese people who have lived here a long time and are actually Canadians," says high-powered real estate agent Andrea Eng. "But I would say that's probably increased to 7 to 10 percent, because the Expo lands are so massive." The top offshore investor remains British: Grosvenor International Holdings, part of the mighty fortune of the Duke of Westminster.

Mention the rich and formerly foreign, and the talk, even among some of the people who welcome the new money at the airport with open arms, and would be mortified to find themselves lumped in with the I've-got-nothing-against-these-people cab driver, frequently turns to the conspicuously visible Asian consumers flaunting their status at the top of the capitalist food chain. You hear about how little the so-called "yacht people" do in pursuit of their fortune-protecting Canadian passports; about how much real estate they're accumulating;*; about what lousy (often absent) neighbours and good shoppers they make; about how the local Mercedes dealer can finally afford that winter place in Ibiza or Hawaii, alongside the lucky luxury home builder.

And somewhere underneath the pat assumptions about who comes here and why—a step or two below the genuine anger over the fact that Canada does indeed peddle citizenship to some economic refugees while stiffing others who can't meet the price†—lurks an abiding sense of unease about the arrival on our doorstep of all that money bundled in distinctly un-Anglo packages and what it's doing to our cherished old values.

The people who feel this unease might never consider themselves racist, and even a few of the newcomers themselves would admit that some Canadians' concerns are

---

* Although some people have trouble believing it when they look around their neighbourhoods, Asian newcomers accounted for as little as 3 to 4 percent of annual home sales at the peak of the Toronto property boom. In Vancouver, where Oriental faces seem to be buying up everything, the Laurier Institute found in 1989 that the market was being squeezed by normal population growth and migration from other provinces. "If we seek someone to blame for this increase in demand, we find that the enemy is us, not some unusual or exotic group of residents or migrants," reported a study commissioned by the institute, a non-profit organization set up to combat racism by explaining why cultural diversity is good for us.

† A normally civil servant who's a strong booster of Asian investment and immigration (and whose wife is Japanese) said in all seriousness that we should deport one rich Hong Konger for every Vietnamese refugee forcibly shipped back to Vietnam by the callous colonials; the only difference between the two being a few million dollars or so. Another time, a lawyer who banks the bulk of his income from wealthy immigrants said it was ludicrous for Canada to let in his rich clients for as little as $150,000 (under certain investor rules in have-not provinces). "If you've got $8-million, $150,000 is the type of money you might spend on a vacation for the family."

understandable. But the fact remains that many Asians feel they are dealing with racism—subtle, quiet, even polite, but nonetheless palpable. To varying degrees, all Orientals must face the problem, and they do so in different ways.

It creeps edgily into the conversations of older Asian immigrants, who themselves hate making waves, but are unwillingly caught up in the giant one sweeping in from the Pacific.

"I've felt the locals feel threatened," whispers a wealthy Hong Kong émigré who came here a scant decade ago. "Canadians are very tolerant, civil. They don't say anything, but the quiet resentment is there. I have my resentments too [about the new arrivals]. The neighbourhoods are changing too rapidly. It's not a comfortable pace. The typical Canadian reaction would be to say nothing and just move away. But that's not healthy. It's up to people like myself to try to tell my fellow countrymen to be sensitive to Canadian values. It's to my interest to preserve a good image for my people."

One affluent suburbanite is hopping mad about the "ignorant" Hong Kong immigrants who've moved to his quiet street. "There were three empty lots. The front lawns were shrinking progressively for each house that was built, to the point there was no lawn for the last one. It was all paved! I find that repulsive. Imagine if everybody paved their front lawn. What kind of streetscape would that be?"

It sounds like the plot of a bad horror novel ("Slowly but surely, the living asphalt buried the unsuspecting town. . . .") or maybe an old Joni Mitchell song ("They paved paradise . . ."). What it isn't—though it sounds like it could be—is yet another diatribe about people with different habits, culture, language and . . . well, you know . . . skin colour coming in and ruining the neighbourhood. The speaker is a wealthy Hong Kong immigrant himself, from an old moneyed family, as worried about the aspersions he fears will be cast his family's way, as he is offended by the uncouth *nouveau riche* from the colony parking on his street and on their lawns. "I wanted to do something about it, but my wife said, 'No, no, let it be.' That's typical also of the Hong Kong mentality," says the entrepreneur, who asks not to be identified, for obvious reasons.

Kenneth Cheung, a frugal (he prefers Ponys and Pontiacs to Mercedes) Hong Kong-born operator of a busy Montreal real estate brokerage and a leading member of the Chinese community in his city, isn't crazy about the way some of the new arrivals display their success either. "I'm not an advocate of their lifestyle. In fact, I think much of it stinks. They come from a totally capitalist society which glorifies those who are very rich. By and large they don't have a social conscience."

He faults both the federal and provincial governments for not doing more to integrate immigrants into Canadian society—a complaint of many newcomers who say Ottawa washes its hands of them once they're consigned to the political ghetto of multiculturalism. But the second generation will be different, he promises. "They watch *The Journal* and go to hockey games."

The taxi turns on to a quiet, leafy street in a sedate, upper-middle-class district near Stanley Park and pulls up in front of a well-kept, concrete-grey apartment tower just before the dead-end. The owner, though the cab driver-guide obviously doesn't know it, is another wealthy person from Hong Kong, Lieutenant-Governor David Seechai Lam. When they're not at the official residence in Victoria, he and his wife, Dorothy, live here, where the two twenty-fourth-floor penthouses have been joined to give them an unrivalled panoramic view of mountains, water and bustling city—a Hong Kong kind of scene, minus a few million faces.

Lam is the ultimate symbol of what we like to think of as success Canadian-style. He's proof positive to the new money that, when all's said and done, we're truly an open-minded bunch with hearts as big as the prairie sky; that anyone here, regardless of where they come from or what they look like, can make it—if not to the pinnacle of power, then at least to the ceremonial outskirts. Of course, the powers-that-be must be smart enough to recognize the public relations value of appointing, in Lam's case, the perfect pitchman for the kinder, gentler, colour-blind Canada that's as alluring to the nervous money of Asia as the prospect of anguish-free immigration at bargain prices.

David Lam is a stocky, grey-haired man with broad features and the air of a studious bulldog. Thoroughly unpretentious, the Queen's rep puts guests instantly at ease with his warm, relaxed manner. The only thing missing is an accompanying smile, the unfortunate result of a case of Bell's palsy.

The illness struck in 1983, right after he announced his retirement at the age of fifty-nine from his lucrative real estate business, he says, laughing heartily at the jest played on him by the gods of work. It partially paralysed the muscles on the left side of his face, but had no other lingering effects. In fact, the energetic Lam is about to sail his forty-two-foot sloop up the B.C. coast with his less-than-thrilled wife in tow. "I was very afraid of the sea. He made me take courses. I get over the seasickness in half a day now," Dorothy Lam confides later.

Ensconced in his modern but scarcely ostentatious living room, Lam reflects on what his 1988 appointment as the first lieutenant-governor of Chinese origin—and an immigrant to boot—means to others coming here. "This is historical, a milestone not only for myself but for Canada," says the one-time Hong Kong banker, who rejected the job twice before deciding its symbolic significance outweighed any other considerations. Symbols can be awfully powerful, as Lam fully understands.

"Canada wants to tell the world that here we really do not care about your bloodlines, aristocracy or otherwise. Or whether you're born in this country. What we do care about is that you're a Canadian, that you serve the country and its people. And we will honour anyone. This, I believe, is the message, and it has been received very loud and clear."

He's right about that. Those who long for the days when white was right, and yellow, brown and black knew their place in the colour scheme called his selection Ottawa's admission that it is ready to hand over the country on a silver platter to cash-carrying Orientals. Nothing personal, mind you. But then it's never personal.

Lam, who immigrated in 1967 at the age of forty-three, with his wife, three daughters and enough money to buy a small house and a Japanese car, wisely steers a wide berth around anything that could land him or his position in hot water, though he's by no means muzzled himself. In his effort to build footbridges across the social and cultural chasms separating frenetic Far East from laid-back Far West, he's waded into controversy more than once. A couple of years ago, in response to the fever in the Vancouver housing market and a rising backlash over property purchases by absentee Hong Kong buyers, he suggested mildly that a home isn't a speculative commodity, and that one should be enough for anyone. This practically smacked of socialism to the colony's business buccaneers (but then so does anything else that doesn't give them free rein to do what they please). Hong Kong tycoon Cheng Yu-tung, who had not yet met the lieutenant-governor, called him "quite unfair. Maybe I have much more money to buy more than one house." (Ironically enough, Cheng—one of the investors in the huge Expo lands deal and the owner of the New World Harbourside Hotel, among other Canadian holdings—doesn't own even one house here.)

That could be why Lam hesitates to talk about issues like racism and the response to the Asian newcomers. "It's a touchy subject for me to be involved in," he says, skiing deftly between the flags. "I tend to believe that Canada has certainly come a long way away from blatantly racist practices, that we have come to be a role model for tolerance and understanding and harmony."

You can almost see the mandarins of multiculturalism smiling down as he speaks.

The words are comforting, and it's tempting to buy the role model routine; but there is too much barely concealed pain and frustration among some immigrants. For instance, the young Hong Kong-born woman who packed up and left Vancouver a couple of years ago: "You come across older people from England or whatever who feel they are superior. They are threatened by ethnic groups, you know, the Asians buying up all the property. So I moved to Toronto. I still run into a lot of problems because you're not a native Canadian. You haven't built up the connections. They don't want to know you. You don't come from their schools, UCC [Upper Canada College] or whatever. So you make up your mind to succeed without their help. They don't have to do anything for you. It's harder, that's all."

But even this businesswoman would admit it's not nearly as hard as it once was, when our sorry record would have discouraged all but the most desperate from trying their luck in a forbidding climate.

The Asians started coming here, some more willingly than others, during the days of the Cariboo gold rush in British Columbia in the late 1850s. From 1882 to 1885, Chinese were imported by the thousands to clear land and lay track for the new Canadian Pacific Railway line. They were nation-building, except that the nation wasn't ever supposed to be theirs. When the railway was done with them, it was hoped they might do the decent thing and quietly fade away. But many stayed on, scrounging work and trade where they could, joined later by Japanese, East Indians, as well as more Chinese; a handy source of cheap, transient labour permanently outside mainstream society—and a highly visible target when economic times turned sour.

The violence and intimidation, the seizure and destruction of property right into the 1940s would have been bad enough without eagerly supported government measures, like head taxes and other regulatory impediments, consistently thrown up by the "None is too many" crowd to keep Asiatic faces out of our midst. These included the federal Chinese Immigration Act of 1923, so effective that only eight Chinese officially made it into Canada between 1925 and 1944, compared to more than 27,000 between 1910 and 1914.*

"The Chinese in this country have always had very low positions," says Susan Eng, an outspoken Toronto tax lawyer and the city's first police commissioner of Chinese heritage. "So long as you knew your place, you could always be accepted. So long as you held those kinds of positions, serving others. But God forbid that they should procreate.† God forbid that they should go to 'our' schools and educate themselves at public expense, notwithstanding that they also paid taxes. God forbid that they should get into a university and take up all the places that really belong to 'us.' God forbid that they should become doctors, lawyers, poets. All of these things were denied the Chinese in this country until the forties."

As long as the numbers remain small and the immigrants relatively poor, "it's non-threatening. And the non-threat allows a level of communication and mutual exchanges that promote understanding," says Eng, born and raised in Toronto, an activist who couldn't mouth a politically pious platitude if her life depended on it. "So now if you have a whole bunch of people with a whole bunch of money, a lot of education, coming in as business people

---

* The odious act was repealed in 1947 and the gates were unlocked; but they weren't opened particularly wide until the 1960s. Nearly 48,000 Chinese arrived between 1963 and 1970, the bulk of them after the 1967 riots in Hong Kong and the easing of Canadian regulations that year. From the repeal of the 1923 Act to 1965, only about 36,000 Chinese came in, most of them relatives of earlier migrants.

† Chinese as well as East Indians were for many years prohibited from bringing in their families. Japanese immigration was virtually cut off by about the start of the First World War.

and professionals, it's a whole new world in Canada. That's a threat.

"Suddenly, everywhere you turn everybody is like somebody else. Alien. 'There are all these other kinds of people with whom I don't share values, and they are taking over. They are outvoting me. They are outbuying me.' So there's that community threat, where we see a lot of people all at once belonging to this other group. And we consider, of course, that this other group is totally homogeneous because they all look alike."

Kenneth Cheung of Montreal doesn't believe in lying low in the hope such fears will blow away. "Having a low profile just plays into the hands of the racists. If we Chinese help to develop Canada and make a few dollars at the same time, that's okay. We create wealth for the society."

Hemmed in by protocol and his own old-country reserve, David Lam wouldn't utter such sentiments in public even if he agreed. "I'm an optimist, so you're talking to someone who would not go out to look for problems. I always believe that if people go out looking for problems, they will find them every day," he says, reaching for a tall glass of iced orange juice brought in by his wife, Dorothy. A diminutive woman of considerable charm and simple tastes, she's far less comfortable in the spotlight than her husband and doesn't stand on any more ceremony than she has to.

Despite David Lam's politically proper public posture (you don't get to his status by shooting from the lip) he's no ostrich with his head in the sand. Aware of the tensions spreading from Shaughnessy to Scarborough, he pleads for patience with the newcomers and retreats into the brothers-beneath-the-skin school of race relations. "In the neighbourhood, it's only the visible minority that stands out. Two families is already an overwhelming majority." He measures his words with the care of a cleaner in a dynamite factory, repeating that the subject is a delicate one. "When the light is turned off, everybody looks the same. Then you assess without the help of your eyes. You just look at what they have done, what they are going to do, what kind of taxes they are paying, what kind of employment they are creating."

Lam, who cashed in his real estate business to devote his time and wealth to community work that cuts across ethnic boundaries, has long forced people to jettison favourite stereotypes — especially the ones about the money-obsessed Hong Kongers who only look after their own. A multimillionaire, he made his fortune through shrewd real estate buys for himself and powerful Hong Kong investors who'd come to know and trust him when he was still a senior banker in the colony.

So far, the clichés string together like pearls on a society matron: Hong Kong money, connections, real estate. Then Lam goes and ruins the comfortable picture when he starts giving his cash away and applying his considerable fund-raising skills to persuading others inside and outside the Chinese community to dip into their own bank accounts as well.

He's not alone. Listen to this wealthy Hong Kong immigrant who's disgusted by some of the tightwads (including a certain media magnate) who lord it over Canadian society: "There's one thing I will never understand. It bugs me and bugs me and bugs me. The rich people in this country are so selfish when it comes to donations to hospitals or to universities. They make all their money from this society. They should give something back. But they just keep on collecting [profits] until their sons or their grandchildren are all spoiled."

He tells of one well-known national retailer who gave $2,000 to a university for which he was raising money in the Chinese community. "That's a big insult. The people I contacted, I said, 'Don't give anything less than half a million dollars.'"

Lam tells a story designed to show the generosity of

the Chinese,* not to mention his own talent as a pump-primer. One day, he was sitting in a gym at the University of British Columbia, one of the major beneficiaries of his beneficence (to the tune of millions of dollars), waiting to pick up one of his honorary degrees. It struck him that the school needed a proper auditorium to do justice to such august occasions.

"I phoned my friend [in Hong Kong] and said, 'I want you to do something for UBC.'

" 'What is UBC?'

" 'University of British Columbia.'

" 'Have I been there?'

" 'No. I want you to build an auditorium. Give me $10-million.'

" 'I'm not even wanting to go to your country as an immigrant. Why should I be giving that?'

"I started explaining the importance of education and everything. He said, 'I'll send you a cheque.' I said, 'Don't.' I'm afraid that he'll send me a million dollars and that's it. I want ten. On the third phone call, he agreed."

The largest single private donation in the university's history was announced in the summer of '89 and quickly became the subject of intense speculation. Some observers said it must have been given by billionaire Li Ka-shing, possibly to assuage concerns over the controversial deal in which he and his friends acquired the huge Expo '86 lands.

But the $10-million donor to the university's new arts centre was later revealed as the Chan family, Seventh-Day Adventists known like Li for designating large sums

---

* "The Chinese," says Lucy Roschat, part of the hugely wealthy Shaw clan of Hong Kong and president of Cathay International Television in Vancouver, "are famous for three things. They love spending ... are very fussy about food [and] have a history of being very good charity-givers." Roschat won't divulge all of her family's holdings here because "we want to have a low profile, there's quite a lot of negative press." She also worries about jealousy in the community, and adds one other convincing argument for reticence: "I don't want to be disinherited at this point."

to charity. The patriarch, Chan Shun, who spun part of his fortune from making shirts with little alligators on them, had invested in North American real estate through Lam. His sons, Tom and Caleb, own the Burrard Building and the Hotel Georgia in Vancouver. They revealed their identity, with extreme reluctance, at the request of the school, which was seeking matching government grants. Newcomers are surprised by the backlash against them, Caleb Chan told *The Globe and Mail.* "What we are doing [with the donation] is saying: 'Hey, you are part of the fabric of the community and it's okay to do things. You are part of this community and you have to take some responsibility for it.' "

Their father was one of several high-powered Hong Kong investors who helped make Lam a success in the property game. The lieutenant-governor says he didn't plan it that way, but the only banks that offered him jobs would have shipped him back to the colony. That would have made the whole immigration exercise somewhat pointless, unless he'd only intended to pick up a Canadian passport. Instead, he took real estate courses at night school, starting a whole new career in his forties.

Once Lam decided it was time to cash in, he disposed of more than $100-million worth of property, mainly in California and Arizona, where he'd made the bulk of his money buying at low prices in a depressed market. "I didn't make my money in Canada much." So much for the made-in-Canada, rags-to-riches story we love so dearly. "Looking back, it was kind of lucky that I had no job," he laughs. "Fortunately I had made a lot of friends. Some of them had decided to make some investments here. I suddenly ended up with quite a number of companies that I served as president and a number of investments that required constant management."

When his rich buddies found out he didn't have his own cash to put in the deals, they financed his portion. The profits and the goodies rolled in, including homes in Vancouver, Calgary, San Francisco and Tucson. But he had other life goals that had more to do with

Confucian principles of moderation and harmony than with principles of accounting. "I didn't want to make the last dollar. I've seen too many people riding up high and crashing down. Not everyone is money-obsessed."

Lam set up a charitable foundation, intent on giving back some of what Canada had given him.* He says he was merely following in the family tradition. His father, a Hong Kong businessman who devoted his later years to education (he was the founding president of Hong Kong Baptist College) and church work, helped organize homes for the refugees who poured into the colony from mainland China in the wake of the Communist Revolution in 1949. "He has been my role model. He was never a rich man, but he had such a rich life." There's genuine passion in his son's tribute.

"I liquidated basically, much to the chagrin of my tax consultant. He said if I want to give my money away, make provision in the will. But that was quite against my desire to do something while I am alive and in good health."

He still rubs his hands with glee when he describes the sale of one particularly valuable building in San Francisco. Under a Canada-US treaty, the Canadian Lam wasn't required to pay taxes on his profit either there or here because he didn't own more than 80 percent of the property. The rules had just been changed to close the loophole, but wouldn't take effect for a few months yet. His advisers thought it a brilliant stroke to sell when he did, but it was pure chance. He'd bought the property for

---

* Lam's not the only wealthy Asian immigrant who claims such noble goals. Kenji Nose, a Japanese fish exporter, insists he'll eventually walk away from his enterprises to fulfill his long-time ambition of setting up his own charity. "I'm going to spend my money to help handicapped people. That is the duty of people who have good health. Right now, I am very sorry to say, I doubt that all the charity I am sending goes to the people. That's why I will do it myself." This road has already been taken by Stephen Sander, 56, who has turned over apartments worth $100-million to a charitable foundation he has set up. The Vancouver real estate entrepreneur came to Canada as a poor immigrant from India, and says he never acquired "the habits of the rich."

$5-million (US), using $1-million in bank financing and taking a mortgage on the rest. When he sold out, he picked up almost five times that amount — tax-free.

"Oh, how I remember that day," Lam sighs. "I made arrangements for my accountant and manager to come to my condo up on Nob Hill for dinner. My wife and I left the lawyer's office, and I said, 'Oh, we closed the deal. All cash. And we're putting all of it into the foundation. It makes me feel happy.' "

He suggested they take a taxi. But the ever practical Mrs. Lam said she'd rather go home by bus. "So I grabbed the first bus that came. It turned out to be the wrong bus. I said: 'Now what? We're even further away. Surely we'll take a taxi.' And my wife said, 'No. It's such a beautiful day.' So we started walking."

The lieutenant-governor pauses for a sip of juice. Meanwhile, I'm forming a picture of this couple wandering like lost travellers around the steep streets of San Francisco, carrying a cheque worth millions in a briefcase. Later, over dinner, his manager couldn't believe his ears. "You just pocketed twenty three and a half million dollars, and you took a bus?" Dorothy Lam says simply, "I find it very interesting to take buses. Don't you?" The fact they were worth millions never entered her picture. It helps explain why she didn't hesitate to encourage her husband's plan to give away what they don't need to keep the wolf away from the condo.

"Actions speak louder than words, always," David Lam says, summing up his philosophy. "It is no good to tell people, 'You have to be Canadian first. And you have to give, you have to serve, you have to care. You have to pay attention to the environment, to culture, to social problems.' You cannot say all that and make it stick unless you can add: 'Like me.' "

On the surface, P.K. Lui seems to epitomize everything cliché-clouded Canadians dislike about the new money: a skinny little rich guy who indulges expensive tastes, including the usual Rolex, top-of-the-line Cadillac and a suburban home with gland trouble. He wrestles the language to a draw on his best days and spends a good deal of his time back in the Far East. He denies it, but he likely moved his family here mainly because of the distinctly unnerving prospect of slipping under the of a Communist Chinese government.

What we don't see, what Lui won't show us without great prodding, is the gritty survivor who arrived in Hong Kong in 1975 as a twenty-five-year-old homeless immigrant from mainland China with exactly one dollar (HK) in his pocket and a fierce determination to make a better life for himself. Hard-working, humble, dedicated to his family, he was the embodiment of all our notions of what the proper immigrant to these shores should be like — with one important exception: He'd already made the startling transformation — from uneducated, poverty-stricken newcomer in a strange, unwelcoming land to multimillionaire entrepreneur — by the time he arrived here in 1984.

"In the history of Canadian society, the immigrant must always go through hardship and then things get better and better," explains Michael H. K. Wong, a Macau-born, Canadian-trained architect and developer with busy offices in Toronto, Calgary and Houston, who's designing projects and working on other deals for some of the highest and mightiest of Hong Kong, Singapore and Taiwan.

He rhymes off the travails of the early Chinese and Japanese, Ukrainians, Jews, Italians and others who clawed their way up the Canadian ladder. "Everybody thinks that's the only way to be a Canadian. And then a rich Hong Kong immigrant comes in and says, 'First, we're going to buy a big house. Second thing we're going to buy is a Mercedes-Benz. The third thing is to go to a prime corner. I want that corner, that corner.' Canadian society is not used to that kind of thing. Suddenly, this five-foot-six, 120-pounder, that's my boss. I don't want to say that's jealousy. It's not their custom. They're not used to it, because they already expect that somebody has to suffer to get it better."

The son of a manager of one of Hong Kong's powerful family empires, Wong was a rare specimen in the University of Manitoba's architecture department in the mid-sixties, a time when most children of the colony's comfortable class were heading to the States or England for such schooling. He was told when starting out here that his was a name better suited to a restaurant than an architect's office. Advised to take a Canadian partner and appellation, he remarked, "If that's what it takes, then I picked the wrong country." He'd already made a concession by turning his Chinese given name, Hung-Kai, into his middle initials.

"In the old days, people always thought being Chinese was a handicap in Canadian society. I feared that in the early years. But later on, I learned to accept it as a part of life. And then in the last few years, I learned that being Chinese or a Chinese-Canadian was more advantageous then disadvantageous. Because we know both worlds, we are ahead of everybody." Wong laughs the last laugh.

P.K. (as he calls himself) Lui, who stands barely taller than five feet but looks smaller, is used to being typecast at one end of the money spectrum or the other. "I already had some experience with discrimination coming from China to Hong Kong. You have to expect some discrimination as part of the environment, rather than expecting the environment to change to suit you," he says reasonably. Unsure of his English, which is functional but inadequate to express his complex thoughts, he sticks mainly to Chinese, relying on his interpretive assistant, Eva, and later her replacement, Alice.

Lui's fine-boned frame, immaculately garbed in dark dress pants and a crisp white shirt, slouches in one of the pink chairs arranged around a pink-and-mauve marble-topped table in the conference room at the snazzy Canadian headquarters of his busy STD group of computer and electronics companies. Models of his computers sit at one end of the room. Photos of other STD products lining the walls are the only other decorative touch.

His shiny new building is located on a barely finished street in the mushrooming industrial parkland that's eaten up some of the rich farm country north of Toronto. Evidence of construction dots the moonscape; buildings unfinished . . . roads unpaved . . . lines undrawn. Altogether a fitting location for someone whose biggest dreams remain to be filled in. In fact, with the black and white uniform, the unlined, worry-free face and short black hair parted on the side, Lui looks more like someone just out of school than the chairman of a group of companies that employs 1,000 people in North America and the Far East.

Lui's no Alex Chan or James Ting (whose own International Semi-Tech offices are nearby), who've built their corporate worlds from scratch here, with the helping hands of powerful door-openers in the Orient. Working without the aid of a safety net in the dog-eat-dog capital of free enterprise, Lui converted raw energy, enthusiasm and nerve into a respectable little empire in a period of time that would seem unbelievably short anywhere but Hong Kong.

Just after going into business for himself little more than a dozen years ago, Lui frequently had to sleep on boxes in his tiny factory, because of the long hours he was putting in to keep his business running. Today, his fledgling Canadian operation alone brings in sales reaching eight figures annually; and he's determined to goose that amount, producing whatever will take seed in what many of the natives have written off as an entrepreneurial wasteland.

"In Hong Kong, you can make snap profits," explains a banker from the colony. "Here you have to have patience. Things don't evolve as quickly. Even if you want to move fast, everybody else has to do the same. Canadians aren't the slowest, but they are slow. They [the immigrants] can't change the system, so they have to adapt."

Lui is proof of that. "In my fourth week here, I set up my company and hired an English-speaking manager. We drove from Montreal to Vancouver and then to America — New Jersey, Dallas, Ohio, Indiana — to do market research. I went to the government, to libraries, to electronic industry associations. All this took about seven months."

His careful homework showed him he couldn't make the tranformer coils he'd planned, because there was no one to sell them to on this side of the ocean. Always flexible, he turned to battery rechargers instead, later distributing the batteries (from Japanese giant Matsushita) as well. Within a year, he figured he knew enough about the North American market to jump into computers, selling 4,000 his first year.

So much for the stereotype of the wealthy Asian citizen-to-be who does nothing but lounge around in his pyjamas, taking a breather from the hyperactive pace of business life back home, idly flipping through real estate ads and jewelry catalogues. A few do fit the role, admitting when cornered that their lives and work are still on the other side of the world. "Most are not equipped or not willing to start businesses here, except as an extension of their business in Hong Kong," a rich immigrant says of his countrymen. But eventually, they too get itchy to test their mettle here, especially as it becomes increasingly evident that their families prefer life in the slower, wider Canadian lane. Besides, their free-wheeling days back home may be numbered anyway.

One entrepreneur with a burgeoning business back in

Hong Kong makes the most quintessential of cheap Asian products — disposable toothbrushes for the hotel industry. He only intended to stay in Canada three years, take his passport and run. Instead, he found he could make the throwaway plastic items at about the same cost here, with lower rent and hydro and more automation. Today, he owns a large factory and employs ten people turning out a product for which there is as yet no serious market in North America.

"A misconception is that money just falls off trees in Hong Kong," says a former school teacher in the colony who's now a senior banker here. "They work very long hours and really take risks. With every risk, there are successes and there are failures. What we see in Canada are only the successful ones. Because if you are not successful, you cannot leave."

The perpetual optimism of people like Lui, the banker tells me, is part of the very make-up that enables them to rise above the horde in the first place. "It's a big decision to move thousands of miles to a strange culture. For someone to make that sort of move they have to look on Canada as something very positive. Having worked so hard all their life, they want some place sure for their money, something more stable, a place good for the next generation."

Lui's formal schooling ended in China in 1966, when he was sixteen and the Cultural Revolution turned his life, and the lives of so many other unfortunate young urbanites, upside down and inside out. For seven long years, he laboured on a communal farm far from home, setting up a power-supply station and broadcasting information for the peasants. He then made his way to Hong Kong, where freedom, sweat and opportunity in a plastics factory awaited at $17 (HK) a day. To survive in one of the world's more expensive cities, he took a part-time night job at the same place, toiling 112 hours a week to support himself.

After three months, he landed a better job at an electronics firm, giving him the time to take night courses in electronics engineering, management and English — essential to get ahead in the colony where he was making less money than his assistant, who could speak the language. Within two years, he was in charge of the design and maintenance of the company's equipment. But he knew that at twenty-seven, he'd get no further without going out on his own.

Still studying by night, he started an electronics venture, Standard General Electric (later shortened to STD General Industrial and then to STD), sleeping on top of those boxes in his rented 500-square-foot factory. He didn't have much of a life apart from work and school, but did manage to squeeze in two dates with the company accountant. She must have liked the bottom line, or the movies they saw on those dates, because she agreed to marry him. They have a nine-year-old daughter and two sons, aged seven and six — who are, without a doubt, the three main reasons the immigrant from Communist China picked up and moved again. With his experience in the Cultural Revolution still etched in his memory, Lui was determined to settle in a country that offered maximum freedom and where his children could get the education he never had.

He landed here late one cold night, eager to get started in his exciting new home, to build a future for his young family. After a few fitful hours of sleep at a friend's house, he rushed downtown to be on time when the bank opened its doors. It was 7:00 A.M. "I'd had some money sent from Hong Kong to the bank in Chinatown and I wanted to make a withdrawal," he says, alternating his own halting English with fluent Chinese filtered by his assistant. "But there was nobody there. I waited and waited, but nothing was open. I paced up and down the street for hours. It was March, so it was still very cold."

Canadians don't seem to work as hard as people in Hong Kong, he now says. But, ever the pragmatist, he's not knocking us for it. Hong Kongers have to work without benefit of the Canadian social safety net. "It's like a rich family that has left its children many assets. They don't have to work as hard as children from a poor family."

Just when he seems to be on the verge of serving up some fresh insights, the Eastern stoic skips right to the newcomers' paean in the immigrants' hymn book, Page 1: "In Canada, it doesn't matter where you are from. If you can prove you are hard-working and can stand on your own two feet, you will be accepted." Maybe they hand out instructions with the immigration forms: Repeat this at least ten times every day, and you too will be eligible for honours, awards, seats on multicultural boards, maybe even a government appointment.

Somehow it seems unlikely that Lang Chee would ever mouth the right words. The Indonesian-born businesswoman is too aware of the barriers that may still loiter, like a surly street gang, to greet the unsuspecting new kids on the block. Her advice for neutralizing them isn't the kind you'd hear from David Lam or some of the other older, don't-rock-the-yacht immigrants.

It's a sure bet that no one who's ever met Lang Chee can ever again think of the new Asian money as a bunch of filthy-rich, neighbourhood-destroying passport collectors who can hardly wait to get back to their life of luxury back home; she could single-handedly bury just about any set of clichés ever cherished about immigrants from the Orient.

Too busy turning what is traditionally a man's world on its ear, this fast-talking bundle of raw nerve and nuclear energy avoids such unprofitable self-indulgences as examining why some people look down on others because of their skin colour or their sex or the size of their bank accounts. Chee, who deals cars and develops property in the vast desert of outer Toronto, flips stereotypes upside down even as she refuses to acknowledge those who cling to them for comfort like Linus to his security blanket.

"I feel sorry for them because they're so narrow-minded," exclaims the no-nonsense entrepreneur in the no-nonsense wire-framed glasses and short dark hair just starting to turn grey. People who try to fit complex, rounded people like her into simple, square holes won't find seats at her ringside.

She starts counterpunching at the bell, hammering cheap prejudice into the ropes as if it were some flabby, over-the-hill fighter who couldn't carry her gloves. "They've got no knowledge of the world around them," she says, firing an upper cut. "They'll be small businessmen all their lives." A left hook to the moneybelt. "It's the big people who are open-minded who are the leaders. It's only small-minded people who feel this way. It's their problem, not mine." The knockout blow of indifference.

"Nothing really bothers me in life. Why bother worrying about what people think of you? They can call me all kinds of names. I just ignore them and laugh it off. If you believe something strongly enough nobody can stop you — not the government, not your neighbour, nobody," says a woman who's made a career of barrelling through every obstacle ever put up between her and her destiny.

Impatient at the thought of wasting even a precious second on people who count for less than zero in her scheme of things, Chee talks in staccato bursts, clipping off the ends of sentences, often throwing in a "Don't you agree?" to make sure the listener's on her hectic wavelength. She works the way she speaks — at warp speed. It's exhausting just watching this mid-sized dynamo firing on all cylinders from behind a cluttered wooden desk in a small, unadorned office tucked away at the back of her huge Toyota franchise out here in car dealers' heaven, a vast suburban shopping zone inhabited only by the tigers and the lambs.

One diamond-ringed, gold-braceleted hand dials and faxes, while the other, worried about being left out of the fun, sifts and organizes papers. When Chee is put on hold, she jumps quickly to another line, starts reading her mail or calls up something on her computer screen —

sometimes all of them at once. But when the phone finally cooperates and stays silent for a few moments, she visibly relaxes, laughing frequently as she returns the balls tossed her way — most of which are lighter than the bird's-egg-sized chunk of diamond-decorated jade descending from a gold chain over her silky black-and-blue, short-sleeved dress.

"It's no good to blame the world for your lack of success, because who will listen to your complaints anyway?" she smiles. "You shouldn't let setbacks bother you. If you really want to be successful, you can be. You just have to keep trying. If you want something, go for it."

It sounds as if she's sat through one too many car sales meetings in her day, the type where the troops gather in an overheated hotel ballroom to boost their cholesterol levels, swap sheep-fleecing tales and nod off during pep talks from the head office. But Toyota executives, who wish a journalist luck trying to get a word in edgewise with her, say Lang Chee could have given Norman Vincent Peale lessons on how to bolster his self-confidence; and after listening to her self-edited life story, it's easy to believe them.

Chee was born in 1940 into a Chinese family of considerable means on the Indonesian island of Sumatra, just before the Japanese swept in and forever changed their quiet life. Her father, acting on his belief that "you have to have a country before you have a home," worked in the (mainly) Communist underground against the Japanese, and later, when they didn't keep their promises, against the British.

He was arrested as a Communist and shipped back to China when his daughter was only thirteen. "He had taken me everywhere with him, so I knew his beliefs. After he was gone, I did what he used to do. I carried messages for the underground and distributed Chinese propaganda. I had a stencil machine and I used to write what I thought he'd like. I knew the British could search the house, so I buried the documents in the backyard."

Despite her precautions, the precocious subversive was

nabbed by British soldiers and tossed into jail — at the age of sixteen. Her mother, also not the sort to let impediments stand in her way, bribed the corrupt local government; and Lang Chee was soon on her way to safety in Singapore, returning only after Indonesian independence three years later.

"My mother had a very strong character," Chee says. "She always believed if you want to do something, then do it. And I believe the same thing. I'm a very strong-headed and stubborn person. If I believe something can be done, nothing can stop me."

Chee proved it shortly after buying, in 1981, the Toyota dealership that now serves as her headquarters — one of several franchises she accumulated after the Japanese auto giant made her its first female dealer in 1976. Personally supervising extensive renovations to avoid hiring an expensive contractor, she bumped heads with the tradesman assigned to install the ceramic tiles. He tried to take advantage of a tight schedule by charging her ten cents more per square foot than the $1.25 she thought they'd settled on. That was a mistake. Chee told him she'd do the work herself. He was sure she was bluffing, and others told her she was crazy. But they didn't know this woman, who'd grown up listening to her grandfather expounding at the dinner table on the trials and tribulations of running a business empire in a society where he was a complete outsider, who'd faced down far bigger challenges before she was out of her early teens than most of us would ever dream of in a lifetime.

She worked on her hands and knees until 1:30 in the morning, learning as she went along. She came out of the experience with a sore back and bruised, cut hands, but with her tile floor, her principles and her iron will firmly in place.

How on earth did a messenger for the Communist underground in a strife-torn Asian country come to be laying floors here in the first place; to acquire not one, but six lucrative Japanese auto dealerships (the others have since been sold at fat profits), in a high-pressure world traditionally dominated by loud men with clothes, cigars and bellies to match; to make a killing on the stock market when a lot of smart people were getting killed; to break up with her husband of twenty-two years because "life is too short to be unhappy" — but still get him to do her taxes?

When the teenaged Lang Chee's forced exile in Singapore ended, she went to work in Kuala Lumpur with a large company that supplied furniture for the newly developing Malaysia. Her ambition brought her considerably more than she bargained for when she was promoted from bookkeeper to buyer: the money and gifts poured in almost immediately. There was jewelry and cash and deposits into her bank account, all of which, she quickly realized, were bribes from suppliers designed to ensure she'd make the correct decisions. Barely nineteen, only a couple of years removed from her underground existence, she had a chauffeured ride to and from work, and was taking home some $2,000 (Malaysian) a month, more than many workers would see in a year. She worried, though, about how to get herself out of what could turn into an extremely sticky situation. And she had other troubles to contend with.

Chee had fallen hard for a lecturer at the local university and wanted to marry him; but her mother didn't like his dialect and ruled that his family wasn't wealthy enough for him to qualify as a suitable suitor. Like any good Asian child, she'd been taught that her parents' word was law, and had been completely obedient — to the point of risking her life to carry on her father's work. Now, trapped between love and duty, she took her problem to a trusted family friend, a philosophy professor who played his proper academic part.

"My dear child," he intoned, "you can't worry about pleasing everybody. No matter what you do, you can never be right. It's better to please yourself first."

Chee still recalls that scene vividly; rarely has such

mundane advice been acted on with such utter finality. "It's so true, so very true. From that day onward, I never bothered about pleasing anybody but myself," she exclaims. Leaving behind both mother and boyfriend, happy to be away from a life of white envelopes stuffed with illicit cash, she headed for Australia.

Finding a lowly job as a junior bookkeeper — at twenty-five dollars (Australian) a week, with none of the perks of her previous work — she set about trying to get into night school to study accounting. It wasn't as easy as it might sound. She didn't have her high school graduation certificate, and the Aussie bureaucrats wouldn't let her in without it. Just another obstacle she'd have to overcome.

Every evening for three months, Chee showed up to bug the same hapless administrator to let her try the entrance exam despite her lack of credentials. "I can do it, I can do it," she'd plead. Finally, he gave in just to be rid of her; and she was on her way.

Moving with typical what-have-I-got-to-lose boldness into the strange corporate world of Caucasians in pinstripes, she became a tax specialist, working for appreciative bosses who helped her obtain valuable stocks. She cleaned up when their value skyrocketed during the boom years of the late sixties, reaping a return of up to 500 percent. It wouldn't be the last time Chee would make a big score in the market. The day after the October '87 crash, she rounded up as much Canadian Imperial Bank of Commerce stock as she could afford, having spotted a bargain in the conservative bank known for its Asian business connections.*

---

* The CIBC has close ties to Hong Kong kingpin Li Ka-shing, who likely owns under 5 percent of its shares, although published reports have often placed the figure at closer to the maximum 9.9 percent allowed a single investor under Canadian law. They first got together when Li, then a little known plastics manufacturer, contacted the bank's rep in Hong Kong in 1969, seeking advice about investing in a B.C. shopping centre. He bought the plaza. An irritated rival banker calls the link-up "a stroke of brilliance, but it had some luck to it. When they struck their deal, everyone was asking; Who's Li Ka-shing? He wasn't even regarded as a rising star at that stage."

The smart player jumped in at about seventeen dollars a share and left the game when the price hit thirty-one dollars. She won't reveal how much she raked in from either her Canadian or earlier Australian coups. But she didn't come here in need of bottom-rung clerical work.

Lang Chee arrived in the summer of '71, attracted by the low real estate prices and the usual immigrant's shopping list of "clean" and "green." She noticed a helpful ad in the subway that advised: "Buy a piece of Canada." And that's exactly what she did. Intending to return to the more agreeable climate of her home down under, she was only hunting for a quick in-and-out investment of the kind that turn critics of foreign real estate speculation red with rage. But Chee just kept adding to her property portfolio and never did leave.

She obtained part-time work with an accounting firm, because she preferred staying home with her two-year-old daughter. There was also a husband in the picture somewhere, a fellow numbers-cruncher she met in Australia. But he doesn't figure prominently when she talks about her life and times. The two live apart, though it's obviously an amicable arrangement. He still does her tax returns, while she gives him investment advice.

Her mother came to stay after the birth of her second child, a son; and she jumped back into the labour pool, signing on as an accountant at a floundering Toyota dealership. She was shocked to discover the inexperienced owner couldn't even read a financial statement, but agreed to do what she could to bail him out of his mess — until a better offer came along from an Italian builder friend, who was urging her to go into business with him. When the car dealer realized he was about to lose his lifeline, he offered her the whole business.

Chee agreed to the purchase (for $315,000) — before consulting her husband or her mother, who by now must have been used to it.

Things worked out so well that Toyota asked her to run a new dealership, the jumbo franchise where she's now comfortably based, hand-laid tiles and all. She is also a partner in a couple of property development ventures, owns six and a half acres around her dealership and was the leading player in a major car-leasing operation, until selling out 40 percent of its assets for $27-million in mid-1990.

"I worked for big firms in Australia at a very young age, and it's a very chauvinistic country," she says, launching into what still drives her. "Women were always second class or whatever you want to call it. But it never bothered me. I always got the job I wanted. I always wanted my boss's job and I always told my biggest boss I wanted my immediate boss's job. If you're good, if you're clever and you're worth the money, you should never be afraid to speak out. Nobody can do something for you if you won't do things for yourself. It doesn't matter if you're a man or a woman." I'm starting to feel sorry for the bosses.

She practises what she preaches, refusing to give her daughter, a commerce graduate from the University of Toronto, a leg up in the business world — in the belief that she'll be stronger if she learns the ropes the hard way. And she sent her son off to Upper Canada College, bastion of the old guard, so he could be schooled to be a leader instead of a follower. A questionable strategy at best, but one rooted in her refusal to acknowledge the barriers that might keep her child from taking his rightful place among society's elite. I suspect the old philosophy professor would have approved.

Like P. K. Lui and so many others, Lang Chee can and will take huge risks without fearing the consequences; she will try things the older, less assured generation of immigrants wouldn't have dared. As long as the barriers can be shunted aside, as long as their children have a secure future, this generation can laugh at whatever's thrown at them. "These are very stoical people," a banker says. "They train themselves to be. They make a decision and accept it. They understand that it's not going to all be smooth sailing."

As Lui says, it's just part of the environment; you adjust because you have to. Once they've scraped the bottom and survived, everything else seems like a breeze. If they lose it all, they'll just dust themselves off and start again. "It wouldn't matter what job I had — even a housekeeper or a maid, it wouldn't bother me. If you can find peace within yourself you'll be okay," says Lang Chee, turning back to her desk full of work.

CHAPTER 4

The Sun Also Rises on Canada

THE WINDSOR ARMS is a historic little Toronto hotel, redolent of old money. A national institution for a good part of its sixty-one-year existence, it's been home at tea time to the carriage trade; rest stop of the literati and glitterati; and, in more recent times, the preferred choice of the "let's do lunch" set and power breakfasters who bask in the reflected elegance of the Courtyard Cafe. It seems only fitting that this proud emblem of class and gentility, tucked away on a quiet side street off the bustling midtown intersection of Bay and Bloor, should be run by a cultured person with a taste for the finer, nobler—preferably British—things in life. It is. But that individual and the group of investors for whom he purchased the hotel in the fall of 1989 are actually Japanese—a bridgehead for the wave of new private money washing over the Canadian landscape from the still cautious and conservative land of the rising yen.

That Japanese citizens should own a Canadian landmark is not so strange these days. Loaded with more cash than they know what to do with, and looking far beyond the remarkable export successes that have

aroused so much bitterness among their trading partners, the Japanese have been on a global shopping spree
unprecedented in modern times. They have left both the
haters and lovers of things Japanese (few people ever seem
to be neutral about this ambitious people) gaping in awe at
the trillions of yen that have been gobbling up soaring office towers, illustrious brand names, historic icons, glitzy
casinos and resorts, castles, vineyards, even entire hotel
and store chains in Europe and North America.

While other Japanese investors have picked off some
well-known Canadian hotels, among them the Harbour
Towers in Victoria, the Nancy Greene Lodge in Whistler,
the Banff Park Lodge, the Harrison Hot Springs Hotel
and the Bow Valley Inn in Calgary, as well as a slew of
small shopping centres and apartment buildings (preferably furnished), Mitsuhiro Kuzuwa has much more ambitious plans. The self-made billionaire, who picked up
the Windsor Arms for a group of friends—and on his own
acquired about $30-million worth of real estate in and
around upscale Yorkville, the yuppie version of heaven
in midtown Toronto—remains something of an anomaly
among his ethnocentric countrymen. Few of the other
investors, if any, would ever actually think of moving
abroad, leaving behind their relative security and social
and cultural certainties for the risks inherent in far-off
places, full of strange people with irritating habits and
impossible languages. Yet that is exactly what Kuzuwa
appears determined to do.

Apart from the intrepid few, individual Japanese of means
rarely ventured or moved money abroad until a few short
years ago—and were restricted from doing so until the
mid-1960s. What the rest of the world has usually seen
is the impersonal face of Japan Inc: the pinstriped samu-
rai helping corporate Japan reach across the globe in
a remarkable display of manufacturing, marketing and
financial might. Then, marching behind the Toyotas,

Mitsubishis, Toshibas and the rest of the corporate elite guard, has been a lengthening column of smaller firms, driven overseas by the demands of their major Japanese customers and the soaring value of the yen, firms which even six or seven years ago would never have dreamed of leaving their own backyards.

Now, the first individual investors like Kuzuwa are wandering out of the dense and protective Japanese forest, perhaps tentatively and nervously at first, unlike their more adventurous—and often more desperate—counterparts from elsewhere in Asia. But they will inevitably mark the course for a vast wave of new money to follow, all dressed up but with no place to go at home anymore. In a country where many home owners are millionaires, at least on paper (tiny condos run about $800,000 apiece in Tokyo, and a modest suburban home might cost $5-million or more), once-humble family fortunes have soared into the multimillion-dollar range and beyond, creating new wealth independent of the giant corporations. In a society where there has tended to be less disparity in incomes than elsewhere between the bosses and the fabled "salarymen" who keep the system functioning, and where the lifestyles of both have been pinched by high costs, crowding and the real and imagined lack of resources, these newly rich are as eager as other Asians of influence and disposable cash to find a safe haven; a nice, secure investment overseas at what they consider bargain-basement prices.

"We're just starting to see the emergence of a wealthy class in Japan," says Michael Goldberg, an authority on Asian investment and head of the International Finance Centre in Vancouver. "My guess is that the Japanese pattern will follow the pattern of other wealthy families. It's still very new. The Japanese have strong family units, but the dominant unit has always been the corporate one. That made it different from Chinese and European investment, where it's largely been family-based." The Japanese, he says, "are going to start to do much more private investing the way the ethnic Chinese invest," buying condos in Vancouver or small shopping centres in Toronto "just for portfolio diversification."

It's already happening. A kimono manufacturer plunks down $100-million (US) for a resort in southern California without even blinking at the price. The owner of a traditional inn, or *ryokan*, on the outskirts of Tokyo, sells a sliver of his land and uses the excess cash to pick up a hotel near Banff. The operator of a simple *pachinko* parlour (*pachinko* is the Japanese version of pinball, a national craze) goes shopping in suburban Toronto for a tasteful little plaza for $15-million. Their property in Japan alone makes them no-risk borrowers in the eyes of their bankers. A golf broker (only in Japan could someone who trades solely in golf club memberships even survive, let alone grow filthy-rich) spots some too-good-to-be-true bargains in Hamilton, where he and his investment buddies take over the Sheraton and go hunting for places to play some cheap golf.

Real estate people like to tell of the Japanese family that went shopping for a golf course and asked the price of one they had taken a fancy to in a rural area. "$4.5-million," came the reply. "You don't understand," the head of the family said politely. "We don't want a membership. We want to buy the whole club." The story has taken on legendary proportions, because it perfectly matches the new Western image of the Japanese as people whose pockets are spilling over with gold, and who find prices for everything here—with the exception perhaps of fish and cigarettes—so ridiculously cheap they seem unbelievable. There are problems with this image. A lot of Japanese would consider themselves fortunate if they could afford a weekend outing to Mount Fuji. The image, though, does fit a growing moneyed class looking for opportunities abroad.

Most such investors still have no intention of following their money. Like the wealthy European families, they prefer to ship their cash to trusted advisers or loyal retainers who hunt down the hotels, office buildings and other investments, and who stay around to manage them for fat fees or a piece of the action. Sometimes, the investors get ripped off, as in the case of the wealthy Japanese high-tech speculator who placed $39-million with a Quebec entrepreneur and wound up in court to get his money back.

Mitsuhiro Kuzuwa, philosopher-developer and self-confessed lover of art and culture, fits the new image of the wealthy player to a tee. Eager to expand into North American real estate, but lacking the international knowledge or experience of the major corporations, he had a tough time getting started here, even after he had settled on Toronto as the place to be. He has said he wasted five years relying on bad local advice, proceeding by trial and error in the unfamiliar market, before finally settling on a set-up to his liking. Now he obviously intends to make up for lost time. He isn't merely looking to diversify out of his overpriced homeland, where his still lucrative property investments—mostly in major provincial centres like Fukuoka and Kumamoto in the south and Sapporo in the north—are increasingly hemmed in by incredible land and construction costs.

Kuzuwa's fledgling Canadian property empire, which could be worth upwards of $300-million when projects now on the drawing boards are completed in the next few years, is not the last redoubt of a refugee fleeing the nightmares of Communism or, as is the case for some wealthy Japanese, the grasping clutches of the taxman. He has, it seems, peered into the future and doesn't like what he sees happening in his native land. A large chunk of his family's future, he has decided, must rest outside Japan.

"In his case, it is entirely different from Hong Kong people," says Fumihiro ("just call me Fred") Shida, a former Sony executive who runs the show here for Kuzuwa under his corporate cloak, Jasmac (for Japan Store Management Corporation) Canada. "He did not come because he is afraid. His strict reason for coming to Canada, I figure, is his understanding of economics. Kuzuwa is always looking for the effectiveness of the return on his investment. The return is not necessarily to his pocket. He always says business should be a social asset, creating opportunities for people. Profit is only the catalyst to keep that social operation going." And in overcrowded Japan, where high costs are increasingly outweighing rental incomes that would have Canadian landlords drooling, energetic developers like Kuzuwa are quite simply running out of room and profit margins. They know full well that they can get a far bigger bang for their buck just about anywhere else.

Shida-the-middleman is as close as most of us will ever get to his spotlight-shy boss. Like other wealthy foreign investors, Kuzuwa needed someone who knew the local ropes to protect his interests here. But individual Japanese are newer to the game than the Europeans or even the rich Chinese families, and lack their networks. As a result, they tend to ship over employees who, they hope, can learn on the job. The Okabe family, for example, buyer of the Coast Hotels chain in British Columbia, sent an affable employee, Eiichi Tomita, from the Chicago office to run things. His only previous experience was in the family's main business, selling industrial fasteners.

Fred Shida was already here, but his experience in real estate was minimal. He got around the problem by turning to Tina Robertson, a real estate consultant with a silver Rolls-Royce and a clientele to match, whom he had met when he was in marketing with Sony and she was a fashion model. "I frankly told her my frustrations when we met. She said Jasmac is the spearhead of Japanese [property] investment here. If we do a bad job, other Japanese won't come."

Shida's small, cluttered, temporary headquarters is in one of the historic houses Jasmac has purchased around the corner from the Windsor Arms. There is barely enough room in the narrow front office for the electronic lifeline to Tokyo—the Sony microcomputer, the Toshiba copier, the Epson printer, the requisite fax machine—let alone one visitor. Kuzuwa's niece, Satsuki Aikawa, bustles in with some green tea. The jeans-clad business school dropout helps with the office work as she begins learning the business ropes from the bottom. Aikawa plans to stay in Canada, where she has a better chance of rising at least a few rungs; unlike in her homeland, where a woman's place is still not in the executive suite. She shares a condo on the waterfront with her cousin, Nobutaka Kuzuwa. One day, he'll probably be running things here for his father, but his immediate task is to get through his own studies at the University of Toronto. He is not involved in the business yet. His father considers it far more important to be steeped in art and culture at a young age: Business knowledge, he says, is easier to acquire and can come later. The elder Kuzuwa stays in the condo—the family's only residential property in Canada so far—on his infrequent visits to Toronto. He'll be sorry to see his niece move into her own apartment. She makes a good miso soup.

It's one of the few personal notes Shida drops about his boss. Shida himself remains friendly but nervous throughout a lengthy interview, punctuating his comments with a surprisingly boisterous cackle. The picture he does draw is of a tycoon who doesn't much act like one. He never flies first class, for example. But he does have a large house near Shibuya, in one of Tokyo's most fashionable districts, and another just for guests. A photo in one of the company's Japanese-language publications shows a somewhat formal, grey-haired man, but with an open, friendly smile revealing a set of rather crooked teeth. "He's worth over a billion dollars for sure, but he doesn't show it," Shida says, smiling as he points out his boss amid the glossy shots of his latest projects. Kuzuwa himself shuns the limelight to the point where even the gossipy local Japanese community knows little about him or his plans. He appears to have toiled obscurely in the trading business until he found his true niche in property development some sixteen years ago, at the age of forty-two: just one of countless Japanese businessmen who have cashed in big on the domestic real estate boom. There are, however, a few interesting differences.

Shida, like his boss, has a deep distaste for publicity of any kind. When *The Globe and Mail* was about to reveal the $30-million Windsor Arms purchase by Edoken Canada, a group of Kuzuwa's friends whose interests here are managed by Jasmac (which gave the previous flipping owners a tidy profit of $1-million for each of the eight months the hotel was in their hands), Shida was mortified. "You don't have to write an article, do you?" he pleaded when called to verify the scoop. He didn't want to talk partly because the deal hadn't closed yet. But he was also well aware of the bad press the Japanese had been getting for their acquisitive ways, and he wanted no part of it.

Taking over American cultural icons like Columbia Pictures, Rockefeller Center, 7 Eleven stores and a few carats' worth of Tiffany's brought down a wrath the always sensitive Japanese should have anticipated but obviously didn't; and it may have been why they dropped out of the bidding for another big trophy, the Sears Tower in Chicago.* When they started buying up hotels, restaurants and gift shops in the Banff area, they provoked a backlash from some Albertans who feared they were about to be squeezed out of their own tourist industry and national park, both over-run with Asians.

It's easy to dismiss such reactions as racist—as they often are in Japan-bashing exercises—but that doesn't mean there were never any grounds for concern. Michael Goldberg, a big booster of Asian investment in Canada, was furious when he heard that a Japanese government official in Calgary had been scolding the business community for being too parochial in its attitude to the Banff investments. "Somehow, it was almost like an American producing pax Americana. This was pax Japonica,

---

* Though it didn't stop Matsushita from going after Hollywood giant MCA in a $6.1-billion (US) deal. Arch-rival Sony already had Columbia, and Matsushita wasn't about to let U.S. sensibilities stand in the way of its global strategy.

that they had the right to do this. It was very insensitive, and given the Japanese record on the Gold Coast in Australia,* the concerns that people have in Banff are legitimate."

More than one Canadian-based Japanese executive was irritated as well by the buying binge in Banff, saying off the record that they wished their countrymen would show more consideration for local feelings; and expressing their fears that the natural surroundings, glutted by tourists, might be harmed. One disgruntled expatriate said he used to enjoy going to Banff when there wasn't a Japanese tour group everywhere he turned. At the same time, he and others in the Japanese community reminded me that the Banff "problem" was caused by unsophisticated investors who simply didn't know any better. That was not the case in Los Angeles, New York, Washington and, most of all, Hawaii, where powerful Japanese companies began buying up property at a clip that turned them into major U.S. landlords virtually overnight. Hawaii, labelled by some economists now as nothing more than a "recreational colony" of Japan, has attracted the bulk of the big real estate players, including the biggest of them all, Yoshiaki Tsutsumi, whose name usually comes with the tag: "the world's richest man," excluding royalty (estimated worth at least $16-billion (US), down from $18.9-billion a couple of years ago, because of an unfortunate shift in the yen-to-US-dollar exchange rate, according to *Forbes* magazine).

---

* The Japanese turned the resort beaches of southern Queensland and northern New South Wales into a virtual extension of their domestic travel industry, a point obscured by the racist backlash provoked by the property purchases. "The typical tour to the Gold Coast goes from Japan to Brisbane by JAL," Goldberg says. "You're picked up in a Japanese-owned bus that's typically made in Japan. You're conducted to a Japanese-owned hotel, where you're going to play golf with Japanese clubs and [which will] probably import a fair amount of Japanese foodstuffs. You're going to hire domestic Australian help, because you can't afford to bring Japanese in. But there'll be Japanese management. Very little money in that system leaks into Australia."

Tsutsumi, fifty-six, whose fortune is based on an inherited commuter railway and the land under and around it, controls a vast web of companies in Japan, which pay so little corporate tax that the normally quiescent Japanese press has begun sniping at him. What is less well known is that he was an early private investor in both Toronto and Montreal, including property and a couple of Japanese restaurants. His best-known Canadian foray is a single sixteen-year-old hotel in suburban Toronto, part of his huge Prince Hotel chain, the largest in Japan. Oddly, despite the hotel's success, the always conservative Tsutsumi has yet to expand elsewhere in Canada. Rumours persist that he built it only to have a far-off place to send a black-sheep relative.*

In any case, the climate toward Japanese property investment was growing cool when I first spoke to Shida; and, if anything, it's worse today. U.S. politicians have begun talking seriously about restricting foreign investment—with the Japanese as the specific target, even though Europeans remain by far the dominant foreign players—after demanding for years that other nations open their borders to American money. But that's what happens to the rich kid on the block whom everyone else loves to hate. And the Japanese, with their unsurpassed global financial power, have replaced the Americans as that kid.

Shida emphasizes that Kuzuwa has no intention of joining those of his countrymen who've become Japanese versions of the "Ugly American." For him, globalization

---

* Tsutsumi, a traditionalist, would know about such things. He is a son and principal inheritor of Yasugiro "Pistol" Tsutsumi, who had six other children. Yoshiaki's older half-brother, Seiji, infuriated his father by joining the Communist Party as a student in the 1940s. He was cut out of most of the Tsutsumi property and railway fortune, but built his own multi-billion-dollar department store, real estate and hotel empire. Not on good terms with his richer younger brother, whom he only met at the age of 14, Seiji controls Inter-Continental Hotels, among 100 or so other companies in his Saison Group. It manages and has a stake in a new Toronto hotel that bears its name.

is more than a buzzword. Unlike other Japanese corporate leaders, who extol the virtues of creating manufacturing and marketing bases around the world while continuing to make all the important decisions and many of the minor ones back in Tokyo or Osaka, Kuzuwa has come to Toronto with an entirely different mission: to build something of deep and lasting value for generations to come. He is laying the foundation for a made-in-Canada fortune.

Apart from his initial investment, "he won't do the Canadian business from Japanese funds," Shida says, gesticulating with his hands to make sure the point comes across. Hockey-stick thin, he is full of nervous energy. "He told me: 'You have to create something which is useful to Canadian society.' His representative, either his son or myself, has to make the decisions in Canada and be Canadian. His son is going to start here, he will stay here and he will die here. He doesn't like the idea of Japanese going overseas and controlling another country. He is investing in Canadian society. A Jasmac investment has to be a social asset." It may be just the party line, but it's a good one, and Shida appears to believe every word of it. The former Sony man insists it was Kuzuwa's enlightened approach to investing here that drew him to work for Jasmac in the first place.

"Please wait to write," Shida urges, "until we can show we are good corporate citizens. We just want to be good citizens of the community." It is a refrain heard countless times from other Japanese, even from some whose employers have been busily pillaging resources and fouling the environment in various parts of the world for years. Most of the executives who spout similar lines are here only on temporary assignment. In another three to five years, they will be dishing out the same pablum in a different country—if they are unlucky enough not to be recalled to head office. What they often really mean is that they don't want to make any waves or get anyone riled up during their brief stints, lest it cause problems for their companies and hurt their own chances of promotion later.

In Jasmac's case, though, being a good corporate citizen may actually be more than a stock phrase contained in some Japanese handbook on how executives should behave overseas. Shida's below-the-collar hair, his mustache and flashy clothes—his expensive light brown suit is quite a contrast to the standard dark Japanese business uniform—give him a rakish air that would make him most unwelcome in a Tokyo boardroom. You instantly accept his word that he and the Kuzuwa family are here to stay and would not want to have to live with the consequences of an unpopular project. "Imagine if our name is on such a building." Inquiries reveal that Shida has been taking great pains to reach the kind of community consensus and support so beloved by the Japanese, well before submitting any of the company's development plans for official approval. Shida says, "We go to the neighbourhood people first. If there's a problem, we will change it, if it makes sense."

He has apparently done such a good selling job that some local business people are eager for Jasmac to get on with an ambitious proposal to redevelop an entire Yorkville block into a major retail and residential project. An influential local businessman who has bitterly battled other major developments that threatened the "look" of the low-rise area says he is deeply impressed by Jasmac's apparent commitment to the neighbourhood; and with Kuzuwa's instructions to high-powered architect Boris Zerafa to design the best project possible, regardless of the cost. Kuzuwa also requested the maximum residential component, when it would have been more lucrative to build offices or additional stores. "He wants to do a quality development," says the businessman, pulling out an artist's rendering of the proposed six-storey complex. "It might be one storey too high, but look at the streetscape. It's level with the neighbouring buildings. All of the height is in the middle of the property. I have no quarrel with that."

Kuzuwa, who employs about 2,000 people in his various Japanese projects (mostly run under separate corporate entities), is not your everyday Japanese real estate billionaire who throws up a building and then sits back to watch the rent money roll in, as the property value shoots skyward. He actually avoids office buildings, the cash-cows of the business, and concentrates instead on hotel and retail developments, like the one planned for Yorkville. Typically he will both own and operate 75 to 80 percent of the boutiques, galleries and restaurants in his projects—giving him a much more active role, and more control, than most developers would ever want. Normally, they are the deal-makers and rent collectors. That's not how Kuzuwa sees it, as Torontonians will discover when he eventually opens his large, exclusive shopping and residential centre in the heart of Yorkville, on a site that includes the original Mount Sinai Hospital.

Shida makes two fists to explain the company's strategy. One holds the assets which, as in every other property business in Japan, have been rising meteorically. But gathering rents and watching assets appreciate is passive, and uninteresting to Kuzuwa. The other fist contains the sizzle: the ever-changing shopping, gallery and restaurant mix that gives the real estate whatever freshness, vibrancy and allure it's ever going to have. Shida clasps his hands together to show how Jasmac seeks to combine both elements. "We buy land like other developers, but once we have built it, we work hard to operate it, to create something," he says proudly.

Kuzuwa has refined tastes, perfectly suited to a spot like the Windsor Arms. For his recent developments in Japan, he has flown in British and Italian architects. When he purchased an aging, Western-style building that dated from the heyday, sixty years ago, of the old commercial port of Otaru on the northern island of Hokkaido, he kept the facade. Inside, his English architect and interior designer carved out an elegant hotel, with a huge restaurant but a mere thirty rooms—each one different and some with ceilings triple the standard height. In another project, a shopping mall in nearby Sapporo, he discovered a natural hot spring at the site and had it included in the design. It must be one of the few malls in the world where a shopper can stop for a sauna. In Toronto, he intends to combine the talents of Zerafa, a top Canadian architect introduced to him by Tina Robertson, with those of Japanese interior designers. The old Windsor Arms will apparently remain as it is, at least outside; but it will be neighbour to a large new condo project. When a similar plan was broached by the hotel's previous owner, it provoked local anger. But Shida promises that under Jasmac's guiding hand, the condos will not be so high or obtrusive, and will fit in better with the district. The early evidence is that Jasmac will seek to do just that.

After the Windsor Arms story appeared, Shida was swamped with calls from real estate agents from as far away as San Francisco, peddling everything from top-notch hotels and shopping malls to empty fields. He wasn't interested, and in fact never buys anything that way. But after having operated in virtual secrecy for a couple of years, he suddenly learned what just about every Japanese banker, broker and trading company executive here already knows. An exasperated Japanese banker put it best after fielding yet another pitch to invest in some business venture: "They think that because I am Japanese, I must have lots of money or that I must know someone with money. It's not true, but they never believe me. Canadians and Americans should not complain about foreigners buying up their land, because they are bringing them in." He pulled out a stack of letters and feasibility studies designed to attract foreign investors for projects ranging from industrial condos to golf driving ranges. One not-to-be-missed deal offered some vacant land near Niagara Falls for a mere $15-million.

Despite occasional appearances to the contrary, the Japanese do not buy just anything that's nailed down. They love collecting prestigious baubles that show the world they've made it. They are after what everyone else thinks of as top of the line, the Van Goghs—of art, office buildings, herbal remedies, laser technology and shopping districts—and they are willing and able to pay remarkably high prices to get them. Shida promptly dumped Jasmac's first piece of Canada—a vacant lot bought by his predecessor on the funky part of Toronto's Queen Street West—when he decided it was not going to turn into a prized retail block that might also attract wealthy residents. He found that spot in Yorkville, where a lot of the new money is settling, with little regard to the asking price.

Real estate pros are sometimes astounded at what Japanese buyers like Jasmac are prepared to pay for property they want badly enough; although most agree they are shrewd and cautious negotiators who happen to have different motives than local investors. Several developers admitted they would have given their custom Porsches for the choice Yorkville block assembled by Shida for Jasmac, but no one was going to try to match the money he was offering. "It's almost as if the Japanese won't touch it unless they know it's been flipped a few times," says a Toronto lawyer who has grown fat off such deals. "Maybe that reassures them that they're buying the best." Or maybe, he muses, the Japanese just feel better knowing that a few Canadians are getting rich before they move in. Because, as more than one expert on Japanese buying habits can attest, once they're here, they're usually here to stay.

Not all Japanese new money takes the shape of absentee investors gobbling up real estate. A short walk from the Windsor Arms is an unobtrusive little Japanese restaurant called Okonomi House. The eatery, which serves a Japanese-style pancake (*okonomi-yaki*), was the starting point of the thriving business constructed in Canada by Kenji Nose, a Japanese entrepreneur of more modest means than Matsuhiro Kuzuwa, but of perhaps even greater ambitions as he sinks his roots deep into Canadian soil. Nose, who came to Canada to stay in 1977, is in many ways a throwback to the poorer Japanese immigrants of earlier times: tough; independent; determined to break away from the yoke of family tradition or to escape a life of dreadful hardship. But the small man with the big dreams and the fax machine in his basement is also a symbol of the new landing gentry—immigrant investors who have money jangling in their pockets even before they get off the jumbo jets ferrying them over from the Far East. Nose, the only son of a self-made Osaka businessman, is just as intent on carving out his own empire in his adopted homeland as any of the gut-busting workers who came decades ago to work the West Coast logging mills, fisheries and orchards. The difference is that this unorthodox, energetic entrepreneur happens to have access to a nine-figure family fortune to eventually back up his bigger-than-life schemes and dreams. And, as Canadians are coming to realize, he is not alone.

Nose (pronounced no-say) is so casual in dress and manner, it's sometimes hard to believe he has singlehandedly built from scratch a company that annually rakes in more than $25-million. Most of it comes from fish exporting, which quickly supplanted the restaurant business as Nose's main interest; but he still calls his company Okonomi House and still owns the midtown restaurant, which is licensed to another operator for a monthly fee of $2,000 plus all costs. He will eventually collect royalties from another Okonomi House, opened in uptown Toronto by the manager of the original spot, but not until it's in the black. When we first met, his small real estate portfolio included his unpretentious split-level home in northeast Toronto, amid the suburban sprawl of Don Mills (favoured nesting ground of Japanese expatriates*

---

* It's somehow fitting that these most orderly and cautious of people should be irresistibly drawn to Don Mills, Canada's first planned community built some thirty-five years ago by the late E. P. Taylor. Back in Osaka, a typical suburban lot the size of Nose's would easily hold two large houses.

and a stone's throw from Tsutsumi's cannily located Prince Hotel); and three condos in Mississauga, two of which were on the block. He was looking to acquire a thirty-five-unit apartment building, and had bought and sold other properties. But for Nose, like many entrepreneurs, real estate is just a game to throw some idle cash at. His real business goal is to become Canada's fish marketing king—sort of a Shoppers Drug Mart of herring peddlers—as he sets about his personal mission to teach people of the world's greatest fishing nation how to buy, cook and eat their own catch.

In his headquarters, incongruously located in one of the gold-clad Royal Bank towers in the core of Toronto's financial district, this rumpled, relaxed-looking man is talking business with the local condo pusher, who figures that if the target is Japanese, he is worth pursuing. In his preferred attire of sports shirt, slacks and a pullover, with his sleepy Peter Lorre eyes and a ready laugh, Nose looks anything but the aggressive entrepreneur who is already a millionaire in his own right, and who will one day inherit many more millions—even after Japanese estate taxes.

In fact, what Nose really loves to talk about is his long-planned, three-to-five-year, 'round the world sailing voyage of personal and family discovery—a lifelong dream. With other topics, he quickly becomes restless, his mind wandering to the next deal or a golf game somewhere. He doesn't much like conversing in English, and avoids it whenever possible. He happily concedes that his children know more about his adopted country than he ever will.

"Sometimes I go to Canadian parties, but I always feel like going home right away," he says with a laugh, stubbing out his cigarette in a full ashtray and lighting yet another in an endless chain of Rothmans. "With Japanese people, there's no problem for me when others are speaking. With English, when you get used to it, you don't listen to what they are saying, just what they want. When a salesman telephones, I say, 'I'm sorry. I can't understand,' so it's easy for me [to refuse]. I'm not saying I don't like non-Japanese. Nothing like that. Just simply, it makes me tired out and nervous to be with them, to listen to English all the time and try to understand. And I try to explain, and they say, 'Pardon, pardon' all the time. It's too inconvenient. I understand the minimum English which is necessary."

But ask him about something really important—his dreams and aspirations—and he immediately comes alive, dropping his inhibitions about English, leaning forward to make a complex point. Sailing around the world is no idle daydream for someone as driven as Nose. Drawing on his training as a naval architect, he designed his own sixty-foot aluminum-hulled ketch, choosing the appropriate name *Dream.* When the company he had hired to build his $800,000 pride and joy, Aragosa Yachts of Unionville, Ontario, teetered on the edge of bankruptcy, he promptly bought a 60 percent stake, talking the boat builder's remaining four customers into buying up the rest and leaving the former owner in charge. He walked away from the unprofitable investment after his boat was finished. It was a typical move from someone who could not let his dream be beached by mere technicalities after coming so far. "If you have a dream, you're not going to give up, never. You will find a solution," Nose says with the confidence of someone who has risked and lost before. "Once you have a dream, once you make up your mind what you want to do, you think about that all the time. All the time!"

His dream—not just of making the meticulously mapped voyage of discovery but of building something important before devoting his later years and all his energy to charity—is the driving force underlying everything he does in business; and it goes a long way toward explaining how he landed here in the first place. "If something goes wrong, then that [dream] reminds me: 'Kenji, if you do this, you cannot make your dream. You will not be able to finish.' That pulls me back. Without a dream like that, it would have been easy to stay in a comfortable job, like most Canadians and Japanese. It makes a big root in your heart. You cannot destroy it and you cannot give up."

The dream has been setting his course since he was about ten, and his father would take him down to the fish market where he did his daily shopping for his restaurant. It led him to study fishing technology in Japan; and, as a twenty-two-year-old graduate student in 1965, it brought him to St. John's, where his Canadian saga first began. (The bittersweet tale of love found and lost, of two irreconcilable cultures, of family loyalty, of obligation, honour and responsibility unfolds later, as he sits devouring piece after piece of what must be the most expensive sushi in Toronto. He occasionally eats at his own restaurant, "but that's fast food, for young people.")

About seven years before Nose's arrival in Newfoundland, his father—on the advice of his doctor—had retired at the unusually early age of forty-five, selling off his busy restaurant and three public baths, but wisely retaining his property investments. "He was told he could either keep the business and die or give up the business and look after his body," his son says of an iron-willed father who is still alive more than thirty years later. With no active business to inherit, young Kenji was left with two options: to work for someone else or go off on his own. The decision was easy. His father, the second son of a farmer, had been on his own since he was sixteen, and Kenji was going to prove he could do it too. Besides, he'd never achieve his dream any other way.

· In his characteristically straightforward way, Nose explains why, of all places, he ended up in St. John's, where the culture shock was immediate. "My hobby is to sail boats. I don't like to buy a boat someone else has designed. You cannot be 100 percent happy. The only way is to design the boat yourself. My professor [of naval design] came to Newfoundland. So I came too." There, he turned up his nose at the food ("They threw away the crab. They were eating spaghetti in cans! They didn't know how to eat"), but found the women much more to his liking. He married one from the tiny fishing hamlet of Fairhaven, much to the distaste of his family—and hers. After his father cut off his money supply, Nose left school and moved to Calgary as a draughtsman, figuring he would never be accepted back into the family fold. But less than a year later, the old man, perhaps softened by the birth of a granddaughter, asked him to come home with his family to Osaka.

There, he started a restaurant business and other ventures, all with his father's backing. But his Newfoundland-born wife, unable to speak the language and pregnant with their second child, couldn't quite cope with the move from a village of maybe twenty homes to a city of dizzying neon and noise, with huge throngs of people jamming the sidewalks from morning till evening, looking for all the world as if they are waiting for some popular parade to march by at any moment, when all they really want to do is cross the street. It was as though a harp seal had been suddenly thrown into the shark pool, a frighteningly alien world marked by a pace considered aggressive even by Japanese standards. The first Mrs. Nose lasted all of two months before heading home to have her baby. She never returned; Nose stayed in Osaka and the marriage unravelled, the victim of a huge cultural and economic gap.

About two years later, at twenty-seven, he hooked up with his former Japanese high school sweetheart, Junko, who was a year older. Finding that Japanese law didn't recognize his Canadian union, he remarried. This was unusually late for a Japanese woman to be tying the knot.

Discussing the differences between the way women are treated here and in Japan, one expatriate businessman said that, even nowadays, if a woman is still working in Japan in her late twenties, she is considered a "leftover. Regardless of her skills or abilities in the workplace, people think that if she is still working, it's because she has no place else to go. And once they are married, they are not wanted in business." One married businesswoman with no children says she was fortunate to find part-time work in Tokyo when her husband was transferred back there.

(In another disturbing case that reveals how far women still have to come, a Japanese banker in Toronto sought to fire his Japanese-born receptionist when he found out she had a child but was unmarried.)

In Osaka, the Noses had three children, and proceeded to raise a happy family. All the while, though, the fate of his Canadian kids gnawed at Kenji. "The longer I spent in Japan, and the more money I made, the more I suffered thinking about my son and daughter in Newfoundland." A subsequent visit convinced him that he should be in Canada, at least while they were growing up. Not coincidentally, it would also give him a chance to work on his own fortune far from his father's disapproving eye. Nose returned to Canada for good in 1977, settling in Toronto—along with the majority of the new money.

Like Nose, many immigrant sons of wealthy families are driven by the desire to get out from under their fathers' thumb—although few will voice it quite that way, especially when they are looking forward to a large share of the family money some day. "When I was young, I was very much against him. And then I learned the hard way. About seven or eight years ago, I had $15,000 in my pocket. That's all the money I had. I thought to myself: 'My father is a millionaire and he never helped me, he never gave me anything.' " That isn't quite true, as Nose freely admits. One of his ventures in Osaka, a roller-skating rink and bowling alley, slid into the gutter, sticking his father with about a $1.2-million loss. "It was my business, but we cannot tell people, 'Sorry, we cannot pay,' because we had the money," Nose says, revealing much about how a proud and honour-bound Asian family conducts its business. "So my father paid the debts. Since then, he has shut his purse like an oyster."

Without his father's signature, it's doubtful a Japanese bank would have given Nose a free calendar, let alone the financing to set up his own business. It was time to seek his fortune elsewhere. "In Canada, I felt like I was on solid ground. In Japan, I felt like I was moving up a creek and on ice."

He goes on to describe, as so many Japanese do almost by rote, life in a resource-poor country with too many people, too much red tape and too few entrepreneurial opportunities. The myth of the poor nation that must always sacrifice to survive endures, even as the Japanese accrue unbelievable wealth and material success. The Japanese ambassador to Canada once told a conference in Newfoundland that one of the few differences between his country and the island province was the latter's incredible wealth in natural resources. The Newfoundlanders must have been delighted to learn how rich they actually were.

Nose has his own version of the national mantra: "Canada is different from Japan. There's lots of room, lots of resources and many things you can do. Japanese have to struggle to survive. Canadian people are happier. They don't have to work hard. In Japan, you have to work and work all the time only to support yourself. In Japan, it is very difficult to have a dream."

The younger generation is no longer buying this line, and that poses its own political, social and economic problems inside Japan. Tsutomu Iwasaki, an independent Japanese consultant and former mining expert with Sumitomo, is from the old school that believes wealth should be the result of accumulated years of hard work. He disdains the new trend among Japanese people of jumping into quick-buck speculative investments and property purchases, the way it's done in North America. "One young girl, a university student, told me, 'We are richer than those Canadians.' This is terrible, terrible," he moans. "This is not the attitude that helped Japan build itself up."

Among the older Japanese expatriates, he needn't worry. They recite the proper refrain at the appropriate times, often accompanied by an insulating layer of superiority, a deeply ingrained belief that other people, especially the rich Canadians, are soft because they have not been shaped by the same crucible. If only—they sigh wistfully—Japan had had this vast, empty land to shape, instead of those crowded little islands. "In a sense, we feel so sorry

for Canadians not to know the Japanese way of thinking,"
Nose says, summing up a national view.

Nose, who started off modestly as owner-chef of his
fast-food restaurant, didn't exactly follow a carefully designed life plan to become an ace East Coast fish exporter.
In true Asian fashion, he had wanted to set up a business
that his Canadian-born son from the first marriage, who
was living with his mother in Newfoundland, could one
day inherit from him. "I thought I had to do something
with him, so I started a fish business. There was nothing else in Newfoundland, for my eyes." The venture,
a dried-squid processing plant, went belly-up for lack of
one simple ingredient—the squid. It seems they were simply not cooperative joint-venture partners, disappearing
from local waters just as the plant was being finished in
1980. Nose bailed out, selling to another processor in exchange for taking over the mortgage. The ill-fated venture
cost $150,000. "We lost entirely what we spent. Still, we
had to do something to survive, so we started buying fish
and selling to Japan."

The fact he knew nothing about minor details like trading, shipping or marketing was hardly enough to deter
Nose for even a minute. He had a friend in Newfoundland who would supply the fish, and he knew his Japanese compatriots were always in the market for suppliers
they could count on. Starting with a borrowed desk in
the downtown Toronto travel agency owned by another
Osaka native, Sam Fujii, Nose began hunting for customers. "The first year, I remember, I spent more than
$15,000 [in expenses] and got only $2,700 back [in com-
missions]. But I knew it was going to be growing. If I stay
in my restaurant, I may have a guarantee to make some
kind of living, but it's no progress. And even though I lost
money, I just bet my life on this business."

Luckily for Nose, he had done considerably better with
this gamble than in his weekly mah-jongg games, where
friends say he typically—and cheerfully—loses large sums.
Nose sold $372,000 worth of fish in 1981, his first full year
in the business, nearly ten times what his restaurant had

brought in the year it opened. The next year, he raked in $1.8 million. By 1986, he was counting up $11-million worth of exports and thinking of designs for his dream boat. By 1988, when Nose was shipping $25-million worth of East Coast fish to eager Japanese buyers, it was time to plan that long-delayed trip to romantic isles in faraway places, as pictured in his beloved collection of *National Geographic* magazines, fifteen years' worth of which lined the shelves in his office—near the oil paintings of New-foundland derrymen and the outdated map of the world.

Not every wealthy Japanese immigrant investor wants to leave a mark on Canada or Canadians. Some would be just as happy to blend into the luxury neighbourhoods of Van-couver and Toronto, never to be heard from again. Take the case of Fred Shida's predecessor at Jasmac Canada, Elizabeth Edo, and her developer husband, James. When Canadians think of conspicuous Asian wealth, they are very likely to form a mental picture of a James Edo, who scored big and fast at home, and who has parked himself in Canada where he can enjoy a pleasant lifestyle at a remarkably low cost. Blue-suited and starched-collared, the gregarious Edo and his glamorous wife live quietly but luxuriously in north Toronto and, occasionally, in the Caribbean at their handsome winter hideaway on the Cayman Islands. A rich developer, he showed up in Toronto a few years ago, single and looking for property and a wife—not necessarily in that order. Elizabeth Edo was then a real estate star who specialized in peddling com-mercial property to Japanese clients.

Nobody has anything much to say about the Edos for the record. There is perhaps no other Japanese couple of such wealth about whom so little is known in the tightly knit Japanese community; unusual for a group that loves to trade juicy tidbits around the bridge and mah-jongg tables and in the karaoke bars that now speckle downtown

Toronto. There is a lot of speculation about Edo's past, though, among those who have met or heard about him. They wonder aloud how he could have amassed so much money so quickly.

Publicity-shy, even by Japanese standards, the Edos stay determinedly out of sight. Elizabeth Edo, who speaks excellent English and seems to do the talking for her husband, flatly refuses to be interviewed and is extremely agitated to be reached at her unlisted home number. "We do our business and we don't want anyone to know," she says in Japanese. "My husband is not interesting to you. He brought his money from Japan. This time, we would like to pass."

Besides her obvious charms, Elizabeth Edo apparently had at least two things that appealed to her future husband: Canadian status and a real estate licence. It couldn't have been her cooking. Acquaintances say Elizabeth, who decided to stay in Canada with her daughter when her first husband was transferred home by his Japanese employer, hated cooking so much she wouldn't even make coffee. Instead, she preferred to buy her morning cups the night before at a donut shop, and reheat them the next day. Edo and her private-school daughter became favourites of restaurateurs around town.

She is said to have been determined to remarry, to help maintain the style to which she had grown accustomed. "She seems very quiet, like a little China doll," says one of her non-admirers. "But they're perfectly suited to each other." James Edo was equally determined to find a bride here, and is believed to have approached at least one other Japanese-speaking real estate agent, who was surprised when the dinner conversation turned from potential property purchases to matrimony. They had only met that evening.

According to the sketchy accounts of people who have met him, James has a deep and abiding interest in fast cars and motorbikes, the good life and complete anonymity. "All Japanese are a little bit puzzled about her husband," says one of Elizabeth's acquaintances.

The Edos, both of whom are in their forties, recently sold their custom-built home in the fashionable Bayview-York Mills area of north Toronto, for one that would park at least eight cars, one of the several luxury residences the Edos' own construction company was putting up on the northern fringes of the city.

James Edo's business interests appear confined to property development. Besides the Toronto luxury houses, he has bought and sold commercial and apartment properties in Toronto and smaller communities nearby, including what was likely his first big acquisition—an apartment building near Eglinton and Yonge that has become known as the "king of the flips," having changed hands about five times in the eighties. It was apparently Edo, though, who got stuck with massive repair bills—mainly for a new elevator system—when he came into this new market, with all the usual pitfalls awaiting unsuspecting foreign investors. At least one disastrous deal is almost the price of admission for the unwary. "It's as if these really bright business people leave their smarts at home," one incredulous real estate veteran said of some of the exorbitant deals he has witnessed.

Edo's other investments, which stretch across a half dozen countries, have fared better; these include residential developments in southern Ontario and a couple of office buildings in downtown Seoul. But possibly his most ambitious project is a $100-million casino and hotel rumoured to be planned for the Turks and Caicos, not far from the Edos' winter hideaway in the Caymans. (The islands are a favoured Japanese tax haven that drew $2.6-billion (US) or 5.5 percent of Japanese money placed abroad in 1988. Another preferred destination that year was Panama, which drew $1.7-billion (US). It must have been the stable government under much loved ex-leader Manuel Noriega that drew the law-abiding Japanese. The United States was by far the choice of corporate and private investors alike, drawing $21.7-billion (US) or 46 percent. Canada, considered a tax burden by every foreign investor who ever set foot here, picked up only 2 percent of all Japanese investment abroad in 1989—$1.4-billion (US)—and most of that in major industrial projects, such as the big pulp and paper mills in the West that have aroused the ire of environmentalists.)

Wealthy Japanese like the Edos leave little behind them. Like some of the other Asian, Middle Eastern and European money in Canada, they are just pitching their tents here as a matter of ease and convenience. They bring no grand visions to the table, the way Kuzuwa or Nose do, and their passing to retirement hideaways in warmer climes will be little noticed. Like their money, they are constantly on the move, global haven-hunters who move to the high ground at the first sign of flooding down below.

The Noses and Kuzuwas are different. They will weather the storms that toss about their golden dreams, secure in the knowledge that they have found the right place to live out at least some of them. "Where would you rather be?" Nose asks, after comparing the usual Canadian attractions with life in Japan. That neither Nose nor Kuzuwa has much use for incidental things like the English language or Western food or customs is of little consequence. Their children are already taking care of that.

CHAPTER 5

The Great Fortunes of Europe

THE ASIANS MAY be attracting more attention here—they're
visible, their new wealth is obvious and they've been
pouring billions into Canada in the past few years.
But the Europeans have been here a lot longer—with
considerably more money. Until the recent political sea
changes in Europe made their own backyards much more
attractive, a steady stream of marks, francs (Swiss, Belgian
and French), lire, guilders and pounds made its way here,
including some of the greatest fortunes of Europe.

The cream of high society gathered one pleasant June
evening in 1986, to celebrate the sixtieth birthday of Johannes Baptista de Jesus Maria Louis Miguel Friedrich
Bonifazius Lamoral von Thurn und Taxis,* better known
to the world by the slightly less tongue-taxing Prince von

---

* Thurn und Taxis died after a heart transplant failed in December,
1990, as this book was going to press. It's unlikely there will be any
impact on the family's Canadian holdings, at least for the foresee-
able future.

Thurn und Taxis—probably Europe's wealthiest businessman, certainly Germany's biggest private landowner
and most famous aristocrat. If you looked closely among
the magnificent period costumes, among the diamond-
studded wigs and the bigwigs, among the royal glitter and
the gold, among the Rothschilds, the Mick Jaggers, the
Khashoggis (before the criminal charges) and the rest of
the 600 guests, you might have spied Rudolph Frastacky,
an elderly bald-domed gnome from Canada, mingling effortlessly with the millions-to-spare set at this romp on
the Danube.

The three-day feast at the prince's Schloss St.
Emmeram, the intimate Bavarian hideaway where
you'd need a map and an expert guide to find the
right dining room, cost mere millions (estimates range
as high as $5-million)—pocket change for an eccentric
billionaire who would spend a king's ransom on the celebration of the 500th anniversary of his family's entry
into the business world back in 1490.

There was even a small savings on the birthday entertainment, when his young jet-set wife, Gloria, better
known to the Monte Carlo crowd as Princess Pop or
TNT, pluckily pitched in with her own rendition of an
old Marlene Dietrich tune (wearing Marie Antoinette's
favourite tiara, but apparently without the support of her
own $500,000, custom-designed brassiere encrusted with
725 carats' worth of diamonds).

One of the enthralled guests, the head of a major
American record company, averred that his gracious
twenty-six-year-old hostess, a slim, attractive blonde with
an aristocratic pedigree even older than her husband's,
could well have a future in music. There's no record
of what Frastacky thought, nor is it likely he would
have said, if asked. And you can bet he wasn't one
of those responsible for the slight shortage of family
cutlery (seventeenth-century Augsburg silver's so hard to
replace). That's not the way discreet, conservative bankers
behave in public. Besides, the prince remained a valued

connection: He had once been an important client who sank millions into Canadian real estate on Frastacky's advice.

The prince was not alone.

What the great fortunes of Europe have spent their money on here in the past thirty years is property. Vast tracts of farmland in Nova Scotia, Ontario and Alberta, forests in British Columbia, industrial buildings in the unlikeliest of places, apartments and offices in the likeliest: All have fallen into the vice-like grip of white-knuckled European money seeking shelter from economic tempests at home; and convinced, at least until the late eighties, that their capitalist castles were about to be stormed by Communist or, heaven forfend, even socialist hordes. No one of prudence and conservatism—and these people are walking definitions of both—would chance keeping all their golden eggs in one basket during such perilous times, particularly when far better returns and glorious tax breaks awaited in a nice, safe, uncrowded place like Canada.

The bulk of private European money has been guided here by a handful of talented and energetic middlemen, most of them immigrants with carefully honed contacts and impeccable credentials in the old country. And of this hustling breed, none was better at the game than Rudy Frastacky, a short, dapper ex-Czechoslovakian cabinet minister with a name and reputation far bigger than he was.

Frastacky, who died in harness in 1988 at the age of seventy-four, had a list of clients, contacts and connections that ran through the moneyed who's who of Germany, Switzerland, Austria, Italy and the Netherlands. He hunted with princes, dined with dukes and barbecued for billionaires (his mother-in-law made the sauce). His former lawyer still remembers accompanying the master on one of his regular pilgrimages to keep up those all-important personal ties. "Frastacky was held in great esteem. He would set up shop in the major hotels and people would stand in line in these sitting rooms. These

were influential people, and there they were, making ap-
pointments for a half-hour of his time. It was kind of like
a papal visit."

If there was a European aristocrat with spare cash in
his riding breeches, this principled pope of property—a
true believer in his adopted homeland—could, with velvet gloves of old world charm, slip it out and send it
winging off to Canada, where much of it still remains
today. The amount can't be tallied with any accuracy,
says an accountant who has been helping Europeans find
tax loopholes here for years. "My guess is that it must be
tens of billions of dollars."

The nightmares that prompted the original flight have
long since vanished. In fact, the pendulum has swung back
the other way. Like every other foreign player, Europeans
find Canadian tax rules a real pain in the pocketbook;
and the pickings back home look better than ever, what
with the approach of a truly common market in 1992 and
the collapse of the Soviet empire. But this ever-cautious
bunch are no lotharios, out for a quick kiss and then off to
romance their suddenly sexy neighbours. There may not
be nearly as much European money coming in, but there's
little of it going out; and what's here is being churned
steadily into new ventures.

Frastacky counted among his satisfied customers an
assortment of barons, princes, the odd Bavarian duke
or two and some run-of-the-mill rich doomed to live out
their lives without a title on their calling cards. There
seems to be a bottomless well of the blue blood to go
around, especially in Germany, where no corporate board
meeting would be complete without at least one noble
nodding off in the corner. But some aristocratic investors, notably Thurn und Taxis and Gerald Grosvenor, the
Duke of Westminster—whose family has been investing
in Canada since the 1950s (without Frastacky's help)—are
genuinely powerful businessmen who've been aggressively
expanding their family fortunes globally, like any other
smart corporate chieftain these days. They just happen
to favour a lifestyle more suited to a much earlier time,

when titles and subtitles ruled the land.

On the rare occasions when Frastacky's clients had to leave the comforts of their walled estates and private forests to endure the hardships of the New World, they would often end up at a modest rented farmhouse north of Toronto or an unpretentious two-storey brick home on a quiet street in the city itself. The latter is the first and only residential property in Canada ever owned by Rudy Frastacky; the man who talked hundreds of millions of dollars into Canadian real estate had scarcely ever acquired any for himself.

The farm (rented from a client who'd bought it on Frastacky's say-so), a place of relaxed, Slavic-style informality, where scions of mighty fortunes would roll up their monogrammed shirtsleeves to help with the dishes, is gone. Yet today, sitting in the comfortable Frastacky home, with its warm touches—its floral couches and its memories in every corner—it's easy to picture the rich of Europe unwinding here after a tiring flight, settling in for an amiable visit.

Viera Frastacky, Rudy's widow, remembers many a weekend when she received the high and the mighty in her good-sized but hardly ostentatious living room; names that still dot the magazine lists of Europe's wealthiest families. "In this business, if somebody comes from Europe, what can you say: 'It's Sunday'?" She laughs. Unlike the Chinese or Japanese, Europeans like to do their entertaining at home. How can you expect people to trust you if they can't see how you live? If you can't hold up your end of a conversation long into the night beside a warming fire?

Elegant in a black dress with a black-and-red scarf peering out of her breast pocket, the slender, aristocratic-looking woman appears far younger than her seventy-one years. Properly formal, she serves tea and fruit custard tarts on fine china, lugging over a tea table to do it right. You can see why visitors like the starchly correct Thurn und Taxis or the imposing but charming Baron Albrecht von Trockau would feel completely at ease in this most

European of Canadian homes, despite the vast differences in their lifestyles.

A well-connected German lawyer, von Trockau preferred life on his medieval estate behind high walls. When he absolutely had to come to Canada, he refused to journey directly from Frankfurt. Instead, he decided he would go by way of Paris so he could fly Air France, just for the wine selection.

To investment managers, aristocrats like the baron were as valuable for their ability to unlock the cashboxes of Europe as they were for their own money here. It never hurts to have a little blue blood in the bank when you're going after European capital. Legendary property syndicator Hans Abromeit constructed a huge Canadian group (with some $5-billion worth of real estate under its wing) on a foundation of European money at least partly lured by the prestigious name of his partner's aunt, Countess Lehndorff, on the letterhead.

A former Frastacky associate says von Trockau "had nothing substantial in Canada, maybe $8- to $10-million here at the most." But he had friends even wealthier than he was (one married into the Mercedes fortune), sat on influential boards and did international work for Simonbank of Düsseldorf, which in 1960 teamed up with Frastacky to set up Minerva TransCanada Investments, the first important Canadian real estate fund for European money.

"It was the most organized investment vehicle being marketed in Europe at that time," says a Toronto lawyer who worked with many of the Europeans, until deciding to concentrate on his own real estate endeavours. "There were never more than fifty to sixty shareholders, but they were all substantial. Frastacky would recommend investments for them."

Worried about managing so many millions as a one-man band, Frastacky started up Metropolitan Trust Company in 1962, with $1-million—half from his European backers—after first pleading with a couple of big trusts to take on his European clientele as a going international division. What, the great Canadian financial brains wondered, could they possibly do with foreign money that was actually busy looking for Canadian real estate? Clients like Thurn und Taxis, von Trockau or Hamburg billionaire Werner Otto carried little weight with the cosy Rosedale and Westmount crowds.

That wouldn't be the attitude today, but it still prevailed as recently as 1979 when a vastly larger Metro Trust ($2.2-billion in total assets) was bought out by Victoria and Grey Trust Company, controlled by Toronto financier Hal Jackman. The Brenninkmeyers, an immensely wealthy, unbelievably secretive Dutch family with a stake in Metro, liked Jackman's deal; and the other European investors quickly came on board once Frastacky—always dedicated to the bank balances of his client friends—backed the offer.

One of the first things the new owner did was to dump the international real estate arm. Some observers say it was just further proof of the Wasp establishment's natural dislike of non-English foreigners, and a typical failure to grasp the true value of land. "They had no patience for Frastacky's traditional client base," says someone close to the family. "At the time, the Belzbergs had their eyes on it, and they lit up when they saw it. They understood real estate." But a Bay Street expert on financial institutions says, "Metro Trust was a disaster. Its books were full of bad mortgages and speculative investments. It was very much a European investor hotplate."

Nevertheless, the business was eagerly sought by the people who knew how to play the European game, including Frastacky himself. He was outmanoeuvred by Abromeit, who had started in the early 1960s managing investments in Canada from Hamburg. Abromeit's Lehndorff group, which pioneered syndicated Canadian property deals for smaller European investors through limited partnerships, bought 80 percent of what became Metro International. Frastacky, who still had a valuable client list, took the rest, but was later bought out by Abromeit after an apparent falling out between the two men.

Mrs. Frastacky doesn't seem the type to chat idly about such goings-on, or to toss off colourful anecdotes about Thurn und Taxis or any of the other remarkable people who've come into her life. She isn't.* "I am not a name-dropper," she cautions, laughing. Finally, though, she reveals some of her thoughts, through a haze of Rothmans smoke that filters out anything resembling distasteful gossip.

Thurn und Taxis "was very often in this house. Whatever they write about him, privately he is a wonderful person. They trusted my husband and we were often there." Yes, she was also at the famous birthday party—their last visit to the prince's home at Regensburg—and at his wedding a few years before that. And what is it she likes best about St. Emmeram, one of the world's great showpieces, a museum curator's idea of heaven? "The thing I really love is that every day it is cleaned. There are 600 rooms.† It's bigger than Buckingham Palace, but every day it is cleaned."

The prince, whose family built its vast fortune from a postal monopoly in the Holy Roman Empire and kept the cash coming as a private version of Canada Post for

---

* Her influential father was president of Slovakia in pre-war Czechoslovakia. Her husband, the son of a miller, became a state banker, head of the national sugar monopoly and a risk-taking courier of microfilm through Nazi territory for the Czechoslovakian government-in-exile. Once, he was carrying a microdot in his fountain pen, but somehow managed to switch pens with a Gestapo agent riding in the same train compartment just before a search. After the war, Frastacky settled down to life as a government minister until the Communists seized power in 1948, and he was forced to flee.

† No one seems to have counted all the rooms lately in this one time monastery, the largest of eleven castles owned by Thurn und Taxis. A visitor told me there were 300. One magazine came up with 350, but must have forgotten a wing or two. Another magazine, *Paris Match*, tallied 653 "livable" rooms, but it's not clear if that includes the part used as headquarters for the family's far-flung business empire. British author Robert Lacey puts the number at 500 in his 1983 book, *Aristocrats*.

the various German states,* started his Canadian portfolio with the farmland so beloved of German and Swiss
investors. But he soon shifted his attention to office buildings, and timber on the West Coast—prompting one B.C.
legislator with boot polish on his tongue to label him the
prince of British Columbia.

The family first began acquiring farm and forest lands
in a big way in the 1700s as part of an earlier diversification strategy, in places like Poland, Bavaria and what are
now Czechoslovakia and Yugoslavia. In the mid-1800s,
when they began turning the Thurn und Taxis postal services into government bureaucracies, the German states
insisted that the family take even more property as payment. This provided a seemingly rock-solid, inflation-
proof base for their money, until the Second World War
came along to shake the family out of its complacency.
Losing a few castles and two-thirds of your land will do
that to even the most blasé aristo.

It was to prevent such vulnerability in future that Johannes embarked on the thoroughly modern corporate
strategy that eventually brought him to Canada. He would
move into North American forestry and commercial real
estate and Brazilian ranching, while forging an industrial
empire (mainly in metallurgy and electronics) that goes
way beyond the old family business. Even now, the final

----

* The family originally came from Cornello, near Bergamo, in northern
Italy, where it was known at the start of its remarkable rise in the
fifteenth century as della Torre e Tasso, and whose members delivered
messages for royalty through the Alpine passes. The name had been
Germanicized by the time good old Franz von Thurn und Taxis (also
affectionately, and accurately, called Franz the Rich; such are the joys
of a private monopoly) started Europe's first sanctioned postal service
under the Hapsburg rulers of the Holy Roman Empire in 1490, eventually building the largest service business of its time. The Thurn und
Taxis were the most honoured postmen in history—barons in 1608,
counts by 1624, and hereditary princes before the century had ended.
Johannes likes to point out that his ancestors were nothing more than
robber barons who worked the protection racket on merchants going
through the Alpines, before becoming the Federal Express of their day.
He believes similar stories lurk beneath the foundation of other great
fortunes.

piece of the tapestry is being woven, with the development of full-scale financial services targeted especially at other members of the silver-spoon set.

Like other European heavyweights, Thurn und Taxis soon decided his Canadian investments were too large to leave in Frastacky's busy hands.* "They got big and spun off. Father wasn't happy about it, but he always got his invitation to go hunting with old Fürst [prince]," says Frastacky's affable son, Fedor. He runs Frastacky Associates, the family real estate business set up by his father from scratch in 1984, in partnership with yet another aggressively entrepreneurial German aristocrat, Count Albrecht Matuschka—builder of a booming, American-style financial group based in Munich.†

"When this company started, we had one telephone, no desks. Within six months, we had a portfolio of $150-million, nice offices and a staff of six," says Frastacky the younger. "Father said, 'I'm starting a new company, please send me your business,' and they did. We're dealing with the grandchildren in some cases of the original investors."

Thurn und Taxis and most other Europeans prefer the U.S. property market these days (who wouldn't, when the average pre-tax return on their money's been running five or six percentage points higher than in Canada?) or their own promising turf, but he hasn't exactly folded his

---

* Fürst Thurn und Taxis Bank did retain 916 shares in Metro Trust until the latter's takeover. The family bank, started after the First World War, and with assets of close to $700-million, is only part of the Thurn und Taxis financial services empire. The family controls five other companies in finance, leasing and investment management, as well as a key minority stake in Butcher & Company, a Philadelphia merchant bank.

† A third partner, the Constantia group of Vienna (assets well over $1-billion), subsequently decided to go its own way.

tent here. The prince's group still lists expansion of real estate in Canada as a continuing part of its global strategy. His Canadian holdings, not counting the extensive B.C. timberlands and related real estate, are worth about $100-million, a drop in the silver champagne bucket to a man like TNT, whose fortune has been pegged as high as $4-billion; which is why he and even bigger private investors here don't bother taking profits out, and probably won't in the future.

"That's not only unlikely, it's almost inconceivable," says Manfred Weidner, one of the prince's real estate advisers. "They just don't do that. They don't need the money. These are people of great cash flow. Their North American investments are just a fraction of what they own. They construct their investments with the intention not to make huge profits, so there's no speculation in any of this. They benefit from slow growth—sometimes not so slow."

Fedor Frastacky agrees. "None of it is repatriated to Europe to support lifestyle." Speaking of his own clients, he says, "What happens is that the revenue is kept here until there's enough to buy the next property." But neither man could predict what will happen once the mega-rich become completely convinced it's safe to stay home again; and both have seen a definite shift of investment focus back to Europe as 1992, with its promise of an economic superstate, fast approaches.

Weidner, a bluff, wavy-white-haired man of fifty-seven, has his offices in a small building on a less than fashionable part of Bay Street, north of the high-priced towers of Toronto's financial district. The plain door on the third floor bears three names: Interras Real Estate Consulting, Interras Real Estate and Regin Properties.

Regin is part of the web of companies set up to manage Thurn und Taxis' holdings. Interras (formed of the Latin words for "between countries") is Weidner's own firm. He's got only three clients: the prince and two other families he won't identify, but who don't have to worry about where the next pfennig's coming from. A sensible man, he's not out beating the bushes for more business. "I'm very much keeping this on a personal basis. My clients are more or less my friends," says Weidner, who's handled the prince's Canadian commercial property interests since late 1979.

It's a bit hard to make the mental leap from Weidner's functional, unadorned offices and his casual, slightly rumpled appearance to his unsmiling (even in birthday photos) boss, with his Savile Row suits and opulent lifestyle. It helps to remember that Weidner spent a good many years, as an auditor and tax specialist, looking for ways to gain marks for his long-time former employer, Werner Otto—a modest man who built an industrial colossus out of a humble homemade mail order catalogue.

Surprised that anyone has discovered his connection to Thurn und Taxis ("He is not known in this country. How did you find me?"), Weidner has nevertheless agreed to confirm what he can about the family's holdings. He immediately denies that the prince is no longer active here. "We are not mushrooming wildly, but there will be steady growth. He bought an office building in 1989 and one in 1988."

The list includes a building at 41 West Georgia in Vancouver; a parking lot in downtown Edmonton; and a couple of properties in Toronto. A subsidiary called Texada Logging runs the forest-covered end of the business from Victoria, while the industrial division (electrical equipment, metals) has a branch in Mississauga, Ontario. "There's nobody here who can give you the full spectrum of what the picture is," Weidner says. "They have holdings all over the place. There are companies that I am not even completely aware of."

Two doors down Bay Street sits the more expensively appointed office of Regentor IC Properties, another Thurn und Taxis company that reports independently back to headquarters in Regensburg, about an hour's drive from Munich. Regentor sounds like a logical combination of the family seat and the home of its Canadian affiliate. "It's actually very funny," laughs a German official.

"*Regen tor* means 'rainy door' [in German]." Rainy Door is the Canadian arm of what used to be RWI, a real estate fund operated by Westdeutsche Landesbank, a large savings and loan bank, until the prince acquired 60 percent control; the fund's top managers own the rest. A syndicator and manager of real estate for wealthy European investors, Regentor operates like Hans Abromeit's Lehndorff just next door, though on a smaller scale. There's a branch office on Drummond Street in Montreal, where RWI started out, and where the Europeans first fell in love with investing here in the sixties and early seventies.

In the past decade, Thurn und Taxis has disposed of only three properties: the Concord, an aging office building in Ottawa that faced high vacancies and repair costs—sold only after he had attempted to refurbish it; a suburban building in Calgary that was 70-percent vacant after its government tenant pulled out; and a farm in Scarborough. His company also reduced a small building in Edmonton to a parking lot, but plans eventually to do something with it. "They are holding on to property for 300 to 400 years," Weidner says. The prince once went into battle here to prove it.

He was enraged by Ottawa's attempt to hit him with heavy taxes, after the Ontario government had expropriated 201 acres of rural land for a satellite city that was never built (because it was linked to a second Toronto airport that also never got off the ground). In a related move, TNT had sold the province another 442 acres when they were rezoned to provide a green belt around the never-to-be community. Regin Properties had bought into the area not because the prince had a sudden urge to become a nobleman farmer here but because shrewd advisers like Frastacky had persuaded him and other wealthy investors that Toronto's urban sprawl couldn't help but eventually spill over its borders, paying huge dividends for anyone patient enough to wait for it. And these may be the most patient investors on earth.

The prince was sanguine about the expropriation: After

all, it had happened before, and this time he would at least make some money out of it. But he wasn't prepared to live with the tax collector's assessment that he had been sitting on the land (acquired in various parcels in 1966 and 1967) for nine years only for speculative reasons, and therefore should pay the maximum levy on his modest gain of $4.16-million.

How dare anyone suggest his family speculates! So angered was TNT at the thought his reputation could be sullied by some pipsqueak Ottawa bureaucrat, that he came to Canada in 1979 to testify personally at a Tax Review Board hearing. His patrician appearance and spellbinding recitation of the family's illustrious history going back to the Middle Ages (he apparently left out the days when his ancestors were virtual brigands) made quite an impression on the appeals board.

He explained the family philosophy of land acquisition—really the *raison d'être* of any European or Asian investor here—as the best and safest way to preserve capital. Among his contentions was that investing in a place like Canada was crucial to a family that had often seen its wealth jeopardized by political upheavals and the erosion caused by soaring inflation. A Thurn und Taxis simply did not, ever, acquire land here or anywhere else with the thought of reselling it.

The sole witness, he won only a partial monetary victory but vindicated his honour, proving it was political stability that had motivated his investments, not the prospect of a quick buck. "His personal attendance cannot be attributed only to the amount of income tax involved," fawned the appeals board chairman. It "is also a clear reflection of his character in accepting responsibility and speaking for himself, so vividly demonstrated in the background family information he volunteered and in the responses he provided to questioning. . . . His evidence regarding the purpose he had in mind for the property is accepted without question."

Carl H. Ladeck, a Frastacky aide who acted as interpreter during the 1979 case, describes the prince as "a very outspoken witness, very temperamental. He presented the chairman with two picture books of his castle." Another observer at the proceedings still laughs when he recalls the testimony. "He was asked whether the family ever sold something. He said, 'We usually don't. But let me see, I think in 1675, we sold some land.' "

Werner Otto, a quiet, publicity-shunning tycoon, was, characteristically, much more reluctant to appear at his own Canadian tax hearing a couple of years earlier. The case, involving a piece of downtown Toronto land acquired in 1968 for $750,000, turned into a parking lot and sold three years later for $1.6-million, sheds further light on the thought processes of the super-rich Europeans who, not so many years ago, were still fearful of losing it all. (Even Thurn und Taxis, who admits his family could afford the loss of a few castles, says, only partly tongue-in-cheek, that he's ready to flee if *glasnost* doesn't work out.*)

Otto, in his early eighties now and pretty much retired to the postcard Alps town of Garmisch-Partenkirchen, started his first mail order catalogue in Hamburg in 1949, putting together the pages by hand, cutting the items out of magazines. Today, the company, Otto Versand, employs about 20,000 and chalks up annual sales of about $8-billion (US). A few years ago, when the German mark soared against the U.S. dollar, Otto shot past mighty Sears to become the biggest mail order house in the world. The

---

* "With the Czechoslovakian border only eighty kilometres away, I don't believe in taking chances," the prince told *Connoisseur* magazine in January 1988. He prefers portable treasures, like his Marie Antoinette jewels and rare family postage stamps. "Thus if my major domo, Willy, were to wake me one morning and say, 'Your Serene Highness, the Russians are coming,' I could pick up my goodies and run." Instead, today he's contemplating one day putting in a claim for the return of his former lands in Eastern Europe.

Spiegel catalogue of Chicago, which always seemed to provide the loot on every U.S. quiz show ever made, belongs
to Otto; and there are other affiliates in Japan, France,
Britain and elsewhere. "It's one of the most successful
companies in the world," Manfred Weidner says. "I know
because I audited the books."

Otto had spent time in jail as a Hitler opponent,* and
had seen the family nest egg (his father was a food wholesaler in Brandenburg) disintegrate amid economic and
political chaos. The one-time war refugee told the tax
appeals board—once his aides managed to talk him into
appearing—that he wasn't about to let the same fate befall
his children. It was vital to move money into property
and out of Germany; and Canada was his choice for security and stability. He later moved into the U.S. as well,
but solely for the profit potential.

"That was a big thing, to get him to testify. I had a
big argument with him over that," says Weidner, who
had been chief of the tax department of Otto Versand in
Hamburg, designing the complicated structure for Otto's
Canadian holdings, with at least five investment companies—one for each child—and another to manage their
affairs. "He said, 'No, I don't want to testify,' and flew
away to New York. Two million dollars didn't mean anything to him." Weidner finally convinced him he had to
fight the taxman—who wanted to treat the property sale
as income instead of a capital gain—for the sake of his
children and as a matter of principle. Otto did manage to
prove he was investing here solely for the future benefit
of his children, and not looking to sell any of his holdings, apart from the occasional property to finance other
Canadian investments.

---

* Otto isn't the only anti-Nazi who teamed up with Rudy Frastacky
in Canada. The Thurn und Taxis family, too, was known for its less
than sympathetic views toward the Nazi regime. Nonetheless, Viera
Frastacky points out, "After the war everyone said they were not Nazis.
I said to my husband,'If no one was a Nazi, who was doing all that
shouting in the streets?' " Did he ever meet anybody he refused to do
business with? "Yes, but I don't remember the names."

By then Weidner was in Canada himself, having moved here in 1972 to run Otto's burgeoning real estate group, earlier managed by Frastacky through Metro Trust.* He took care of the tax and legal ends until going on his own in 1976, while Otto's former son-in-law, Klaus Vogel, now a major syndicator of European money, handled the acquisitions.

Otto was pouring millions into apartment blocks, farms, industrial parks, new residential subdivisions and offices from Hamilton to Oshawa, and was seriously thinking of immigrating to a country he openly admired. He "always loved Toronto. There was an instant smile on his face every time he came to this city," Vogel says. "He watched it grow from a small provincial city to a major centre." Otto actually went as far as buying a mansion in Forest Hill, Toronto's premier neighbourhood of the day, for $600,000, a huge price in the early 1970s. He never moved in, though, and it was sold at a small loss six months later when his staff convinced him he'd be unhappy here.

Weidner says, "We told him 'You don't speak the language. You are in your late sixties with two young children [the others were grown up]. You can't watch television here. You can't read the papers. You have no friends except us.' I think his wife probably would have preferred it, because they would have had a lower profile. He was not ready for retirement, [and] it would have been impossible for him to run his business from here. He would have been very frustrated."

In the seventies, other rich investors obtained landed immigrant status "very quietly"—just in case, says an accountant well-versed in the ways of European money. "Most of them never really took up residence, because the political and economic situation changed so dramatically."

---

* In the tight little world of German money, Hans Abromeit worked as a real estate adviser to the Otto family in the early 1960s. The current Mrs. Abromeit was a valued Otto director at the time.

The Otto organization, run by Otto's increasingly influential forty-eight-year-old son, Michael (who removed fur coats from his catalogues in response to environmental concerns and the consumer mood), hasn't stopped buying in Canada. "Basically, all the money generated here is invested here," says Klaus Vogel, who made some big deals for the family over the years.

Otto, who liked to conduct meetings in his office from behind a lectern and was known as a demanding but fair employer, does not have an unblemished record of success here. Like Li Ka-shing and other elite investors, he's occasionally made the kind of blunders we usually associate with mere mortals whose income isn't in the stratosphere.

In 1978, offered the huge portfolio of Y & R Properties, a company that controlled about 13 percent of downtown Toronto's office space, Otto declined—only to kick himself later. One of the properties, a large building offered at twenty-three dollars a square foot, is worth at least a dozen times that today. To compound his error, he rushed into another purchase that turned out to be a mess. Of course, they didn't all turn out like that or he wouldn't have become one of Europe's richest businessmen. He once paid $160,000 for a hundred acres in the Markham area. It was sold a couple of years ago for development. The price: $8.7-million.

Otto's substantial stake in our territory exceeds a cool half-billion dollars. Thousands of Canadians live in Otto-owned apartments—which account for the bulk of his holdings today (there's never a problem finding tenants, though a lot of other investors fled the market when rent controls came in)—without ever knowing who their landlords really are. Park Property Management, an Otto company, runs the buildings out of a suburban Toronto office. The Toronto phone book's list of the company's residential buildings alone covers a third of a column. Sagitta Development and Management, the Ottos' main real estate division, responsible for industrial land and office projects, is at the same address.

There's no indication the Brenninkmeyer family ever got involved in a tax dispute with Ottawa. But if it did, you can lay odds it would forfeit the cash before ever publicly revealing anything about the way it operates. The huge, close-knit Dutch family's been going about its business here for some thirty years; but few people know who they are, and the Brenninkmeyers would be perfectly happy to keep it that way. More Canadians come into contact with their business on a daily basis than with any of the other serious money that has shifted here; but the family is scarcely known beyond the elite social circles in which its members are highly regarded as gracious, charming and usually up for a good charitable cause.

The quest for more information starts and ends with Peter Bloemen, a hardnosed Dutch native who's president of Trucena Investments, the family's Canadian investment wing. A man of impeccable old European manners, Bloemen always returns reporters' calls . . . to tell them he's got nothing to say about the family or any of its activities here. "We are private, and we will stay that way."

That's unfortunate because, unlike some European investors, the Brenninkmeyers are big employers, with a considerable stake in the future of this economy. It might not hurt for Canadians to know a bit about what value they're adding here; about the benefits of foreign money. He might agree, he says, but "the person you referred to" (from long habit, family retainers avoid using the "B" word in conversations with outsiders) isn't about to break a code of silence that goes back five generations. Not even the Vatican has had such unbroken success shielding its darkest secrets; the papal functionaries should take lessons from the Brenninkmeyers. Bloemen says he'll go as far as checking what is written for accuracy. People who know the family say that's a major victory.

Like most other foreign investors (which they hate being called), they're into real estate, buying and developing property out of Canadian cash flow;* and they've got plenty of other investments on the go—notably in finance, often in the company of local money like financier Hal Jackman. They were, for example, key players in Jackman's takeover of Frastacky's Metro Trust in 1979. But their true global business—and the basis of their remarkable wealth—is retailing.

"They're everywhere," says the vice-chairman of a huge Dutch multinational in Amsterdam. "I don't know how big they are because they don't publish any figures, but I would make a bet that they could well be one of the biggest retailers in the world. But nobody can prove it, so how could I collect?" A senior Dutch finance ministry official says he would love to know how rich the Brenninkmeyers are, "but even the tax forms cannot reveal the truth."

This idiosyncratic family, whose minimum net worth, based on the sketchy information available, has been estimated at somewhere over $6-billion, owns dozens of well-known stores across Canada, selling mainly clothes, shoes and handbags to middle-of-the-road women in their middle years with mid-sized budgets—women who probably wouldn't be caught dead in a miniskirt or tight leather pants. Their stores include chains like Brettons, their costly eleven-store national flagship, and less flashy, but steady, regional money-makers like Irene Hill, Clark Shoes, Robinson and Ogilvy department stores; good and solid, like the family itself. All are run by a company called Comark Services, from modest Mississauga offices—a short drive from the home owned by Derick Brenninkmeyer, the family's low-key Canadian commandant until his death from cancer in August 1990, in the Bahamas.

---

* They like to point out that they're not passive foreign investors, but a Canadian development company, no different from any other small to medium-sized local company in the industry. A favourite line: "Every company you can come up with started somewhere else."

A call to Comark just to confirm the stores it operates is deflected by a secretary, who declines even to take a message. "Just please drop us a line, tell us who you are and what information you are looking for."

Apart from a handful of graduates from the Thurn und Taxis if-you've-got-it-flaunt-it prep school, the rich families of Europe—and just about anyplace else—put a high premium on discretion. And while terrorism seems well under control in Mississauga these days, it isn't hard to understand the genuine Dutch concerns about possible kidnapping or assassination (after his own narrow escape from death, Freddie Heineken stopped going anywhere without armed bodyguards, hired from the crack Dutch police squad that saved him). And with so many millions to protect, who couldn't relate to their loathing of the taxman?

But when it comes to the Brenninkmeyers, the passion for secrecy borders on the pathological. The tight steel curtain around this staunchly Catholic family and its business affairs has helped make the Brenninkmeyers (they only call themselves that outside Holland; at home, they're the Brenninkmeijers) one of the true puzzles among the great fortunes of Europe.

In the early 1840s, there were a couple of door-to-door peddlers in Mettingen, Germany, brothers named Clemens and August Brenninkmeyer. Making a reputation for themselves in textiles, sometime in the mid-1800s they migrated across the nearby frontier into northern Holland. From there, they built their thriving schmata business into a European department store chain carrying their initials, C&A.*

The Brenninkmeyers have since spread their tentacles

---

* The tradition-loving Brenninkmeyers usually stick these initials somewhere in their corporate names. The 'cena' in Trucena is Dutch for C and A. The holding company in the U.S. is Amcena. Then there's the English version of C and A, as in Tascanda, which operates in Australia, Necanda, which has directed investments to Canada; and just plain Canda, a large clothing manufacturer.

around the globe, relying on close family control of all operations. A Brenninkmeyer is always in charge in every single country in which they operate, and even lawyers and other retainers are often cousins or brothers-in-law (the family motto, according to *Forbes*, is "Unity makes strength"). They also rely on an unbelievable myriad of holding companies and cross-holdings, preferably based in a tax haven like the Bahamas or in a Swiss canton where, at one point, fourteen separate Brenninkmeyer companies, including the Canadian Cavendish Trust, based in Prince Edward Island, were registered.

Stories of the family's legendary conservatism, iron discipline and just plain quirkiness abound. There seem to be two approved vocations: the family business or the priesthood, each requiring about the same degree of devotion. "It's amazing how they do it," says a Dutch executive with another large company. "Apparently, they have a system whereby those members of the family who, for one reason or another, should not be in the business are being bought out or whatever, so there remains always a relatively strong group."

One observer admiringly calls them the "Dutch Reichmanns," possessed of the same kind of no-nonsense approach, secretiveness and orthodoxy. No driver's licence allowed before a certain age. Close scrutiny of potential mates. Holidays taken at the same time, to ensure harmony among family members who might otherwise fret about a relative getting the jump on them while they're away from their desks. Retirement from a foreign post at a designated age, with replacement by younger blood.

No Brenninkmeyer is promoted or sent abroad without an extensive apprenticeship, begun from the bottom up. The former head of American operations (about 1,100 stores in eight chains, including Uptons Department Stores in the South and Eastern Mountain Sports in New England) began his foreign duties as a window dresser in London; then he became a buyer—before being sent to the United States for schooling in marketing. Even then, he

was recalled to the Netherlands to make absolutely sure
he was suitable managerial material.

It's the family secrecy, though, that lives on in myth,
legend and reality. One long-time European employee
said that after thirty years he still didn't know which
Brenninkmeyer was his boss. The huge German operation
buzzed with Bs in management jobs, all calling themselves by their first names—except that they apparently
weren't using their *real* first names, a perplexed journalist
once wrote in *Capital*, a respected German magazine that
in the early eighties took a couple of cracks at unravelling
the company's spiderweb of holdings.

German corporate law requires more disclosure than
other jurisdictions in which the family operates. But the
reporter soon discovered that no one was better at shuffling assets (apart from certain holdings that were just
too big to conceal) to stay below the minimum required
to reveal financial information. "Whoever tries to lift
the curtain on the Brenninkmeyer business activities,"
the obviously frustrated journalist wrote in 1983, "he en-
counters retainers of the clan who can say 'We never
heard of a family by this name,' without getting red in the
face." The same is true here. One Brenninkmeyer staffer
refused to confirm that the family was even his employer,
though I already knew it.

When Eaton's executive Marcel Lamoureux was personally recruited by Derick Brenninkmeyer to run
Brettons—the family's bold entry into upscale retailing* along the lines of Holt Renfrew—he was an affable,

---

* The jury's still out on the family's biggest Canadian gamble, an
attempt to lure shoppers with fatter wallets by offering them more
personal service. The stores sometimes look as if they've got more
sales help than customers, and even with staff working on commission,
overhead's high. And it's hard to break old patterns in the clothing
business. One woman looking for something trendy and well above
the knees at the first Brettons, in the nation's capital, was quickly put
in her place by the sales clerk: "This is Ottawa, madam." No one can
accuse the Brenninkmeyers of never taking risks. They had to bail out
of a major investment in the New York area in 1986—the twelve-store
Ohrbach's chain.

open fellow who answered his own phone. His personality hasn't changed, but the savvy marketer has become one of the most publicity-shy retail executives around. "Our owners have asked us not to comment on any aspect of our operations," is his terse comment to an innocent question. The Brenninkmeyers' cardinal code of silence has taken hold.

A bit less secretive than the Brenninkmeyers is Gerald Cavendish Grosvenor, the sixth Duke of Westminster, and the wealthiest man in all of England (with a fortune estimated at more than $6-billion, he's outranked only by another big real estate tycoon, the Queen). When he looks at the ever-expanding map of his own overseas holdings these days, the owner of the choicest acreage in London must smile when his eyes come to rest on a spot near the bottom of the West Coast of Canada. It was there, on a small island in the Fraser delta with little appeal to the locals, that his uncle first tested the foreign waters for the family's huge property business back in 1953. The Grosvenors obviously liked what they saw in that tranquil provincial backwater, enough anyway to start amassing land in and around Vancouver for a ring of offices, factories, homes and shopping centres, either on their own or in partnership with other European money.

Now, when Vancouver's been transforming itself into an international metropolis—teeming with new money from powerful Hong Kong and Singapore investors like Li Ka-shing, the Shangri-La Kuoks and the New World Chengs; Japanese investors like the Suns; Malaysians; lately Taiwanese and other Pacific Rimmers; as well as becoming sought-after turf among the big institutional boys—look who's sitting on some of the more valuable real estate around town. You've either got the golden touch or you haven't—and the Grosvenors have had it for centuries, starting with a bit of speculative building in London in the 1700s.*

It took nerve and foresight to decide that some scrub meadowland, the site of a notorious annual spring fair, could be converted into the place to be for any Londoner who was anybody at the time. Yet that's how Mayfair was developed by one of the Duke's innovative ancestors: Wisely, he divided up the lots among small builders on ridiculously short ninety-nine-year leases, unheard of at the time, and let them take the risks.

Vancouver became the cornerstone of a similarly bold family decision to get part of their enormous fortune to safer territory while the getting was good. And it has been carried forward aggressively by the latest in an aristocratic line that traces its roots back to a rather overweight, disreputable buddy of William the Conqueror. Thurn und Taxis would approve of both the heritage and the strategy. Like the German prince, the thirty-eight-year-old English duke has been determined to get the family billions—built up through enormous land holdings in England and Scotland, and held through various offshore family trusts—out working in the wider world.

Today, the foreign portfolio includes about twenty Vancouver area buildings, with more on the planning boards. But the city is more than a profitable place to park some cash; it's also the nerve-centre of the family's international empire, where a small group of executives run a lengthening string of investments stretching from Montreal to Honolulu to Sydney. Grosvenor International Holdings, which develops and manages property across North America and Australia (staying within the English-language dominions makes for an easier night's sleep

---

* While Grosvenor's been buying, another famous British family, the Guinnesses, have been selling. Developers of the British Properties, a prestigious subdivision in West Vancouver, and the Lions' Gate Bridge, they have been steadily shedding their holdings since the tax rules became unattractive in the seventies.

when you're worrying about risking the family money) is headquartered downtown, on West Georgia Street, in an impressive twenty-one-storey office building that bears the family name. This bronze, marbled modern wonder is full of enough computerized communications technology to make it "smarter" than the average tower.

On the top floor, in an office that's all dark wood and plush carpeting and glorious corner view looking northeast over the city (is there a senior executive in Vancouver without a breathtaking view?) sits Nicolaas Blom, senior vice-president of Grosvenor International Holdings. Blom—tall, conservatively dark-suited, bespectacled—isn't as formal as he seems which is probably why everybody calls him Nick. He may just be too busy for formalities.

"Our total portfolio is somewhere in the $2.4-billion range. Of that, 20.7 percent, $450- to $500-million, is in Canada," says the relaxed-looking former lawyer, as he sips coffee from gold-edged china. That includes property owned entirely by the dukedom, and a great deal more managed for ventures in which Grosvenor has a piece of the action, usually with other European investors. "What is there in self-owned? Frankly, I've never worked it out."

One such joint vehicle, Northwest Freeholds, combines Grosvenor money with that of seven British pension funds. In Vancouver alone, it owns the Vancouver Centre, the First City building on Hornby and a downtown parking lot. Then there's a regional shopping centre in Winnipeg, industrial property in Regina and an office tower in Toronto. The family has pieces of dozens of other buildings in Canada, the United States and Australia, about eighty in all—as well as industrial land, housing developments and malls. On its own, Grosvenor owns large shopping centres in Abbotsford and Penticton, British Columbia.

Grosvenor International's $60-million headquarters itself is 50 percent owned by Butlin International Holdings, held by the family trusts of the late British holiday-camp king, Sir Billy Butlin. Sir Billy, who died in 1980, was a South African native with a soft spot in his heart for Canada, where he'd spent his youth and had his first taste of work as an Eaton's delivery boy. He'd also done a stint in the Canadian army overseas. "Towards the end of his life, he was very concerned to get some investments in Canada," says the Dutch-born Blom, who himself immigrated to British Columbia as a teenager, and who practised law for eighteen years before joining Grosvenor about a decade ago.

The Duke of Westminster also has an affinity for Canada, or at least its western side. "He likes the entire scenic layout," says Blom, thinking like the good real estate man he's become. "He worked in British Columbia as a ranch hand on the Woodward ranch. This would have been after high school, maybe fifteen or twenty years ago. He did that for a couple of months." It's not that hard to form a picture of the lean, smiling aristocrat, casual in an open-necked shirt and favourite tweed jacket, herding cattle in his Aston-Martin. Actually, such a life could well appeal to a man who appears totally unpretentious, definitely not one of Princess TNT's A-list party guests. Blom says the duke devotes much of his free time to charity work, or to duty in the military reserve, which takes up about 80 percent of Major Grosvenor's weekends. "It must play havoc with his personal life and his other commitments, but we're all aware that that comes first. His own personal life is not running around investing money."

Like Thurn und Taxis, he leaves day-to-day management up to his skilled team of professionals, but he does keep a close eye on business. "He's not some mysterious figure that we never see," Blom advises. "It's a far more personal relationship than an anonymous bunch of shares." *Fortune* estimates the duke earns $5,100 (US) an hour.

Unlike some European investors, the Grosvenors didn't come to Canada for the great outdoors. They own more than enough open space back home to avoid that cramped feeling. What was missing was a feeling of security about the future if they were to keep all their assets locked up on their little island. "Germany was growing stronger, the confidence in the British economy wasn't that great," Blom says. "The worry about the Russians rolling across the iron curtain was real, so it was a sensible thing to do."

The first Grosvenor banner was planted on Annacis Island, about twenty minutes southeast of downtown Vancouver, in 1953. "At the time, there must have been a fair bit of giggling about those silly English people who were buying this property way out in the boonies," Blom says with a grin. Local real estate types might have cashed in big, had they looked up their history and joined the Grosvenors. Instead, the family was able to acquire all the property on the island, selling off developed land later, while keeping about a quarter of it for themselves—260 acres worth, with a million square feet of industrial space. There's even a Grosvenor Square there, though it's a tad less valuable than the one in Mayfair.

When the Grosvenors settled on Canada, they were following in the historic footsteps of countless British property hunters—peers or otherwise—who've been drawn to the colonies over the years. When the newer money began coming in from continental Europe, they found the old British masters already firmly entrenched, though not particularly aggressive or opportunistic. Most of the early big names retreated from the battlefield long ago, when their political comfort level dropped and local competition picked up—but not Grosvenor.

Blom agrees "it's somewhat unusual to set up an operation, an office with employees and everything else in each country. Lehndorff [a partner with Grosvenor in the Wells Fargo building in Los Angeles, until selling out to the Japanese] and so on, those are people who created a particular fund and then went out and found investors for it, which is quite different from the kind of thing that Grosvenor did. It illustrates a long-term commitment. We've been here now for over thirty-five years." And, obviously, they intend to stay a century or two more. (The duke has already laid out an estate plan well into the next century.) The profits, as with Thurn und Taxis, Otto, the Brenninkmeyers and the rest of the great fortunes, stay here. "The whole point of the exercise was to have money outside of Europe, so it hardly makes sense to take some out, then bring it back in."

CHAPTER 6

The European Middlemen

WHILE RUDY FRASTACKY and others were busy courting the rich blue bloods and powerful industrialists with millions to toss into Canada, it was Hans Abromeit who had the stroke of genius that would turn him into the uncrowned king of the Euromoney set: a real estate fund that would tap not only the deep pockets of wealthy individuals and vast pension funds but the desires of all those average dentists, butchers, tailors and candlestick makers to own their own sliver of safety in an uncertain world—for a mere 5,000 or 10,000 German marks or Swiss francs.

Today, his Lehndorff group, started with Hamburg partner Jan von Haeften,* numbers some 4,000 European investors, manages syndicated properties worth $5-billion (about 25 percent in Canada, 50 percent in the United States and the rest in Europe) and employs nearly 1,000

---

* The well-connected von Haeften has an interesting lineage of his own. His father was a diplomat involved in the plot to blow Hitler to smithereens late in the Second World War. He was executed, along with his fellow conspirators.

people. Rarely in the news—though its Lehndorff Canadian Properties arm is publicly traded—the company controls large chunks of Toronto, Edmonton, Calgary, New York and its U.S. command centre, Texas. It also has stakes in U.S. oil and gas and in European companies that make cassettes, rubber car-parts and grinding machinery, among other things.

Abromeit holds court in downtown Toronto, on the sixth floor of an older, well-kept Bay Street building that bears the Lehndorff name, but includes no directory to guide the uninformed or unwanted. He doesn't often grant audiences. That doesn't mean that the one-time economist with a doctorate from the University of Berlin keeps a low profile; quite the contrary. The honorary Austrian consul and his wife turn up frequently in the society columns; as fund-raisers for this or that favourite cause (the Canadian Opera Company's at the top of the list); or as hosts of lavish parties at their impressive home—dubbed "Little Versailles" by some of his employees, and worth somewhere between $3-million and $4-million—in a posh part of north Toronto next door to the likes of Conrad Black.

His wife has her own assistant at Lehndorff headquarters, and keeps busy in various aspects of the business. One of her assignments was the luxurious and costly redecoration of their Sutton Place Hotel in Toronto. When they met, Abromeit was an advisor to billionaire Werner Otto in Hamburg, and his future wife was on Otto's board.

Outside his circle of intimates, Abromeit may be better known for an undying love affair with the Group of Seven artists, and particularly Lawren Harris (he paid $400,000 for one painting), than for being, say, the biggest land developer in Edmonton or one of the larger landlords in Dallas; and that's the way he likes it. "I saw my first Harris in Vancouver in 1965," he rhapsodizes. "It was beautiful art, which I could not afford at that time. But after that, Harris was constantly on my mind. It's great international art. As a Canadian, you cannot appreciate that. They [the Group of Seven] were painting Canada in a modern way. You see how perfectly they captured the soul of the country. In other countries, artists paint people. Here, they paint landscapes, because in so many parts of the country, there is nothing but landscape."

It was the large open canvas holding out the chance to sketch in great dreams—far away from a Europe still struggling to pull itself together under the Soviet empire's shadow—that attracted immigrants like Abromeit in the first place. Today, we scoff at paranoia about the Soviets and their intentions, particularly in light of what's happened in eastern Europe; but the fear was very real, at least well into the seventies.

Lehndorff's softly lit reception area directly faces the elevators; no one can slip into this place unnoticed. Except for a constantly humming fax machine, you'd think you were in the restful waiting room of an extremely exclusive private consultant, which Abromeit has been in his day. The elusive professor usually avoids journalists, especially those seeking to pry into his corporate affairs or private life.* But when the trim, balding, fit-looking man wearing an impeccably cut grey striped suit, wide-striped shirt with white collar and cuffs, an expensive silk tie and an air of complete authority comes out to greet a visitor, he's all old-world charm.

Adjourning to his suitably spacious, elegant, library-quiet office, he sets the ground rules for the audience: No tape recorder; no discussion of his age (he's in his early sixties, but doesn't look it) or wealth (others estimate his fortune at about $25-million); and he would like to see what's been scribbled "to correct your misconceptions." A nervous visitor starts wondering if a secret trap door opens into a dungeon below, but the floor appears sturdy.

---

* Secretiveness is the universal theme linking the old and new money. One Swiss investment and real estate pro in Montreal types his own messages and sends them personally to his European clients. Not even his secretaries ever get to see what's in them.

Starting with Abromeit's art collection seems safe enough. Asked if he would ever consider putting it on public display, as did Ken Thomson with his Krieghoffs, he replies, "Would you take off your clothes in public?"

"Well, no. . . ."

"I have a pretty busy social life. I just cannot take off everything from my walls and leave them with nothing."

There are few stories about the way Abromeit operates, but people who will never be on his Christmas card list say he divides the world into two groups: those who work for him or are otherwise useful to him, and everybody else. Surprisingly, Abromeit turns out to be a thoroughly benevolent host, eager to talk about what's made this country so attractive to European money over the years, and what's gone so wrong in recent times.

Like most wealthy immigrants, it pains him to see his adopted homeland drifting, without apparent purpose. "The world wants to see some leadership," he says with frustration, noting that when Jimmy Carter was in the White House, it was tough to persuade Europeans to put their money in the States. "In Parliament, there is almost no discussion of necessities. Only: 'What did you say in the last election campaign?' One is always accusing the other of doing something wrong, instead of discussing their vision of the future."

Abromeit's original move to Canada, in 1958, "was absolutely planned. I made an investment study—I was always interested in international investment—and I selected Canada, especially Toronto, as the target area. That was basically researched and did not come about by chance." There's no reason to doubt this; he doesn't look as if he ever does anything off one of those starched white cuffs.

He saw what Frastacky had seen, possibly because Frastacky showed it to him: a land of endless opportunity. In Metropolitan Toronto, it was still possible to buy farms, unheard of back home, where even in the countryside hardly anybody ever sold any land.

His first building was in northeast Toronto. "People

thought there would be no development north of the 401 [highway]." He laughs. It's the hearty sound of someone who enjoys a good joke, especially when the punchline has made him millions. Today, Lehndorff's various investors own more than 300 Canadian properties, mainly in Ottawa, Toronto, Vancouver and urban Alberta, which still holds out the allure of cheaper, wide-open spaces to Abromeit and other handlers of European and Asian money. Lehndorff has more than 2,000 acres in Edmonton alone, "and I think it is justified. The entrepreneurial climate is better in Alberta. We had quite a land bank in Toronto and Ottawa, but we sold out and re-invested in Alberta."

Toronto and Montreal once seemed full of such promise to Abromeit, before political and tax changes, rent controls and soaring prices—and the spectre of instability that always haunts foreign money—came along to dampen his enthusiasm. "There was an interesting investment climate and still reasonable prices," he says wistfully of the long-gone days when he could buy a 200-unit apartment building in Toronto for $2-million—with $400,000 cash and the rest borrowed at 6.5 percent—and still guarantee a return of 9.5 or 10 percent, even after the interest. "Nowadays, if you buy a downtown property even on a free and clear basis, you are lucky if you are getting five to five and a half percent."

Most Europeans can do as well at home, without the currency risks, and considerably better south of the border. As a result, the money "has dried up tremendously. The climate definitely has changed over the years. Even the small print in the tax laws is not very friendly to foreigners investing here."*

These days, Lehndorff is four-fifths fuelled by domestic

---

* Foreigners selling buildings, for example, have to put up 30 percent of the sale price as a guarantee they'll be paying their Canadian capital gains tax. That's true even for Lehndorff, with its huge assets. "They know our history, and we have to give them 30 percent the moment we sell," an aggrieved Abromeit says. There are no capital gains taxes on German real estate held for more than two years.

and U.S. money and is hunting for Japanese and other Asian investors; a far cry from the days when 90 percent of its funding came from Europe. The company has even started to reverse the traditional investment pattern, taking North American money to European cities like London and Frankfurt. Some Euromoney experts say its main problem is that it's outdated, that the kind of old-country investor Abromeit has always served isn't out there in force anymore. The new European money is also much more sophisticated, unwilling to just let Canadian managers shuffle them in and out of investments they never see, and over which they have no control.*

Abromeit concurs that "foreigners do not come in by themselves anymore. You have to make a lot of propaganda, to sell it. Before you get someone to go to Edmonton, you need some persuasion. It needs a special effort." His oldest son, thirty, works out of the New York office, where he helps show the family flag to European investors who like to be reassured that the next generation is on the job. (Another son is still in university.) Abromeit himself spends five months a year outside Canada, keeping up his personal links—even after twenty-five years of running a hugely successful property fund (with occasional blips, like an overly enthusiastic plunge into Calgary when the oil-fired markets there were collapsing; which is a problem only if the owners aren't willing to wait out the bad times).

"Nowadays, you really have to have enthusiastic partners, because the investment business is global. You have to be willing to go through the aggravation of being constantly on the road," he says, the audience over.

---

* Controversial German billionaire Friedrich Karl Flick once bought an office building in Edmonton, sight unseen—even though he was in town the day the deal was closed. He was more interested in looking at a farm for his sons, but ended up acquiring one in the United States instead.

Klaus Vogel may not aspire to Abromeit's mantle, but he has already been anointed by some in the business as the best of the newer players in the Euromoney sweepstakes. He acknowledges that the game has changed dramatically since he started here in the 1970s, when people "were not yet travelling. North America was very foreign to them. Language was a barrier."

A fussy eater and recent fugitive from the dentist's chair, he picks at his lightly grilled catch of the day at a favourite French dining spot on Toronto's Queen Street. "These almost-blind funds [like Lehndorff's] were the right concept for the time."

Vogel—superbly conditioned, immaculately tailored, his thick, fair hair combed straight back—looks far younger than his fifty years, a walking ad for the benefits of an eat-right, cycle-in-the-French-countryside lifestyle. As meticulous about what comes out of his mouth as what goes in, he pauses, a cautious note in those shrewd blue eyes. His words are measured, as if each one has to clear customs before it reaches a journalist's cocked ear. He wants to make it clear he's implying no criticism of the way others operate their businesses—just that, well, times have indeed changed.

"The generation that runs business in Europe now has been brought up internationally. They study and travel abroad. They work in Paris, Brussels, London and New York. They run international operations. They have a completely different outlook than the World War Two generation. They don't need the same type of manager."

Bernhard Kaeser, a Swiss-born former assistant to Rudy Frastacky, who brings in European money through his Atlantis Real Estate Corporation, couldn't agree more. "Twenty years ago, the typical client would be a manufacturer in his sixties, a self-made man. Today, that's all gone. The second generation is now moving in—Harvard-educated guys with spreadsheets. There is no more 'Let's do a deal for old times' sake.' It's more detached now," he says, nostalgia seeping between the lines. The sophisticated new money isn't necessarily smarter, either. "You can calculate everything to death, but if you don't have a gut feeling that you can trust. . . ."

Vogel has that intuitive feel. There's little doubt of that. The Stuttgart native started off here by running the mega-buck investments of Hamburg catalogue king Werner Otto; but he headed out on his own—with the essential well-connected partner back in Europe (in his case, a prominent distant cousin)—when the Otto torch was passed to that more analytical younger crowd, possessed of no instinctive touch for the property side of things.

His earlier divorce from Otto's daughter had nothing to do with it. Before taking the Canadian posting, "I went to him and said, 'Look, I'm going to get divorced from your daughter. Do you still want me to go to Canada?' He told me: 'Klaus, love is love, business is business. If you want to go to Canada, go to Canada.' " An old acquaintance says Vogel's relationship with the family patriarch actually improved after the marital breakup.

Vogel remarried here and never did go back. He and his wife, Annelies, a former art-teacher-turned-designer, have lived quietly with their two sons in the same tree-lined, suburban Toronto neighbourhood for thirteen years: "It reminded me of the house of my grandparents in Stuttgart, full of old trees." Like the Abromeits, they have a taste for talented Canadian artists, though of a considerably more recent vintage and lower sticker price. Annelies Vogel's pet charity is the Royal Canadian Academy of Arts, a 110-year-old national arts institute that's always strapped for cash. "They almost went bankrupt," Vogel says with genuine feeling. "It's a really important institution. Nobody here knows of this."

He too tried to help the academy by talking a renowned plastic surgeon he'd met on a flight to California into donating $10,000 worth of face and eyelift surgery to the academy's annual auction. "No one bid. It was embarrassing, so I bought it for $4,000. It took ten months to get rid of it. A woman bought it for her husband as a

Christmas present." Just in time, too: The prize was only good for a year, and Vogel sure didn't need it.

When Vogel's not out trying to safeguard Canadian culture or cycling with pals in Europe, he puts his considerable enthusiasm into building his company, the Tandem Group, which handles close to $1-billion worth of property for a select clientele. Unlike Abromeit, he never touches the small-fry burghers, and doesn't deal with the European institutions favoured by Kaeser, who teamed up in 1972 with three German partners (one of whom had all the requisite credentials for any such venture—he was a prince*), but has run his own show for years.

Vogel declines to name his own partner, or any of the group of about sixty well-heeled German and Swiss individuals and families who've entrusted him with their spare change. About a third of them are still putting new money into Canada or southern California, the only other spot he's investing in; and even then, he has to swallow his deep distaste for doing business with Americans.

In his decidedly low-key offices (the normal hustle and bustle—with the accent on hustle—that you might associate with real estate types just isn't the kind of reassuring atmosphere that would encourage the serious money) on the twenty-eighth floor of the Cadillac Fairview tower—which holds up the south end of the Eaton Centre—Vogel sips peppermint tea while he ducks questions about the real estate he's purchased. The far wall of his boardroom is lined with tidy framed pictures of buildings: small industrial plazas in the suburbs; the Cantel building at Eglinton and Yonge, high-rise apartments. Nothing recent, though. "I'm glad I stopped that practice," Vogel laughs when he catches his visitor ogling the trophies.

Each of his offerings from the à la carte menu so beloved of Europeans—of offices, industrial buildings,

---

* Like Abromeit, Kaeser wasn't about to waste such a useful aristocratic door-opener. He called the company Hohenlohe, after his princely partner, Johannes Zu Hohenlohe. He changed the name to Atlantis in 1974, when the prince left the picture.

apartments, shopping centres, even restaurants—will typically involve four or five of his clients; and in a departure from the days when a Rudy Frastacky lived on management fees alone, Tandem takes up to 30 percent of a deal for itself (except once when a German investor insisted on the whole enchilada).

Every player has a different reason for being here, but fear's no longer among the top ten. One German industrialist, after selling his company, parked $10-million with Vogel in a span of three months, but removed it all when he saw a golden opportunity at home. The remaining partners took over his share. "They usually know each other and have other business relationships," he says. Ironically, his biggest single deal, worth $186-million, involved no foreign money at all: Tandem took a sixth, with Canadian partners on the hook for the rest. Domestic investors account for about a quarter of the money in his projects today; and like Abromeit and the other Europeans here, Vogel is now looking to take some of them into Europe.

The Vogel smile fades only when the talk turns to his adopted homeland. Like many of the appreciative immigrants here, he's an ardent champion of Canada, its people and way of life, even if he does occasionally see things through rose-tinted glasses. (Unlike some of his real estate colleagues, he's not even sour on buying rent-controlled apartments, calling them a perfectly good investment because you never have to worry about a vacancy problem.) He just wishes we would realize how lucky we are.

Dark shadows of anger cross his handsome, tanned features just thinking of people like Robert Campeau publicly dumping all over his own country (as he was embarking on the borrowing and spending spree in the United States that brought him to the brink of financial ruin). To hear an incensed Vogel—as close to sputtering as this erudite man is going to get—it's almost as if Campeau had personally slapped him in the face.

"Here you can say someone's decent, you can do business with them," he says. "If you do business in the United States, you never can relax. You always have to be on the lookout or someone will screw you. Nobody would say that here. Canadians are honourable." Obviously, Vogel has been remarkably lucky in his dealings, but he thinks there's more to it than that; and other Europeans back him up.

In the States, "anything written doesn't mean very much, because you can dismantle it with a lawsuit. With my Canadian partners, things are so easy. If they agree to something, they honour it." He tells of the president of a California financial institution, who sold him a building and then rented space back, finally deciding he wanted out of the lease. "We said, 'We'll be happy to help you sublet.' You know what he did? He moved out and said, 'Sue me.' That's the way they do business."

Bernhard Kaeser, a friendly, cultured man who sees the world through many lenses (he owns twelve pairs of glasses), explains that "while the U.S. might be more attractive from a purely tax or economical viewpoint, your average European relates better to Canada. Canada is more like Europe in its daily life and culture . . . even in simple things like eating habits."

He goes on to describe what surely must be the definitive difference between us and our neighbours to the south: "A wine connoisseur in Canada is a refined person who knows something about wine. A wine connoisseur in the States is a snob who splurges with money. There is a fundamental difference in the people." If only Campeau had known. . . .

So, despite Abromeit's darker view, Canada will continue raking in its share of the new money, even when it might make more sense—at least according to the computerized printouts—to be somewhere else. After all, we do know our wine. "The problem is not so much raising money in Europe, but finding good deals here," Vogel says matter-of-factly. "But even in this period, they exist."

Another major European player with a Canadian passport who's channelled millions into this country also has
his sights aimed in the other direction in pursuit of his
multinational ambitions. But as Karsten von Wersebe has
discovered, it's not always easy to go home again.

The first time I met von Wersebe, he was in a screening
room one winter's day ... watching a cartoon. There
were wizards in castles and damsels in distress and
a dastardly villain who sounded exactly like Vincent
Price. The technical magic of it all was dazzling, but no
one seemed to care—least of all the stocky, wavy-haired
man sitting stiffly in the dark. These weren't your typical
film buffs sneaking out of the office for a matinee; they
were clutching copies of the financial plan for the still-
unfinished epic, more interested in the bottom line than
the closing credits.

Canadian animator Richard Williams, fresh from his
Academy Award-winning design of Roger Rabbit for
Steven Spielberg and the Disney people, was doing his
damnedest to talk the men in the suits into handing him
the green he needed to fill in the rest of his technicolour
dream. Von Wersebe knows all about great visions and the
passion needed to bring them to life; but he wasn't about
to sink a cent into a hugely risky project in a busines that
was completely alien to him.

Von Wersebe is chock full of contradictions, which helps
explain why he'd have turned up at that animated pitch for
financing in the first place, it being the sort of thing that
usually appeals to overpaid dentists trying to trim their
tax bill.

A deeply private man, he's involved in such public ventures as investing in a pro sports team. A daring businessman, he looks as if he would be more at home behind
an anonymous desk in some big insurance office. Almost
painfully shy, he's labelled in the Swiss press, "champion of the money-raisers" for his skill at luring European
cash into his deals. A gentleman of the old school—the
kind that doesn't turn out many graduates any more—he
seems to enjoy the company of flashy, larger-than-life

personalities. He's a stay-at-home who's hardly ever at home.

Von Wersebe, or KVW, as his junior staffers call him, had tagged along to the catered wizardry at the urging of one of those characters: Peter Thomas, a high-rolling British immigrant, who moved to Vancouver and cleaned up peddling Century 21 real estate franchises. Von Wersebe was in on Thomas's failed bid for disgraced U.S. televangelist Jim Bakker's PTL amusement park in North Carolina—proof that when he's satisfied with the odds and the rules, he's more than willing to roll the dice.

The perpetually tanned Thomas looked perfectly at ease with the sharks who circle anyone with a wallet who comes near the movie business. Von Wersebe, by contrast, quietly acknowledged this wasn't his sort of schtick. That's a good reason for feeling out of place; but in fact, he seems to feel that way most of the time.

A few months later, in the spring of 1989, von Wersebe is in the wilds of Mississauga, where his company, York-Hannover Developments, is unveiling its newest office project. Soon, this muddy landscape—within sight and sound of Toronto's Pearson International Airport—will be filled with gleaming symbols of corporate achievement, some already under construction; but for now the Spar building, named for its biggest tenant—a high-tech Canadian success story best known for its space arm that goes up with U.S. astronauts—stands out like a tree in the Arctic, on the aptly named Explorer Drive.

This is von Wersebe's turf—the world of property development and the entrepreneurs, deal-makers and financiers who people it. Yet even here, among his own kind, he seems out of place, like sneakers in a room full of dress shoes, nervous in any spotlight . . . even his own.

Von Wersebe dislikes the public eye, even in Germany,

where he has constructed a real estate and steel power base that garnered him a string of nasty reviews in the German press for his North American-style wheeling, dealing and borrowing. (One magazine article assailing his business methods was headlined "Russian Roulette.")

Even after becoming a sports investor with the Toronto Blizzard soccer team (which has cost him several million dollars over a decade); the proprietor of Winston's restaurant, a fifty-year-old landmark where the high and the stodgy of Bay Street have been cigar-puffing and power-lunching since long before the phrase was coined; and the operator of such glitzy projects as the Montreal Eaton Centre and Toronto's ultra-chic Hazelton Lanes shopping centre, von Wersebe hasn't exactly transformed himself into a Canadian Donald Trump.

He's far more comfortable in the shadows, concocting his big, complex deals, thinking of new worlds still to be conquered outside Canada's confining borders.

The Mississauga project is typical von Wersebe: an ambitious scheme, put together mainly with other people's money and managed for them. The city was originally thinking industrial subdivision "in a boring sense, and in my view it was going to be wasted," he says, as well-wishers close in on him before descending on the roast beef, raspberry tarts and French wine. "I spent a lot of time assembling a more interesting package."

The city's feisty mayor, Hazel McCallion, seems happy with the "more interesting" (developers' jargon for "considerably more profitable") result. She reminds her laughing audience; "You could have had West Edmonton Mall here, remember?" That was the goal of the Ghermezian brothers, immigrant dreamers who had proposed an eastern version of their giant Alberta attraction.

Reserved as he is, von Wersebe isn't deliberately mysterious or secretive about his background like the Ghermezians, a wealthy orthodox Jewish family that emigrated from Iran a few years before his arrival from

Germany in the mid-sixties. The then twenty-four-year-old agricultural specialist from an upper-class ("asset-rich, cash-poor") family became a trainee at Metro Trust, and later assistant to its chief, Rudy Frastacky.

It was a good place to learn the ropes and begin making the connections that would ultimately lead to a remarkably intricate web of international holdings, which at last count numbered close to thirty companies, in Canada, the United States, Germany, Switzerland and the Caribbean; with interests in real estate, steel, construction, trading, engineering, hotels and entertainment. And that doesn't count small personal investments in several German firms (including a bank), or venture capital efforts like the one with Peter Thomas that went after Jim and Tammy Faye Bakker's old homestead. Von Wersebe has built it on a foundation of borrowed money.

"Karsten, like a lot of other people, believes in totally leveraged deals. He used to say you have to keep people on their toes," an old business associate says. (Translation: Why use your own money when you can do so much better with someone else's?) When his large Munich-based real estate company, Raulino, went on a buying spree, a German business journal opined that as usual, very little of the group's own capital seemed to be involved. Purchasing with no money was something von Wersebe had obviously learned in Toronto, the writer declared.

He certainly didn't acquire his taste for such heady manoeuvres at the knee of his erstwhile mentor. Frastacky was a poor teacher, better at doing than showing, and still very much clothed in old-world fabric: cautious to the core; looking for steady fee income—not an immense personal fortune—from putting his clients into safe investments. "If you worked for Father you couldn't be too aggressive," says his son, Fedor Frastacky. "He also didn't believe in paying anyone anything. When Karsten started there, I think he was being paid $9,000."

Von Wersebe quickly acquired a reputation as a workaholic; but no one who came into contact with the terminally diffident young man could have guessed that he would one day employ thousands and deploy millions in businesses around the world.

"He was Frastacky's real estate assistant," a former Metro Trust client remembers. "If less important European investors would come over, Bodo [von Wersebe's middle name, used by old acquaintances but never by him today] was allowed to take them to lunch. But he was so shy, it was almost painful for him."

Von Wersebe may have an old-world air about him, but strip away the bashful packaging and he's all new money: bold, enterprising, a player for the big pots. "He is extraordinarily entrepreneurial. He comes up with schemes that nobody else has ever done," says one of his former executives, who adds that he still admires him but would rather work in a saner corporate environment. "When you do his kind of deals, you can't be totally a pragmatist. You've got to be very creative. And he is very creative. He loves the deal-making more than anything—oh, something terrible." No wonder he's shaken up his fellow Germans these past few years.

One story goes that, some time after marrying Renate, a fellow German immigrant as reserved as he was, he sought a raise from Frastacky and was turned down, prompting his departure. His own version is rather different, a pointed reminder of his position as an outsider in the clubby little world of Canadian finance. Von Wersebe says he knew it was time to move on after Ottawa decided to limit foreign ownership in financial institutions to no more than 30 percent. At the time, non-Canadians held 70 percent of Metro Trust. With his employer starting to look more and more like just another trust company, "it was abundantly clear that I, as a foreigner, would never rise to the highest rank," he says. "It's part of the history of this country." It wouldn't be the last time a Canadian political decision would drastically alter his career plans.

For an interview, he chooses a small conference room at York-Hannover's headquarters, located in First Canadian Place, the biggest of the downtown Toronto bank towers.

He wears conservative blue (suit, tie, shirt, eyes), which fits the outward image. A handsome tapestry behind him depicts a soothing forest scene.

The ever-guarded von Wersebe is hesitant at first. There's a hint of fear in those clear, savvy eyes, perhaps a result of the aggravation he's had with the German press. Slowly, though, he relaxes, even managing the occasional smile, revealing flashes of pungent humour as he warms to the subject at hand—himself.

He originaly came in 1965, for a brief stay, then returned here in 1967 as a student, intending to acquire some experience before returning to Europe. "My opportunities were substantial and I thought I would go back," he says softly in rapid, lightly accented English. "I was interested in working in the Common Market. Many young people who came over on that basis stayed two years, and then four years and six, and then they never went home."

He didn't become a Canadian citizen until 1984, and has never surrendered his German passport, though he had to fight to keep it. "Now, with present European Community status, I can work in every country in Europe. I would be nuts to give that up." He had to prove he had no choice but to become a Canadian; a requirement satisfied by the federal Foreign Investment Review Act (FIRA), which put curbs on what a foreigner could own, or at the very least required a lot of extra paperwork. He had to satisfy the Germans as well, by proving he still had family obligations back home; easy enough when your name's been attached to the same soil for more than 1,000 years.

"It was not a successful business, but it was a traditional business. The family has this large estate, large by German standards, of 330 hectares. But it was a place where you could barely raise a family, because there was no money." Still, it has been in his ancestors' hands since before the Norman Conquest of England; before Columbus booked the first package tour to the Caribbean; before the Europeans discovered the joys of investing in (and expropriating) the New World. That tradition has obviously meant a great deal to his family. His father was a public figure who avoided party politics, which made him the ideal choice to sit on impartial bodies like the local labour relations or forestry board, always without pay.

"I think he went to a meeting every night," his son recalls. "That's why he didn't make any money. He responded to the noble class environment, where duty to the state was the number one responsibility and profit was a bad word, I guess." Von Wersebe smiles at such a notion today. As he has set about constructing his labyrinthine business empire, his equally low-key older brother, Luder, trained as a lawyer but now running the family affairs on the estate has been responsible for the *noblesse oblige* stuff.

Yet, for all his new-money instincts, you can almost hear the old landed money rustling when von Wersebe voices his fears about Canada's future stability. Or when, like a surprising number of other immigrants, he attacks official multicultural policies and lax citizenship rules—despite his belief in an open door for newcomers and the vitality they bring with them. "How can you control your environment, your heritage, if you overload your society with foreigners who have absolutely no relation to this, and are forced to thrive on their own ethnic backgrounds and languages and cultures?" he wonders. "The whole problem is that Canadians don't know what it means to be Canadian. In my view, as a new Canadian, it's absolutely ridiculous. We're supposed to be all together."

His background may also help explain why he's so determined to make it big in his homeland; to prove he's no upstart who happened to get lucky in some overseas backwater. Had he not been the younger son (there are also four daughters), it's more than likely von Wersebe would still be on the humble family plot near Hannover, making use of his agricultural training, instead of heading off to Canada to manage real estate and other assets for Canadian and international clients.

Von Wersebe left Metro Trust to handle the Canadian interests of the Herzes, super-rich Hamburgers who've

brewed one of Europe's leading fortunes out of coffee.*
They made their first major investment here in 1970,
$1-million in a suburban Toronto building; but they were
after much more.†

Within short order, their Polaris Realty, which von
Wersebe set up and in which he became a partner,
had picked up over $150-million worth of property in
Montreal, Vancouver and Toronto—a sizeable chunk
for the early seventies. "I remember when we had a
press conference on one investment we made and it
was $28-million or something like this, and we had
the whole media of Montreal there. This was big news!
For $28-million, nobody's going to come to see you
these days," von Wersebe says with a laugh—a pleasant
punctuation mark that increasingly dots his conversation
as he gradually lowers the protective drawbridge.

One of the company's more prominent ventures was
the revolving restaurant it built atop its Harbour Centre
(since sold) in downtown Vancouver. "They got burned
on that deal," says a property specialist who knows all the
Euromoney in town. "It needed that great remedy for real
estate, which is time." It was one of the last bold moves
the company would make for more than a decade—not
because it got caught in a tricky market but because of
what von Wersebe calls Ottawa's meddling.

The year was 1974, a year draped in black in the

---

* The main Herz business is Tchibo Frisch Rost Kaffee, a European
coffee trader and retailer with a German market share alone of more
than 20 percent. Their thousands of stores also peddle a variety of other
goods, from videocassettes to tennis gear. Their controlling 60 percent
stake in a big tobacco company, Reemstma Cigarettenfabrik, is even
more lucrative. They also own 26 percent of the company that makes
Nivea cream. One observer says not to discount them when compiling a
list of the two or three wealthiest families with money in Canada. "Don't
underestimate them. In many cases, they own the real estate under their
stores as well."

† Before signing up von Wersebe, the Herzes had invested on a smaller
scale through Lehndorff. Frastacky's Metro Trust had once managed
their assets, but wasn't into the sort of active development they were
eager to pursue.

memories of veteran European investors, a year rank-
ing right up there with those of the Black Death—and
all because of four little letters: FIRA. The Trudeau
government's effort to ensure that foreign investments
would also do Canadians a bit of good sent a pneumonia-
like chill through capitalists born to rail against political
interference of any kind.* Then, to add insult to injury,
the tax advantage of parking cash here began evaporating;
and when provincial rent controls came along it was
like driving a stake through their hearts. "The political
environment was considered very unhealthy," von
Wersebe puts it mildly. "The feeling that foreigners were
not wanted drove a lot of the big property companies out."

The Herzes stayed, but slowed to a sleepwalking pace
until a few years ago, when a young retainer, Rainer
Hackert, came over from Hamburg to breathe some life
back into things.† (The family isn't known for idly tossing
money around. Owed a large sum by a basket-case of a
company in the Bahamas, Michael Herz, who helped run
the coffee interests with his older brother Gunter until a
split in 1989, flew there personally to settle things with
the desperate owner before the matter reached the courts.

---

* FIRA, which lasted until 1984, when Brian Mulroney's Tories took
power and quickly ditched it, didn't turn down many proposals.
Nonetheless it had a powerful psychological effect. Hans Abromeit
remembers a cuckoo-clock maker who wanted to set up a factory
here, but was told he would have to fill out a 250-page document,
including the most intimate details of his business. "He said, 'You're
crazy.' He went to North Carolina instead, and today has about 80
percent of his world production there."

† Hackert, a tall, amiable thirty-nine-year-old, dislikes the limelight
about as much as von Wersebe. Yet, as he's taken the company into
major developments, he's been forced to raise his profile. "I used to
just be the guy who signed the cheques," he sighs. The licence plate
on Hackert's BMW reads TCHIBO, the name of the Herzes' European
coffee empire. "Everybody thinks I'm working for the Japanese," he
chortles.
  The Herzes own the striking Daon Building in Vancouver, bought in
1987. They've also developed a large office building next to the Queen
Elizabeth Hotel in Montreal, and they own other offices and stores
downtown. In Toronto, they've built a huge project near the airport.

They were scheduled to meet at the airport, but missed each other. The poor wretch was waiting the whole time in the first-class lounge, not knowing that these billionaires never travel that way.)

Von Wersebe holds his reading glasses in his hands, to give them something to do as he rests his elbows on the marble table top. "If you didn't have FIRA, I would probably still be president of Polaris." Von Wersebe smiles; the irony of once again shifting career gears because of an Ottawa measure is not lost on him. "I had a 20 percent stake in the company. I already had a number of [outside] investment interests. I had a tremendous team of very nice professionals. Why would I leave?"

He shifted his piece of the Polaris assets to his own company, York-Hannover (he wanted to call it simply Hannover, but his lawyer convinced him it was too German for local tastes), where he got off to a less than auspicious start. A former colleague still remembers him scrambling to complete his deals at the last possible second. "Friday nights, Karsten would be wandering around with his lawyer to try to wrap up the financings. Those nights were life or death." There were five people at the first company Christmas party.

In 1978, he acquired a large amount of undeveloped land, apartments and some offices from John Prusac, an eccentric Yugoslavian immigrant and a one-time partner of Hans Abromeit, who was liquidating his substantial real estate holdings.* Later he added the Skyline hotel

---

* Prusac who started as a house builder, sold York-Hannover the control block in his Imperial General Properties for $18.7-million. He also sold control of the more lucrative Y & R Properties to Oxford Developments. In typical Prusac fashion, he demanded a certified cheque on the spot. The buyers had to wake up a senior banker—at 3:00 in the morning. Hamburg billionaire Werner Otto had turned down the deal, which he later regretted. Prusac's dream was to beat out Conrad Black for the late Bud McDougald's Argus empire. Prusac, who was so secretive even his business associates had no idea where he lived or whether he had a family, was once reportedly the largest individual depositor with the Bank of Nova Scotia. He later took his millions to Geneva.

chain, built up by Bill Hodgson, the wealthy sportsman and former owner of the Toronto Argonaut football club; and both of them were off to the races—Hodgson literally, as he began dabbling in thoroughbreds. Von Wersebe was happier betting on himself.

He had already acquired his formidable reputation for attracting foreign money, and for pulling rabbits out of the hat just when his exceedingly complex deals looked as if they were about to come unglued.

He actually chuckles as he recounts the guessing games that went on in the real estate community over the source of his financing. "I started largely with borrowing from Canadian banks and Chinese business people. The perception was there that my financing came from German investors because of my accent and name."

His days with Frastacky had exposed him to Swiss, Italian, German, Dutch and American money. "I have done business with them all going back to those days." But most of his early European cash was actually Italian.* "When everybody thought I had Swiss money, it was Italian. When they thought I had German money, it was Swiss."

Some of the big domestic financial accumulators were also in early, and they remain favourite partners. Confederation Life, for example, is half-owner of the posh Hazelton Lanes, which von Wersebe bought from French interests. His share: $40-million. "There also, of course, are some big German investors who have invested continuously in various of our projects. That's how we met Raulino. I became a small shareholder, and then

---

* There was actually more private Italian money floating around the big urban markets in the late seventies than from any other European source, say real estate people. Less concerned than the Germans, Dutch or Brits with Canadian tax rules, the Italians were busy trying to hide from their own taxman, and feared that continuing political instability was about to dissolve their fortunes. Euromoney pros say Tito Tettamanti, an Italian based in Lugano, funnelled more cash here through his Fidinam group than any other single money-raiser in Europe.

bought more and more until I had eighty-seven and a half percent."*

The key link to Swiss and German money was Castor Holdings, a Montreal-based company set up in 1975 with a former German banker named Wolfgang Stolzenberg. Essentially a mortgage broker, it proved extremely attractive to the coupon-clipping crowd, because interest from mortgage transactions with German investors wasn't taxed in Canada (a rule since changed). "Castor was very smartly put together," says a real estate expert. The company is still active. In 1989, Castor placed more than $400-million in mortgage loans in Canada and the United States, and it administers more than $1.5-billion worth of such investments. Though von Wersebe's projects represent only a small part of this, Castor's impressive list of prominent German and Swiss investors† helped turn York-Hannover into a major developer and property management company with a couple of billion dollars worth of real estate under its wing; these include offices, shopping centres, condos and hotels in Montreal, Ottawa, Toronto, Edmonton, Florida, Las Vegas, Bermuda, Pittsburgh and much of downtown Raleigh, North Carolina.

Stolzenberg, Castor's chairman, is a close friend of von Wersebe's, despite their seemingly diametrically opposed personalities. Someone who knows both of them once told me that if the two men were combined into one, they

---

* The company's full name is Raulino Treuhand und Verwaltungs. Once known as Messerschmitt, after the old controlling family, it is owned by von Wersebe through his Swiss holding company, with financing provided by the Rothschild Bank in Zurich. Raulino has investments in industrial businesses as well as property.

† Among Castor's Swiss investors is Stephan Schmidheiny, through his Anova Holding, which owns the company that makes Leica cameras. His lower-profile brother, Thomas, owns Holderbank Financière, the biggest cement-maker in the world. One of its many companies is St. Lawrence Cement of Montreal. The family is worth more than $2-billion (US), according to *Forbes*.

would embody just about every conceivable Germanic stereotype: von Wersebe the cool, controlled Teuton, and Stolzenberg the more flamboyant flip side—dashing, gregarious, fun-loving. Yet, ironically, Stolzenberg, the ex-banker, is probably less of a risk-taker than his more conservative-seeming buddy.

Stolzenberg "is the total opposite of Karsten. It's like night and day," says a former associate of the outgoing ex-banker. "One time, I was visiting his office in Montreal. He invited me to lunch. We were sitting in his Porsche, and he said: 'I can get out of this parking garage in twenty seconds.' He pushed the button to open the [garage] door before he started the car. Then he revved the engine and we raced through. The door was coming down. I told him I wanted to live a little longer." Von Wersebe drives a Porsche too, but there's no record of him ever challenging the land speed record in a Montreal parking lot.

Stolzenberg has played a key behind-the-scenes role in von Wersebe's ventures for years. Yet in lengthy conversation with von Wersebe, the name never surfaced, perhaps because he's simply not a name dropper; but he does appear sensitive about his friend's activities. A *Globe and Mail* reporter looking into Stolzenberg's part in a since-resolved legal dispute found himself, much to his surprise, getting an earful one day from an angry von Wersebe. Chewing out journalists is a habit of some self-important executives who like to throw their weight around, but it's totally out of character for someone as press-shy as von Wersebe. It's the only time anyone can recall him making such a phone call.

Stolzenberg is a resident of London but qualifies for plenty of frequent-flyer points. Castor's Swiss sister company, Castor Investment, has holdings here. Stolzenberg has other investments of his own and sits on several corporate boards.

Von Wersebe, Castor's chief executive until May 1983, as well as one of the founding investors, sold his shares in

1987 and resigned from the board. European sources say there may have been a dispute with shareholders over his German investment plans.

The big dreamer rocked the German establishment in 1986, when he came out of nowhere—Toronto, though to the European business elite it might as well have been nowhere—to buy 51 percent of a large, public, former mining company in Dortmund called Harpener. The cost was 500-million marks, of which close to 80 percent was borrowed from banks—simply shocking to the German traditionalists, who feared he was in way over his head and that he was out to strip off pieces of the company to pay for it. But he was gone just six months later, selling out for 565-million marks.

One press account surmised that the banks weren't prepared to carry the heavily indebted von Wersebe any longer; but he had already been totally frustrated by Harpener's board, which thwarted every one of his major schemes, and he wasn't interested in a long, drawn-out battle to get his ideas accepted. He wanted to take Harpener into the international real estate business (there's nothing like raw land to get a developer excited) and that would include the purchase of Raulino; but they couldn't agree on a price. Von Wersebe says that the banks and the press agree in hindsight that his plans were sound, but that they were ahead of their time.

Von Wersebe was also eager to move into another pet pastime: steel. In the early seventies in Houston, he'd started a company called York-Hannover Seamless Tube, a subsidiary of his Swiss-based York-Hannover Trading, which supplies pipe to the oil and gas industry. He had started as a specialty steel trader in a market dominated by a handful of global players. "Back in the 1970s, the development company had a low profile," he says. "Our trading activities [mainly property then, with steel second] were much more flamboyant."

He had recognized early that while Third World countries like Brazil and Malaysia were building magnificent steel plants with western aid and technology, they didn't have the networks needed to trade the finished goods. He wanted to go a step further, providing the venture capital to manufacture steel—a move that had no appeal to the Harpener directors, or to a lot of other companies at the time.

Von Wersebe retreated, saying he was being picked on by the hidebound German banks. He bounced back in late 1988 to buy Coutinho Caro, a big, troubled, public steel-trading company in Hamburg with sales of nearly two billion marks annually. It was available because its American parent had been unable to get its operations under control from overseas.

Already out of Canada about six months of every year, and with his new acquisition badly in need of a salvage job, von Wersebe would spend even less time at his comfortable, traditional-style north Toronto home near the Rosedale Golf Club*—leading to conjecture that he intends to pull up stakes here altogether. Perhaps opportunities in the new Europe are too good to pass up, or the market here has turned too sour. Like many developers in the current market, York-Hannover is paring its costs to the bone and appears to have nothing new on the drawing boards—always a troubling sign for a merchant builder. Or perhaps von Wersebe wants to get away from the painful memory of his teenage daughter's tragic drowning at the family cottage here in the summer of 1989. Perhaps all of the above.

Old associates question such logic. They say von Wersebe's already been running his far-flung businesses from Toronto for years. While he's thrown himself into his European work since the family tragedy, a loyal staffer reminds me that he still has a son, Lloyd, in school here, at the University of Western Ontario—and that his prolonged absences from Canada do happen to

---

* Von Wersebe bought the house in 1973 for $270,000, and has put another $200,000 into it. He says it's worth $2-million today, but an acquaintance insists that if that's all he wants for it, "I'll write him a cheque right now."

coincide with the need to put his expensive new steel toy back on the track.

"That's going to certainly take him away, at least for the time being, from any activities that he was planning here," says a lawyer familiar with the steel deal. "Who knows what he is going to do. He probably will be trying to switch it over into some kind of investment business."

One ex-employee predicts that Stolzenberg will end up with York-Hannover—"or what's left of it." Stolzenberg, through his lawyer, calls such speculation ridiculous. And it must be a standing line in the development community that von Wersebe is overextended.

"Ever since Karsten has been in his business, people have said that he is in trouble, because he likes leverage so much," says another European deal-maker. "That's the way he likes to be. I think he needs to be like that. He held on during the recession [of 1981-82], when everybody thought he would collapse. You have to admire him."

Marco Muzzo, a grey-bearded, balding bear of a man, a poor Italian immigrant who has become one of Canada's most powerful developers, known for his influence in the bedroom communities around Toronto, says that, over the years, "I've never known him to bite off anything he couldn't chew. He's a risk-taker, but one who knows what he's doing."

CHAPTER 7

The Wanderers

IT'S HARD TO picture the earnest, conservative Swiss-born fund manager as a globe-trotting adventurer. He's spinning wondrous yarns of wandering across the dusty Persian trading route from Afghanistan in the company of itinerant merchants and camel-herders; of trekking through Uganda and Ethiopia; of being down but not quite out in Capetown and Singapore; of landing in Toronto and not even knowing what country he was in. But how do you reconcile all that with this tall, dark-suited man who has been entrusted with so much of other people's money?

Peter Cavelti is, after all, a solid family man, cautious manager of hundreds of millions of dollars, who worries about global debt and warns his clients to keep their cash balances high and stick to gold in times of trouble. Yet he was once as nomadic as the Asian tribesmen who sold him some of the spectacular rugs that warm his old stone home in Toronto, unsure where or whether he'd settle down.

Some newcomers to Canada have carefully crafted grand designs for the future, whether it's to put down permanent roots from the outset or merely temporary

170

ones while the tempests blow over back home. A few, like Cavelti, have bounced here almost by accident, in the midst of roaming the globe in search of excitement, challenge, a good carpet or simply a place where they and their ambitions won't seem out of place.

For Cavelti and his fellow travellers, Canada started out as just another stop on the world tour; but for one reason or another, it's reached out and grabbed hold of the imaginations of a remarkable assortment of moneyed wanderers. They could live just about anywhere—and some have; but they've seen the future and decided it's here.

Chronically pessimistic about our prospects; fearful of the overfed but always hungry giant to the south; locked in petty, parochial quarrels that sometimes leave once bewitched newcomers thoroughly bothered and bewildered, we don't often view our land as an enchanted place where dream and reality can still hold hands. Yet some of the wanderers pitching their tents here think of Canada in just that way.

"There's a tremendous amount of freedom, which is very unique in the world," says Dutch-born, U.S.- and European-trained Willem Bijl, who was a senior executive with Inter-Continental Hotels in Paris before coming to Canada in 1975 on a whim and a job offer from CP Hotels. He later built his own hotel- and nursing home-management firm, from "an idea and $2,000 in the bank," into a multimillion-dollar public company. "You're given a tremendous scope to do as you please. You can get things done with a minimum amount of bureaucracy compared with where I come from and the other countries where I have lived."

Bijl flashes a wide smile when he talks of how he started his business, Kanata Hotels, in 1981. (The company was bought out in 1990, though he still runs it.) The notion wouldn't have entered his head anywhere else. "I could never, ever have achieved, dared or tried what I have gone through here in Canada."

Burmese-born Danny Gaw, who sells enough tarts,

doughnuts and other baked goods in Vancouver to bring in a sweet $10-million a year,* would certainly agree. He considers himself to have been a "gypsy, travelling all over the place without a stable country to live in" before landing on the West Coast in 1982. His wanderings had taken him from Hong Kong, where his ethnic Chinese parents had immigrated in the fifties, to the United States for university and a year with an insurance company in Hartford, Connecticut. Then he was off to Singapore, back to Hong Kong and on to Thailand, which held his attention for a dozen years. "Thailand was a nice place to stay, but I still felt unstable, uncertain."

The doughnut king, who doesn't look as if he's ever been tempted by one of his chocolate glazes, laughs easily and with good reason. He says he doesn't plan another move. "That's why we [Gaw and his U.S.-educated wife, Jeannie] bought a house. We've never owned a house before. This is the first time that we are able to make long-term plans. It's a different feeling altogether. You feel a sense of belonging."

Peter Cavelti is cut from similar gypsy cloth, wandering even farther afield before making it here. A Swiss banker like no other, he found his own country too small; the United States too threatening; South Africa too . . . well . . . South African. He tried Singapore and seriously weighed Australia and a couple of South American countries before choosing what he saw as "this oasis" to finally reach for his own dreams.

Knowing his reputation as an international fund manager, I had sought him out in the vain hope he might lead me to some of his private European or Taiwanese clients, the ones who have put as much as $2-million apiece

---

* The money behind his purchase of Superior Bakery (1989), Max's Donuts (early 1987) and Nuffy's Donuts (mid-1988) came from the Windsor Group, a public Hong Kong textile corporation. They've also added a few valuable properties downtown, including the old Province newspaper building, and are on the lookout for more businesses.

in his care. Who would think this restrained, bankerly type—and a Swiss one at that!—would turn out to be far more passionate about the issues I was exploring than any of his gold-brained foreign investors were likely to be?

"Immigrants are people who have to take very, very substantial chances in their lives. You give up things over and over. And I have done this several times," Cavelti says between sips from a giant styrofoam cup of coffee. "My parents were very well off. I could have blissfully stayed in Switzerland and had a mediocre, very predictable, upper-class life. I didn't want to do that."

He's talking about the old days, in his spacious downtown Toronto office a few blocks from the high-powered competition in the glassier bank towers. He's got a good view outside and as good a one within, where his walls hold up some dramatic Canadian etchings, a couple by artists he has helped promote. He himself paints—just one of several passions. (No abstracts, though: "Somehow, I have an inhibition. I guess it's money management that's done that to me.")

The forty-two-year-old Cavelti first revealed his wanderer's instincts after being consigned, as a teenager, to a monastic school for a proper seventeenth-century education. Young Peter told his father to get him out or he'd leave on his own. His father finally complied, delaying the start of his son's global ramble. In four years at the school, Cavelti did manage to pick up a little Greek, Latin, calligraphy and the invaluable ability to scribble, 1,500 times at a crack in perfect Gregorian script, *Silentium aurum est* (silence is golden)—his punishment any time he opened his mouth when he was supposed to keep it shut.

"My father was convinced that this classical education was extremely beneficial. I think I missed part of my youth, but I caught up wildly afterwards," he says, a smile crinkling his handsome features. The words come out smoothly in impeccable English, pleasantly overlaid with an unmistakable Swiss lilt.

Cavelti later dropped out of a prestigious university after only a year of studying economics. "I found the system very autocratic. Maybe I could stomach it now, but it was extremely rigid and very ideologically slanted." Only his rakish mustache and the glint in his clear blue eyes offer a hint of such un-Swiss nonconformity. It's no wonder the amateur artist finally felt compelled to see what lay beyond Switzerland. First, though, he did some time as a rookie gnome with one of the big-league banks in Zurich to scrape together the price of an airline ticket. "I had this vision of travelling, working to earn enough money to see more places, meet more people. My desire from the very beginning was to go and see the world."

He wandered to South Africa, where life, more often than not, was a beach. Then, it was off to roam the rest of Africa and Asia. Even several years after deciding that Canada might be the place to plant his tent pole, he took off in a Jeep across the Hindu Kush mountains (in the days before thousands of heavily armed mujahidin fighters took to the rugged Afghan terrain in their battle to oust the Soviet-backed government) in search of tribal rugs, another obsession he simply had to pursue.

"One of the tragedies of our modern industrial age is that you've got armies of people who will be sixty-five and what they have done during the preceding forty-five years is gone to work at nine in the morning and walked out at five-thirty and had on average x meals at x hours per day. And I don't think that was genetically the imprint that human beings had."

Cavelti's parents weren't thrilled with their eldest son's roving ways (another son and two daughters showed no such deviancy), but had always encouraged him to make his own choices. "I remember my father gave me 1,000 [Swiss] francs, which I thought was extremely generous, because I expected nothing. At that time, it bought you about two or three weeks of rent somewhere and a few hamburgers a day. I was in Capetown, and I rationed myself to two hamburgers and two Cokes every day. I ran out of money after three weeks, because I had to pay an advance on this room I was living in."

The low-nutrition diet didn't last long; he had no trouble

landing a banking job in a country begging for bright, lily-white recruits to join its thinning professional ranks. His employer threw in special management training, helped him polish his English and sent him to university at night to learn the nuances of gold mining. He would go on to become an acknowledged international expert on the subject, penning five authoritative books (one, *New Profits in Gold, Silver and Strategic Metals*, is dedicated to "my parents for always letting me be myself"), making liberal use of the classical training he so reluctantly absorbed, and turning out a monthly newsletter with a worldwide circulation today of 60,000 copies.

Bay Streeters call him a true "gold bug," a heavy metal fan no matter what the economic circumstances. He detests the tag, but comes by it honestly. His firm, Cavelti Capital Management, manages or co-manages almost $600-million (US) in gold mutual funds. (One partner is N. M. Rothschild, the influential London investment banking group.) Two chunks of gold-ribboned ore bask, like prized archeological finds, under lights in his quiet, marbled reception area, which faces a glassed-in bank of computer screens. Brochures shilling Maple Leaf gold coins sit on a side table beside copies of his latest newsletter. "They say you can never crush a gold bug," an acquaintance says. "They keep bouncing back up." The image would fit the irrepressible Cavelti even if he had never tumbled into the metal during his South African sojourn.

He refuses to reveal what he's worth today, apart from grudging acknowledgement that he's a millionaire. "I would not feel good if you say Cavelti says he's a millionaire, because I don't relate to myself in those terms. Money is a very, very important thing to me, because it translates into freedom. But I have come to absolutely despise the way in which other people relate to it. I have nothing in common with that. I believe that what matters in life is that you go and win the battles that you set out to win and realize your dreams. Whether you get rich by doing that is a totally secondary thing."

The former globe-trotter now finds most of the escape he needs in an isolated cabin on Georgian Bay, accessible only by boat "and a brilliant navigator." There's no television, no radio. He does have a phone, but only his closest relatives know the number. He laughs when asked how he survives in this day and age without the ubiquitous portable fax, the executive's umbilical cord.

"The cabin was one of the first things I bought," Cavelti says. "To me that was a dream. After five years here, I came to the conclusion that Canadians were completely ignorant of what they had, complete morons. To be able to buy a fifteen-acre retreat with a mile of shoreline for $40,000 or $50,000 [in the late seventies], you've got to be completely crazy not to have one. That was the first money I ever had in this country." The seller even threw in a motorboat.

Cavelti had his own twenty-six-foot sailboat, but has since shed that luxury item, along with what he calls his other toys. "The more possessions you have, the more they possess you. Everything needs money to maintain—except of course my rugs and my art, which relax me. I have come to the point where I need one automobile and I need my house in the city, because I'm with Carol and the kids and I need room for all my collected works."

He married only in 1985, acquiring a ready-made family with two teenage daughters. He attributes the delay to his workaholic's existence. "I was no swinging bachelor. I really worked unbelievable hours. I still don't have as much time as I would like."

Completely at ease, Cavelti speaks freely, often in a self-congratulatory tone, of the attitudes that have shaped the way he lives—a far cry from most of the new money, who prefer staying in the shadows and rarely pat themselves on the back in public. "When you're poor you have to compromise more. You find it much more difficult to be principled," he philosophizes. "That's why unprincipled rich people are at the very bottom of my personal social ladder."

The South Africans bent over backwards to hold on

to this quick study with the European pedigree, but he was gone after three years. In explaining why, he doesn't single out the racist government—apart from noting that "there were social problems and the dark side of South Africa, which made it unattractive."

While others might be inclined to use stronger language when talking about apartheid, people with wanderlust in their veins don't need excuses to pack their bags and walk away from "what was a very cushy job which allowed me to go to the beach every afternoon. For a young man of twenty-three, I was really having a super time. I had a nice car, I saw nice girls, I played tennis. I had all the material things. But I wanted to see Africa, and I left everything."

He eventually made his way to the Far East, where he ran out of money and took a job in Singapore with his original Swiss employer, a subsidiary of the Swiss Bank Corporation. It was on the way home, after changing his mind about moving to Australia (Perth, where the immigration authorities would have required him to work, was pleasant, but there's evidently a limit to how much sun and fun a Swiss banker can take), that he first stopped off in Toronto. "I thought it was a part of the United States I had never heard of before. I was planning to go to Canada after landing in Toronto. It was very different from what I expected the United States to be like."

Cavelti continued on his journey home, thinking he would return to his old life, only to learn that you can't if you never really fit in in the first place. "I noticed within three weeks that I could never live there again. It's a funny thing, but it just literally happened that way. I had lived in Africa and Asia and seen North America, and here I was back in little Switzerland. It was too small for me, the people were too narrow-minded and too proper. Everything was too conservative. I have since modified my views, as I've gotten a little older."

Cavelti thought next of New York, but changed his mind as soon as he landed there. It was 1972, and he had arrived smack-dab in the middle of anti-Vietnam war protests, anti-Nixon marches, flag-burnings, all of it a shock to his sensibilities. "I expected to come to the industrial powerhouse of the world. And all I saw was complete turmoil and what I felt was a completely demoralized society. I thought, 'Shucks, where am I going to go to now? This is a country with no future.' "

Hoping perhaps it was only nutty New York that had turned its back on order and good sense, he hopped a Greyhound bus to see the rest of what would prove to be a most unpromising land. "I jumped in and went all the way out to San Francisco in a wild frenzy of travel. I saw all of these cities of two, three, four, five million people. They were dumps, nightmares."

In between, he took a short detour to Vancouver, where the only people carrying signs were strikers on a picket line. "They were marching up and down the street, which I soon learned was a major phenomenon in Canada. I got to know these nations at the gut level very, very quickly."

The wanderer finally opted for Toronto as being just about the right size and shape for his dreams. Europeans sometimes sarcastically compare Toronto the Good to a typical Swiss city: clean, smug, orderly and cold, the kind of place where the sidewalks are rolled up at night to prevent anything interesting from happening on them. Cavelti unwittingly reinforces this outdated view when he recites the standard lyrics of the Why-I-love-Canada immigrant's marching song: "You didn't have to worry about getting mugged. The traffic was a breeze. There were parks everywhere. The transit system was the best I've ever seen. So I thought, 'This is where I want to be' "—Switzerland, with lots more space.

Then, to his dismay, Cavelti discovered a clubby little financial community that had no interest in admitting a foreigner with international training. "I was rejected by every Canadian bank and financial institution. They were so closed and parochial. I was really quite desperate. I couldn't even get a teller's job." To pay for his burgers, he began selling oriental carpets on consignment for traders he had met in Switzerland. "I had to do something. I don't think I sold terribly many, but I really got to be very knowledgeable."

He finally ended up as a management trainee at Deak, the aggressive New York currency trader that had expanded into Canada. It would turn into an enormous break for the erstwhile rug merchant, one of those perfect marriages of talent and timing.

Once in the door, Cavelti became head of Canadian operations within two years. "It was just unbelievable. I had become used to the way international banking is conducted in most of the world. If you're a level-K employee after your education, and if you're really, really good, in a ten-year span you can go to maybe level E or F, and then gradually over the next three decades work your way up. In Canada, I saw that there were no such barriers. The system was more prejudiced, but once you were inside it, you could bust your way through very, very quickly."

Good thing he hadn't started at one of the conservative Canadian banks that tower over the nation's financial skyline, or he might still be handing customers their change, or measuring carpets or roaming the high Andes, instead of bringing his humanistic values to a business sorely in need of them.

After four years with Deak, Cavelti did something highly unusual: He quit the firm, but not the country. Instead, he shifted to a tiny, family-owned Montreal company called Guardian Trust, which had ambitions beyond its regional redoubt. Soon, he was on the board and in charge of everything west of Quebec. In 1983, he talked the firm into expanding international operations, with him in charge. He was gone two years later, with a considerably healthier bank account, when Groupe Coopérants, a big Quebec insurance company, swallowed up his employer.

"They were the type of company that I felt would have a very difficult time being entrepreneurial because they were a very large conglomerate, many times our size; and I had come to believe that the insurance industry is a rather structured and bureaucratic one, even worse than banking. I decided that the danger of our cultures not mixing was significant." (Cavelti appears to have been right. By the fall of 1990, the insurer had found another trust company to take over management of its troubled holding, through a merger.) He sold his stake in Guardian—he won't say how much he owned—but continued managing the same funds as when he was on the payroll.

Cavelti says he could manage today from just about anywhere he can plug in a phone. In fact, only 5 percent of the money invested with him is Canadian, dwarfed by his American (85 percent) and more distant (10 percent) contributions. He's fully aware of this country's ingrown inferiority complex—a problem that so infuriates enterprising immigrants. He had to line up a couple of giant U.S. customers before Canadians would even consider investing in him. "I suddenly had absolutely no problem getting Canadian funds, which is very much what every novelist, every painter, every entrepreneur in the high-tech area tells you too."

Nevertheless, he appears to have found what he was searching the world to discover. "I have a very soft spot for this place. If I come across as someone who thinks that Canada is all negative, I don't think so at all. It has many, many advantages over the United States and other countries. But our attitude towards new ideas is not one of those. I still see Canadians as extremely negative thinkers." If wanderers like Cavelti had shared such a narrow view of the world and their place in it, they would never have left their secure little corners in the first place.

Once the members of the petroleum club found out in the seventies just how much the rest of the world was willing to pay for their precious resource, they began raking in far more millions than they knew what to do with, closely followed by a crowd of eager international hangers-on who knew exactly what to do with the windfall. One Hong Kong native who brought his millions to Canada in the early eighties was among those opportunists, landing in Saudi Arabia in 1975 to cash in on the sudden demand for prefab housing by all the Americans determined to bring the civilizing touch of suburban Dallas to the desert kingdom.

"I'm a bit of an adventurer," chuckles the son of a major Hong Kong manufacturer, who doesn't want his father to know he's been talking to strangers. After wheeling and dealing in the Far East, the Near East and the American Midwest, he spends his time more quietly these days, investing the family money in other people's businesses here, from technology to fast food. Like many seasoned wanderers, he says the steamer trunk's been put away for good.

"It was very hot in Riyadh, both the weather and the business. But it was not a long-term place. At the end of my three years, I said: 'I'll take the money and run.' And I did. It's like a casino in these places. If you stay long enough, you're bound to lose."

That helps explain why a slim, aristocratic-looking Dutchman with a fabled name and old-world tastes packed up his bags and left the Persian Gulf for Canada (a rare migratory path for any European, let alone a bird of plutocratic plumage who can read classical Greek without the aid of a dictionary). Hendrik Hooft too had concluded that while the Middle East might have been a good spot for a bit of adventure and excitement, it was no place to try to put down any roots.

Hooft, then thirty-five, had moved his wife and four children to the gulf oil station of Dubai in 1974 to watch a nation in the making, but found it doesn't take long to lay in the modern essentials for a population of only 100,000. "By the eighties, the oil scene started to become less exciting. It got flat because everything had been done by then. It wasn't new anymore," says the scion of one of the mighty merchant families that turned Amsterdam in the sixteenth and seventeenth centuries into a centre of money and power. "It's very fascinating to come to a country that is building. In two years, everything in

Dubai was done, more or less. Also, the children came of high-school age and we decided it was time to move on."

Not that Dubai's ruler hadn't tried to make life pleasant for the drifters. He even built an ice-skating rink, which is where Hooft's kids learned to play hockey. "One day when we came out of the rink with our skates in our hands, we saw seven camels sitting right in front of the entrance. 'Now remember this moment,' I told the children. 'You will never again see this in your life.' "

With no desire to return to a Europe that a decade ago still seemed on the downward side of a slippery slope, and with the kids already being schooled in English, "we decided to go somewhere where the language was spoken. If we'd been in our thirties, we might have gone to the U.S., but since we were in our forties, we decided to come to Canada." This is evidently the way we look to the wealthy, world-weary wanderer: friendly, secure, comforting, a country that's easy on the blood pressure.

Like most Dutch people who remember the Canadian liberation of their homeland from the Nazis, Hooft already had warm thoughts about this place and its people. His patrician wife, Eliane, an athletic sort, had her own special attachment, having gone to school in Ottawa when her father was posted there as the Dutch ambassador. Nonetheless, Hooft is too much the traveller (he doesn't even have to pack when he travels to Europe, keeping everything he needs at his father-in-law's house in Amsterdam) to see himself tied down to any one place. "The world is a smaller place. With the global village, you can live and work anywhere. It is not so divided by national boundaries as in the past. A human being should be between poles. That makes life interesting. You need opposite currents or life becomes very bland."

In his living room Hooft holds court like a country squire. To him, it's no more than a comfortable place where he can read his London *Financial Times* by the fire or amuse himself at the piano. Yet, like most of the rooms in his surprisingly modest T-shaped home on High Point Road (in the luxurious Bridle Path area of north

Toronto, one of the most affluent suburban neighbourhoods in Canada*), it could be transported right to the
middle of Rembrandt's Amsterdam. The old artist himself wouldn't seem out of place here. (Hooft genially cor-
rects me. His family, he says without apology, never commissioned Rembrandt, preferring their own favourites of
the day. But if I do want to see the finest collection of
the Master's work in private hands, he'll happily write
a letter of introduction to the Six family in Amsterdam,
another of the old merchant dynasties and Rembrandt's
great patron.)

Hooft, whose tanned, unlined features and boyish enthusiasm make him seem much younger than his fifty-one
years, would never understand Peter Cavelti's attitude
towards possessions; not when he's faithfully preserving
a houseful that have been in the family for several hundred years. He insists he's no collector (there'd be no
room anyway beside the family treasures), apart from the
purchase of a grand seventeenth-century Flemish tapestry
that blankets one wall. He thought its depiction of water and plants might be a refreshing reminder of Europe
in hot, dry Dubai. The rest may look like glorious
antiques and paintings by Dutch masters, but it's all
really just the old family furniture and a few pictures
of the relatives. The two 400-year-old portraits bracket-
ing the living room—a famed poet and his red-haired
wife, who bears a passing resemblance to Queen Elizabeth
I—are each more than six feet high and four feet wide.

You might expect a gate of upper-crust European
reserve to be guarding this conservative (in the old-
fashioned sense of the word; he actually sees the good
points of socialism, at least in theory) in the well-cut grey
suit, crisp white shirt, navy silk tie and black loafers, his

---

* High Point and neighbouring streets like Post Road, the Bridle Path,
Bridle Heath Gate and Park Lane sprawl with estates owned by the
likes of Conrad Black, Hans Abromeit, Robert Campeau, a couple of
mega-buck Iranian immigrants and Hong Kong movers and shakers such
as super-rich Stanley Ho, Kenneth Lo and the Kwan family.

thick grey hair parted perfectly on the right and silver wire-framed glasses lending him a scholarly air. Instead, he turns out to be a thoroughly engaging raconteur, as amiable and relaxed as his living room, with its well-used fireplace and overstuffed couches, upholstered in a playful blue-and-green-bird motif and with plaid car blankets at one end for the family's Irish setters.

The squire sips a café brûlé, served in an elegant china cup by his assistant, while absently petting the two young dogs whenever they wander over to nudge him. Their mother is sleeping in another room; but the three budgies in their cages by the picture window are wide awake, loudly adding their own comments to Hooft's.

Smiling broadly, he sums up his stay in Dubai as "great fun," a watchword for his whole approach to business life. He'd gone there to do some investment banking for English and Arab interests, later hanging out his law shingle. It seems the no-nonsense Dutch and Germans who'd followed the smell of petrodollars couldn't stomach the tradition-laden Brits—with their overblown opinions beautifully bound in green ribbon—who dominated the European legal business in the region. The newcomers hated paying for the ribbon, and went to Hooft instead.

Someone who goes where the fun is can't really expect to be taken too seriously by many of the staggering workaholics who weave their way here from abroad, and Hooft isn't—though his family name, connections and obvious wealth make him a good catch for dinner parties, do-nothing corporate boards and various arts and education causes. A Dutch immigrant who's lived in Canada for three decades spots Hooft radiating his well-honed upper-class charm at a crowded business reception, where he seems to know everybody who's anybody. "The really important people, the movers and the shakers, aren't here," the grizzled veteran sniffs, looking at Hooft. Does he mean Hooft isn't exactly a heavyweight? "Oh yes. He's a dilettante. Nothing serious."

While it's true that Hooft isn't a driven deal-maker, he does try to keep busy acquiring farmland and real estate for Dutch investors through his company, Woodmount

Head Management (including the property he has assembled right across the street from the King Edward Hotel in downtown Toronto), when he could just as easily be doing little more than clipping his coupons or walking his dogs. His clients, whom he declines to name, include both institutions and wealthy individuals. "I love to be back in a merchant banking type of business. What I'm doing for international investors is close to what you'd do in an investment bank. I find the investment, deal with the tax considerations and the equity financing mix."

He also spends hours on causes like a small, cash-starved chamber music group and the private Toronto French School, both of which put him in charge of their boards. He has helped steer the school, a favourite among silver-spoon immigrants, through some rocky times. Some of the other parents say that he grates on their nerves, but is perfect for the job because he seems to have so much time to devote to it. "I didn't want his opinion," says one parent of Hooft's contributions at a particular meeting. "I wanted to hear from the people running the school. He's just the chairman of the board, but all of a sudden, he's an expert on education." (Hooft, in fact, had started a private elementary school in Dubai, with the help of American expatriates.)

In his spare time, he dabbles at the piano (the talent and tastes are inherited from his singing Swedish mother); and like Peter Cavelti, he paints—along with the rest of the family, on their annual summer sojourn to a hard-to-reach Greek island. The previous occupant was an artist who left behind suitable paint supplies but little else. Everything has to be carried in by donkey, and there are few twentieth-century amenities.

That suits Hooft, who doesn't even have a TV in his Toronto house or at the family's weekend farm (where he grows cash crops such as corn) in southwestern Ontario. He has scarcely accepted radio. Seated beside Barbara Frum once at a charity event, he had to admit that he'd never seen her work. "She was fascinated by this," he says in a slightly bewildered tone. "We had a very animated conversation."

His own family story would make an exciting mini-series. His ancestors were powerful grain merchants—which amounted to a licence to mint guilders during the famines and wars that ravaged Europe during the late sixteenth and seventeenth centuries. They were right at centre stage, along with a handful of other trading families, during Amsterdam's glory years. Two great merchant dynasties laid the foundation of the modern Netherlands, Hooft states proudly. "One of those families was mine."*

The power faded, but not the wealth. By the nineteenth century, the Hoofts were leading the lives of country gentlemen; riding, shooting and gaming. Then, one day, Hendrik's great-grandfather was contemplating his future on one of the family's large estates in central Holland, musing to a relative about the tiresome life of the idle rich. Putting their heads together, they came up with a hobby to keep them occupied: making beer, a favourite pastime of the landed gentry who can't grow grapes.

"Usually, people found companies because they want to make money," Hooft says affably. "My great-grandfather and his brother-in-law already lived on estates. They were hunting and shooting their whole life and they were bored. So they founded a brewery. It came to be called Amstel."

Amstel remained solely in Hooft hands, keeping numerous family members busy off the estates, until it went public in the early 1950s and was later bought out. Hendrik's well-travelled father was in charge of export markets, but his eldest son had no taste for that sort of corporate life. "I didn't think it would be much fun to go into my father's business. I wanted to do something on my own." (He says it's a coincidence that he sits on the board of Amstel Brewery Canada, though the irony isn't lost on him.)

Trained as a lawyer, he opted instead for what seemed

---

* Cornelis Pieterszoon Hooft, head of the family in the late 1500s, is described in one account as "everything that was good about the Amsterdam merchant." Which means he was incredibly skilful at making money, had a talent for politics and a taste for religious freedom. It's his renowned poet son who graces his descendant's living room wall in Toronto today.

the more adventurous life of an international investment banker, going to work for an old Dutch merchant bank called Pierson, Heldring and Pierson. His brother, two years younger, has followed a similar route, working for Royal Trust in London.

Hooft happily admits he didn't have a clue as to what he wanted to do in Canada, but in 1980 he emigrated anyway, certain something would turn up. His old employer, Pierson, asked him to set up an office, reviving a historic connection: The merchant bank had helped finance the building of the Canadian Pacific Railway more than a century ago.

Hooft says the part-time job as a foreign bank representative was a "nice stepping-stone," but it was an even quieter life than he had envisioned. "Having a lot of time is to lead an unhealthy life. I found I was spending too much time at long lunches and dinners." After two years of heavy dining, a frustrated but still trim Hooft told the firm to open a proper banking operation or forget about showing the flag here.

Unwilling to go through basic legal training again after running his own firm in Dubai, he opted instead for a real estate licence, after several wealthy compatriots kept pestering him to look after their investments in Canada. "I was in the classroom with housewives and students. It was an opportunity to see a real cross-section of the people," says Hooft, who makes it sound as if he was on some sort of anthropological field trip among a particularly primitive tribe.

Walking down to the foot of his evergreen-lined property, this least likely of real estate men grimaces as he glances across the street, where workers are framing an enormous mansion for Iranian immigrant Shane Baghai, who's made his millions building slightly smaller versions for other wealthy newcomers.* He bought the property

---

* It would be 30,000 square feet. The homes that have cast a giant shadow over older neighbourhoods in Vancouver and Toronto generally come in at 6,000 to 13,000 square feet.

beside his own to make sure he would have enough room. The house next door to Hooft's is an institutional-looking fortress—complete with indoor pool and enough space for a good polo match—acquired by another wealthy Iranian expatriate, Karim Hakim, who's made his bundle in eyeglasses under the name Hakim Optical.

Ever discreet, Hooft won't dump on his more ostentatious neighbours, especially after they rallied to support his successful effort to block another symbol of excessive progress in the area—curbs on the street. Why, the next thing you know, the municipality might start thinking sidewalks, and who knows where that could lead? "I like the unfinished look," Hooft explains. "It makes it seem like a country lane, and they said they were going to widen the road."

To celebrate the triumph of democracy over the advances of the late twentieth century, this throwback to another place and time invited Baghai, Hakim and the rest of the new money who had joined in his spirited campaign to a dinner amid the old family furniture, while his ancestors, unsmiling, looked down from the walls.

There are no ancestral portraits hanging in Boris Birshtein's office. Getting in to find that out is the easy part; it only takes a couple of months of phone calls and enough luck to catch him in town. Talking to the international deal-maker, who specializes in trade, travel and just about any other venture that promises a few roubles inside the Soviet Union, is an entirely different matter, a bit like trying to put a roof on in the middle of a tornado: you get sucked up before you can nail anything down.

When I finally enter his luxurious inner sanctum at his Seabeco Group headquarters, an oddly stylish mixture of antique furniture, marble-topped desk, hundred-year-old Persian carpet and brooding modern art (a complete surprise in an otherwise generic building in midtown Toronto), the Lithuanian-born entrepreneur is fielding an endless stream of visitors and phone calls in enough languages to send a UN translator into early retirement. I sit down in a corner and wait for things to quiet down . . . and wait . . . and wait.

Finally, the bundle of energy mumbles an apology for all the interruptions and sits down for a good five or six minutes, during which he commandeers a bagel from a harried assistant. It could be his lunch or maybe even his dinner. Time has a strange way of losing its moorings in the presence of this wanderer, who's dragged his family from his Baltic homeland to Israel and then to Switzerland before arriving in Canada, unsure where in the world he should alight.

"So, ask me questions," commands the white-shirted cherub with a taste for showy silk ties. Close up, his thick, carefully styled greying hair and mustache, serious demeanour and smoker's wrinkles creeping around his dark, tired-looking eyes make him seem older than his forty-three years. He doesn't have time to waste on long get-acquainted chats with people who can't make him a dime, so I'd better come right to the point.

What brought him to Canada? The answers to this question are almost always a variation on an overplayed theme of safety, security, space, opportunity—but not Birshtein's. "I remember the day. It was in June 1985. I came with my wife for a business meeting. Each year, my Canadian partners tried to convince me it was better for me to be here than in Zurich. I said, 'You know what'—and it really was my joke—'if I can be here before September 1, because my son starts in school, then we are ready to move.' "

Birshtein, a natural storyteller with the timing of a stand-up comic, says he never expected it to happen, not in less than three months, and insists he wouldn't have extended the deadline. He just didn't realize Ottawa was welcoming rich immigrants with imploring arms, or that he would be put in the hands of a lawyer who knew how to steer him past whatever red tape might lie in the way of such a speedy entry.

The strings were pulled quickly. He found himself the next day in the airy, oversized office of Mendel Green, one of Canada's top immigration lawyers, best known for battling for newcomers' rights, but whose serious income and influence come from quietly bringing in the rich ones like Birshtein or Raymond Chow (whose Hong Kong-based Golden Harvest film company is best known in North America for *Teenage Mutant Ninja Turtles*) and then wisely sticking around to handle their legal affairs later.

"At that time, I didn't speak any English," Birshtein says. The larger-than-life, turbo-charged pair must have made quite a sight struggling to understand each other in their only common tongue, Yiddish.

"He's a very strong person. He starts to scare me, to push me," Birshtein recalls. "I said, 'Listen my friend, I'm sorry, but I'm not a poor immigrant. I have here business interests. I have here partners. They try to convince me to come to Canada. I'm ready to come, but on the condition that I will be here before September 1. If you can do that, okay. If not, that's okay too.'

"He's looking at me. 'You bring any money?' I said I will bring some money."

Birshtein mimics Green's blunt style in his own syntax-mangling version of the language, the fifth one he's picked up without formal lessons. He changes inflection and pauses for effect. " 'How much you will bring?'

" 'How much do you need?'

" 'How much do you have?'

" 'Listen, tell me what you need.'

" 'You can bring a million dollars?'

" 'I will bring a million dollars, if it's necessary.'

" 'Okay, you will be here before September 1.' "

Birshtein says he found himself being shunted off to a medical exam. Then, early the next morning, "Mendel brings me to I don't know where. He made a presentation to some big man from government. I understood a little bit, but not enough for a conversation." After the meeting, the official sent a Telex to the Canadian embassy in

Bern. "Mendel said: 'Okay, done. You are Canadian.' I said, 'Mendel, stop with the jokes.' "

The greying Green, a fast-talking seltzer bottle brimming over with the same kind of brio that infuses so many of the immigrants he has helped bring into this country, says, "Here's this guy who's lived in three countries. He couldn't settle down and couldn't find a place where his wife and children were happy." The lawyer picks up the Montblanc fountain pen from his desk as an expensive substitute for a baton. "You cannot imagine all the contributions that immigrants like him are making to Canada. He's got all kinds of joint ventures going on in Russia with Canadians, all kinds of things! And if you think I didn't have a hassle getting him here, you're mistaken. It's not easy. It's not easy."

Birshtein, still stunned by it all, was indeed on a relatively rapid march to Canada as a landed immigrant—he arrived right on schedule—without really having had time to think about what it would all mean for him or his family.

His wife Natalie hadn't much liked Zurich ("It was so boring. After eight o'clock, everyone closes their doors. I don't know what they do, count their money?"), where her father's wealthy family had once owned a bank before the Russian Revolution.* She would have preferred staying in Israel, where she and the children still spent part of each year and where her parents were living.

"I was worried when he told me he applied to go [to Canada]," she says, pouring the requisite tea and proffering cream cakes and dried fruit in the comfortable, expensively furnished living room of her modern skylights-and-mirrors home (the showpiece is a stunning bathroom with a huge pale green marble tub) in affluent

---

* Natalie Birshtein's family, which lived in a town in Byelorussia, about two hours by train from the Birshtein home in Vilnius, lost not only its businesses but two large homes after the revolution. Her father, a manager of a wallpaper factory, grew up in a small house with other relatives, including eight kids.

Forest Hill, long a parking spot for old Toronto money. A slender, attractive woman with friendly blue eyes, well-placed freckles and shoulder-length brown hair cascading gently over a soft blue-green sweater, she looks considerably younger than her husband despite an age difference of only two years.

"He said, 'Don't worry, it will never happen.' What will I tell my parents? They will die. 'Don't worry, it will never happen.' "

She's used to his antics. "When Boris is coming home, I say, 'When are we leaving again? I want two days' notice.' He says, 'Don't ask me that now.' But I want to know. All of a sudden, he will say: 'Let's go,' and we go."

But the wandering days are gone, insists Natalie Birshtein. She displays a quick, straight-faced wit and enough uncommon sense to make her more than a match for her rougher-edged husband with his candy-floss dreams. Before coming to Canada, "I told him I'm not moving any more. One more language and that's it." Unless he's prepared to retire, about as likely as getting him to sit still for more than two days on one of their rare vacations.

"Boris, he always dreams of something. To leave something for our children. You want to leave a good name. Money is just money. If you are healthy and you like to work, you have money. Boris, he tells me he will just work for a few more years, then that's it. But I don't believe him. I ask him why he does not send somebody else to travel, and he says, 'Because nobody can do what I can do.' "

Birshtein, who presides over about a half dozen companies under the Seabeco* mantle, with offices in five

---

* The Birshtein business in Israel was called Sealon, a combination of the names of their two children, Simona, now a twenty-one-year-old university student, and Alon, an eleven-year-old computer enthusiast. Birshtein then teamed up with two partners who had a company called Ibeco, and they merged the names. Initial capital of the trading company was $200,000 (US), half from Birshtein, and half from his partners. Canadian money came in later.

countries but most of its work inside the Soviet Union in various joint ventures and trading deals, isn't quite in the class of some of the Hong Kong traders setting up here. Nor does he fit Green's gushing description of him as the second coming of Armand Hammer, the legendary U.S. industrialist who had incredible links to several generations of Soviet leaders. (Senior Russian officials certainly admit to knowing Birshtein, though they don't appear to be card-carrying members of his fan club. "I don't like him," says a deputy trade minister. "We have had a few dealings.")

He is a tireless promoter and compulsive deal-maker who brought Molson's beer to Moscow, has teamed up with one of Russia's biggest pop stars in an entertainment venture, is a partner in a charter airline inside Russia and once sat down in Taipei with Chiang Kai-shek's son to discuss building an aircraft factory, without a clue as to how he would go about it should he happen to get the contract. A mere detail like that wouldn't stand in the way of a survivor who has been plunging into new ventures almost as fast as he can think them up, ever since he moved to Israel from his native Vilnius.

The year was 1979, and the Kremlin was opening the gates to Jewish emigration, letting out thousands more than in preceding or subsequent years, until Gorbachev tore down the entire wall. "I cannot say that I was poor in the Soviet Union, that I had a bad type of living. I was absolutely okay. But I wanted a better type of life."

When he saw the main chance, he made his move boldly and quickly—on sheer nerve and gut feeling. This is much the way he conducts his business life, unlike his more cautious father, who was a factory manager of what had once been part of the Birshtein holdings. Or his grandfather, who had made the fateful decision to keep the family in Vilnius when he still had the means to lead them to safety—before the Red Army marched in and seized everything in 1940. "It was his mistake. He wasn't ready to build a new kind of life in a new kind of world. It's very hard. If you have to make the decision today to move to another country, with another language, another culture, another everything, I think you will think twice," says a man who seems not to have thought twice. It took him only five months to get his family out, including his parents and in-laws.

It was in Israel that he had his first taste of the raw capitalism that had once made his family rich; and he didn't waste any time jumping back in at the deep end. He started a souvenir and silk-screening business with part of the money Israel had earmarked for newly arrived Soviet Jews. His father and Natalie, who was trained in plastic technology, worked alongside him. As a factory manager in Lithuania, Birshtein had supervised a similar business. He had been schooled as a lawyer, but "it made no sense to practise law. Now, of course, the situation is different."

Birshtein, who spends much of his time up in the air, even when he's on the ground, could live any place equipped with a decent-sized runway and flight connections to places like Taipei, Tel Aviv, Zurich, Chicago and Moscow, where he might be pushing anything from carpets and electronics to tourism, textiles and rock concerts. Once in a while, the schemes actually work out, though far less often than he would like.

"You can work on twenty-five deals and just one of them will be successful, and you have to be prepared for that," Birshtein says, explaining his operating technique. "One successful deal compensates for all the others. But sometimes, you can make [initiate] a hundred deals, and not do one."

When he turns on the warmth, which he seems able to do at will, it's easy to see why anyone might have an irresistible desire to buy a few hundred cases of Canadian beer or a shipload of Russian rugs or Korean TVs from this man. "He has a lot of confidence in himself. He's a tremendous salesman and I think he'll pull off what he's doing," says Harry Gorman, a respected Toronto builder. The gentlemanly Gorman heads a group of about twenty Canadian and U.S. investors who bought a third

of Birshtein's young trading enterprise in 1984 for close
to $5-million, because "it looked like doing business in
Russia was the coming thing. And that's turning out be
be true."

Not everyone is as sold on Birshtein or his dreams.
One story has it that he once asked a wealthy Canadian
businessman to lend $500,000 to one of his Moscow staff-
ers to buy Russian gold, which would be sold here at a fat
profit. "I asked what guarantees my client would have,"
recalls an adviser involved in the discussions. Birshtein
said he personally would provide the guarantee. What
security did he have? "He said he didn't have any, just
himself. I honestly thought it was a scam."

Another frequent flyer in international financial circles says he has plenty of unanswered questions about
Birshtein. "He's always got these deals, but has anybody
seen any money? He's supposed to have all these connections in Russia, and now I see he started a Polish business
group. [Birshtein was named chairman of the Canada-
Poland Business Council, one of many such bodies that
have sprung up since eastern Europeans began embracing
capitalism.] What is he supposed to know about Poland?"

Harry Gorman sketches a picture of a kid who's suddenly been given a great box full of free-enterprise toys,
and who may have irritated some of the others in the
playground while he figures out how they all work. "There
have been cases where he said he would do certain things
and it was just impossible. He really wants to keep his
word, but sometimes he gets overenthusiastic. If he can
do it, he will. He's learning how to do business the Western way, and he may have antagonized some people in the
process."

Gorman had a big hand in setting up his business partner in Canada, putting him in the offices next door to
his own. Gorman's son, Earl, designed the impressive
interiors. Birshtein had much more modest headquarters
in Zurich, but thought that if Gorman's represented what
successful Canadian offices looked like, he'd better have
one of them. He chose to live in Forest Hill for the same

reason. "He wanted to live like the wealthy people do," says Gorman. A visit to his home or office shows that Birshtein has achieved at least those goals.

When asked how much he's actually worth, Birshtein shrugs and gives this direct response: "I couldn't say I am a rich man. I have a mortgage on my house. According to the value of my shares [in Seabeco], I would say [I have] a lot of money. But in real money, I don't have any. It's all paper. All the money is in the business. One day we will come to a situation where we will have a lot of money—in the bank account, I mean."

Gorman says Birshtein wasn't merely joking about moving here, on that June day in 1985. "I guess he saw what he liked here, a lot of opportunities. He didn't need much talking into." Both Boris and Natalie already had relatives here, and they were looking for a place to raise their teenage daughter and young son in peace and affluence. Moving from place to place is particularly hard on the children, Natalie says. Her husband was also eager to do his globe-hopping on a Canadian, rather than an Israeli, passport.

Birshtein is vague about some details of his past, such as his move to Switzerland—though this is a classic route for Israelis trying to keep an international business from sinking into a sea of inflation, taxes and bureaucracy.

His dealings with the Soviets, which started when he was still in Israel, attracted official attention and piqued the curiosity of people doing business with him. One executive mutters darkly that he thinks Birshtein may have KGB connections, partly because his main activity has seemed to be procuring products from Taiwan and South Korea, with which the Kremlin doesn't officially do business.

This is a ludicrous claim, say Harry Gorman and others who have shared his renowned homemade meat and vegetable soup. "Naturally, we were all curious [about his connections]. But we did some checking on his background through Israeli people, and there were more important people than us who checked into it."

At first, Birshtein asks me not to tell the world that he left Lithuania only in the late 1970s. An odd request, as his departure was legal. Actually, he says, if he had left illegally the Soviets would probably have a better record of him. "When I go back, they don't know I'm an emigrant from there. They look at an emigrant like you did something wrong. You're against your country." I finally persuade him that this attitude must be changing—and that Russian bureaucrats won't read this far anyway.

While Birshtein departed with all his documents in order and with the acquiescence, if not the blessing, of Soviet authorities, there are others of means who have been wrenched from their roots by cataclysmic events, their families placed in grave peril should they have made a wrong decision or failed in their urgent quest for a secure place to weather the violent storms. Having seen a lifetime of effort and sacrifice go up in flames, the least of their concerns today is how they are viewed by their home government. Many expect never to see their homeland again. Many others don't want to, counting themselves lucky to have escaped when they had the chance.

CHAPTER 8

The Escape Artists

THE BUS RIDE itself would have been harrowing enough: forty hours in a jam-packed death-trap rattling over treacherous mountain roads. But the young Iranian couple had other things to worry about: the constant threat that Khomeini zealots would appear without warning to drag the husband, a former soldier, off to the killing grounds of the Iraqi front; or worse, that they would discover what was hidden in the ordinary-looking carriage—at that moment the most dangerous perambulator in the world—of their increasingly restless baby daughter. Then there was the unrelieved fear of the unknown, scarcely charted journey that still stretched before them.

Despite the nightmarish possibilities, everything went smoothly until they reached the Turkish border. They held their breath as the Iranian guards poked around and through their belongings. The carriage didn't draw a second glance. And even if it had, it's doubtful the security men would have noticed that the tubing wasn't quite as hollow as it should have been; it was stuffed with enough illicit German cash* to give the couple a fresh start in another land or lock them away for years in the one they were trying so desperately to escape.

So far so good, but the Turks were yet to come, fresh from their latest military coup, and not exactly the most sociable of neighbours in the best of times, as far as Amir O. and his fellow passengers were concerned. "It was more scary than in Iran. Turks are very unpredictable. We didn't know what they would do with us." (Strangely enough, the Turks say the same things about the Iranians.)

Amir insists on using a pseudonym, worried not about Turkish reprisals but about the safety of relatives who helped in his escape; especially the famed surgeon uncle who offered to fake a stomach operation to keep him out of the war with Iraq; and his aunts (who already sound like candidates for Tehran's Most Wanted list because of their taste for cosmetics—strictly forbidden in Iran).†
The image of flight is still vivid, as if his mind's video recorder has been locked on freeze-frame for a decade; but the story is related in a voice that's matter-of-fact, almost clinical, like a doctor discussing a patient's case with colleagues over breakfast.

The story of Amir O. isn't unique. Many of the 30,000 or so Iranians who have fled to Canada since the 1979 Islamic Revolution and the collapse of the oil-fired economy have similar memories. The wealthier typically departed in jet comfort, with or without legitimate papers, while their less fortunate cousins left through the historic smuggling routes. Amir ended up on the bus because Iraqi bombing had closed off the airway.

---

* The legal limit for any person leaving the country was the equivalent of $60 (US), down from $600 in the last days of the Shah's rule.

† "I remember my first day in Iran. The women all had so much make-up on," says the Indian-born Mrs. O. "I had never seen housewives look like this. It was not to enhance their looks. It was just to show that they had make-up, I guess, and that they could use it. After a while, one of the aunts offered to show me how to put it on. I said no thanks."

It wasn't quite the way he and his wife expected to travel after arriving in oil-slick Tehran in 1975 from Munich, where he'd lived since the age of twelve, gone to engineering school and met his future wife, Nair, a language scholar from India. Until a few months before their hasty retreat, they'd been leading a comfortable existence in the expensive Iranian capital, complete with swimming pool and nanny. But Amir, who represented a German industrial giant cashing in on the seventies' oil boom, had been quietly stashing away money and preparing his family's escape route once he realized that all hell was about to break loose in the name of heaven.

By the time they made their break in late 1980, with only the things they could carry in their hands but considerably more money than the people who normally carry refugee tags on their bags, it was abundantly clear that there would be no room in revolutionary Iran for them or any other Western-looking technocrats, ambitious capitalists or the bureaucrats and hangers-on associated with the *ancien régime* of Shah Mohammad Reza Pahlavi.

Amir and Nair are sitting on the grass behind a comfortable two-storey home bereft of enough family heirlooms to underscore their unscheduled departure from the old country. Gone too are the strains and emotions of their fright-filled flight, the cold sweats and pounding hearts at the sight of uniforms bearing down on them with deadly weapons. Such feelings have been consigned to underground memory vaults beneath the placid surface.

Nair unlocks hers to provide a vignette from their last frantic days in Tehran, when her husband, who freely admits he's not much at planning ahead, was coolly plotting their escape. For five days before the unwanted see-Persia-by-bus tour, "he sat calmly and did a 500-piece jigsaw puzzle. I couldn't believe it. I cracked up. I couldn't stand losing the stupidest things. I remember a vase I had bought when we were getting married.

"Remember that old carpet?" she suddenly turns and asks Amir, who doesn't go out of his way to let the past clutter up the present. "It had a memory attached to it.

I purchased it in a small village. And all my books, my wonderful books. We only carried nappies and children's clothing and the money. I was very upset just leaving the way we had to leave. I remember thinking the whole world was crashing around us."

A voluble sort who now devotes herself to teaching language and other life skills to immigrant women* in Canada, she still shudders at her memories of the Turkish border, where a guard, angry over not being paid his expected *baksheesh*, kept the passengers waiting for the longest eight hours of Nair's life. "We were in this little, ugly room, just sitting there. I'll never forget it. On one side was a portrait of Khomeini and on the other side was Ataturk (founder of the modern Turkish republic). I was so happy to be out of there. I've never seen a more god-forsaken place."

As soon as they got to a town with an airport, Amir took out a knitting needle he'd brought along for the purpose and drew enough banknotes from inside the carriage to pile the family onto a plane for Istanbul. Then he cut up the carriage tubing and they headed to Munich, where an apartment was waiting but where they knew they could never settle permanently, "because Germany is not a country for immigrants. They never accept you." Amir says he had been happy as a student, "but once you want to get into the system, working and paying taxes, then you feel the prejudice."

Figuring they were set financially for a long time to come, they moved eight months later to a strange place

---

* Many of her students are refugees whose experiences make her own departure seem like a pleasant country outing. I once listened to a group of women recounting their horrific escapes from the hell-holes of Southeast Asia and Africa with a kind of distanced nonchalance that's helped keep them sane. One woman, who had walked for days in searing heat with little food or water to reach freedom, asked another, "Were you bombed?" as if it's the most natural thing in the world when you're travelling refugee-class. "We were bombed, two times," the other woman replied quietly, sipping her tea.

on the other side of the world, where Amir didn't know the customs, either of the official languages or even the cost of living. "We thought we were rich until we came to Canada," he says with a smile. "At least we had enough to buy a house."* Making use of his engineering background, Amir found work as a technician, quit to try retailing on his own but returned to the highly technical work he loves with an innovative Canadian manufacturer. Nair administers the immigrant training programs, and both are investing in property, "because you cannot get rich working nine to five."

Amir says he would consider visiting his home-land—possibly even working there again—if the political climate were to change. But he wouldn't uproot his family again, even though he himself never expects to feel completely at ease here. "I want my kids to grow up in Canada. They should have what I never had [because of his family's move to Germany], which is roots. It happens for us that the roots were put down here, and I don't want to pull them out."

The moneyed émigrés naturally do everything in their power to avoid putting their families or their cash in peril. The mere hint of unrest is like a persistent cough at a classical concert: No matter how good the music, the audience can't help wondering whether the whole evening's about to be ruined. Sooner or later, even the most tone-deaf of capitalists start looking for the exits, shopping around for quiet little duchies that take their bank

---

* It's a story repeated often in the Iranian community. Manoucher Etminan, a tall, slim forty-one-year-old with a voice like Rod Stewart's, is best known today as an importer of caviar and a maker of cheese and other specialty breads, a high-priced staple of Toronto's chèvre and olive oil crowd. He came here in 1981 with $80,000, all he could salvage from various businesses in Tehran; but he was still leading his old luxury-class existence, and the cash soon disappeared. "I applied to the *Toronto Star* for a job collecting [paper route] money from the little kids. It was for maybe $4 an hour. They asked me how much money I had made for the last three or four years. I had to put that it had been millions of dollars, and they thought I was crazy." He didn't get the job.

secrecy laws seriously, and for nice, safe, secure places with plenty of space for them and their families.

Canada has welcomed the wretched wealthy of the earth for decades; but only in the last ten or twelve years have the first families of the Third World—people with plenty to lose running for cover in their dusty Guccis and wrinkled Armanis—been picking Toronto, Vancouver, Montreal and Edmonton (if you're one of the downtrodden Burmese royals), over preferred international haunts like Paris, London and New York. The ethnically eclectic list embraces such permanent outsiders as the East Asians of Africa and the Chinese of just about any place, who discovered that years of hard-won prosperity could go up in xenophobic smoke almost overnight; Pakistanis and Bangladeshis on the precipice; Vietnamese and Cambodians faced with the loss of more than their money; Baha'is escaping persecution in Khomeini's Iran (joining Shiite Muslims who might have been able to live with the religious order but not the commercial chaos); Libyans, Lebanese, Iraqis, Israelis, Filipinos, South Africans and the rest just plain exhausted from living in permanent danger zones.

That's why the super-rich of Hong Kong have been so carefully digging their gold-plated escape tunnels here for years. When the Communists from Beijing take over the British colony in 1997, the capitalists want to be sure their kinfolk and a lot of their loot are stashed well out of harm's way, despite all the confident puffery being spouted about the colony's future. (It's no accident that billionaires like Li Ka-shing started shovelling years before the merely mortal multimillionaires. They've simply been relying on the same uncanny, built-in early warning systems that made them so rich and powerful in the first place.)

The Hong Kong Chinese may not be the first custom-heeled refugees to hop aboard the luxury-class airlift to these shores, but they're certainly the ones with the most time to pack their Vuittons. "The Chinese are lucky. They had thirteen years' notice. I wish I had had two years for god's sake," grumbles Saeed Khayami, member of a once-mighty Iranian industrial family whose personal bank accounts were frozen and near-billion dollars' worth of holdings confiscated before the Shah's getaway jet had reached cruising altitude. "It was a surprise to everybody. Nobody could have believed that a disorganized mob can become so powerful."

Sirus Mansouri, scion of a giant construction fortune, insists the upper crust "couldn't predict the revolution, because we always thought that Iran was a sea of stability. We were always led to believe that nothing would ever change and that was the way it was."

The high and the mighty in Iran were living in a dream, often unaware of or indifferent to what was going on around them, says Karim Hakim. Hakim, with his $100-million chain of optical stores, is perhaps Canada's best known Iranian success story, apart from the Ghermezian brothers of West Edmonton Mall fame, who brought a bit of money with them from Tehran when they came looking for security back in 1959. Unlike the Ghermezians, or those fleeing the later Robespierrean excesses of the Islamic Revolution, Hakim (he likes the shorter version of his name, Hakimi, which appropriately means son of the medicine man) started from somewhere near the bottom of the Iranian ladder before eventually moving here via Geneva in 1967, as an eyeglass technician.

"You were on the top or you were nothing. I could not accept or understand that," says the optician, who is always passionate, whether it's about life, work or his Australian-made, $9-million (US) yacht, the *Hakim*. "I see the change in them [his rich countrymen] here. Five or ten years makes a difference. Nobody here buys the hot air, so they change their ways. Back in Iran, there were a lot of buyers for hot air, so they could sell a lot of it."

Sirus Mansouri, member of one of the richest and oldest of Iran's business clans, with money dating back to the 1940s, has been busy since 1981 carving out a new Persian empire on British Columbia's Lower Mainland and in the American Northwest, with the 5 to 10 percent of the family's assets that had been parked in Europe before the Shah's fall in 1979.* (Mansouri is as common a name in Iran as Suzuki in the Tokyo phonebook or Smith in the nearest motel registry, which is why I've chosen it for this Reichmann-like family with a similar passion for privacy and a deep distrust of journalists.)

"Obviously, our wealth wasn't easily transferable, because a lot of it is in the form of office buildings, residential apartments and condominium projects in Iran. Legally, they are still in our name, they haven't been confiscated or anything like that." Today the family is still worth "how do the banks put it? They normally talk about figures. It's nine figures."

The Shiite Mansouris had bravely soldiered on during the early days of the revolution, finishing buildings already on their way up. "I guess we felt we had an obligation because we had presold a lot of the units. There's always fear, because when a country's in turmoil, if you're high profile, you attract a lot of attention, even if you're not in politics."

After six months, they reached the same conclusion as Amir, who'd been trying to pick up industrial contracts abandoned by the Americans: They'd better get out while the getting was good. "It was just impossible to work in Iran anymore because there was no work mentality. It was a revolution, and in a revolution you can't do business. You'd get these people, militias, coming to your projects with machine guns and breaking into your office, asking

---

* A rarity. As a member of another Iranian construction dynasty, all Baha'is, explains: "We got rich from the rising oil price. All Iranians graduated at that time. Iran was really a poor country. A hundred thousand dollars was big money. After [the boom triggered by what was labelled, in the West, as the oil crisis of 1973], some incomes were $1-billion." His family was apparently in that class, as the main road builders for a government rushing to take its place alongside the great paving nations of the world; a source in the Iranian community says they managed to hold on to about 25 percent of their wealth. The family spokesman, a residential developer in the Toronto area, denies this. "I'm not rich. I just have money."

who's in charge and questioning you without any evidence but in the hope of finding something."

When it became impossible to continue, the Mansouris flew to Europe, where the family had a home and business interests, before making their way to Vancouver. Why Canada—when several hundred thousand of their countrymen had settled confortably down the Pacific coast in the considerably warmer, drier and sexier suburbs of Southern California? When they'd been schooled in England? When they had money in Europe and had cultivated such distinctly continental tastes?

"We wanted stability, and also a country where you would be welcome and where you would have a future," says Mansouri, who has constructed a rafter of high-profile projects, bringing him closer to his goal of becoming a major North American developer. The United States, as many Iranians say (some a lot more vehemently than others*) didn't seem likely to provide either the welcome or the future, in the wake of its embassy's seizure in Tehran and the prolonged hostage crisis that made Iran a dirty word in the American lexicon.

"Every time something happens, they pick on people," says Mansouri flatly. He deeply resented being lumped in with pro-revolutionary forces who'd made his own life so miserable. "That's why we decided to come to Canada instead."

Vancouver was their choice, sight unseen, because friends liked the city. This so astonished their Canadian lawyer (the year was 1981, before the big Asian money had started pouring in) he was left speechless. "I told him we

---

* Some of the émigrés blame American ineptitude for the fall of the Shah in the first place, while others share the feeling of compatriots in Iran that they'd have been better off without the pervasive influence of "the Great Satan" (one of the Ayatollah's legacies to the language of geopolitics. The Soviet Union was "the Little Satan"). "Americans are hated all over the world. And besides, coming from Iran I do believe a lot of the country's problems came from the United States," Nair tells me. "The whole Coca-Cola culture was so predominant that Iranians had no respect for their own art, their own music, their own culture."

came to Vancouver to do business, and he said, 'You're the first person who's ever said that to me. Normally, people come for the sailing or the skiing or things like that.' I always remember that," Mansouri laughs. "For a while, we thought maybe we made the wrong decision, but I think in the end we're happy about it."

It may come as a distinct shock to self-satisfied Canadians, but when these developers from the underdeveloped world arrived in our third-largest city a decade ago, they found an unsophisticated industry throwing up second-rate buildings they wouldn't have dreamed of constructing. "Everybody said we were spending too much money [on apartment and shopping mall projects]. They said average-income people wouldn't appreciate some of these features, like a *porte-cochère* and a conservatory swimming pool and a high lobby and very high Italian finishes and formal English landscaping [in suburban residential buildings]." Luckily, the area has grown considerably more cosmopolitan in the ensuing years, thanks in no small measure to the wave of international money, and the Mansouris no longer feel as though they're slumming in the boonies. "You see a lot more taste, good taste. People are doing better projects, and there's generally a much more positive feeling than when we first came."

The Mansouris have also made the painful adjustment to the horrifying drop in their standard of living, for there's no way to match here the opulent lifestyles of the rich in any have-not part of the world. "We had servants and drivers. We were never extravagant, but it might sound extravagant by some people's standards. We had three chauffeurs and two or three people in the [household] staff. A lot of people had more. Here we just have someone who comes in each day."

Accepting their fate and nurturing global business dreams helped ease the anguish of their downward slide into an ordinary upper-class Canadian existence. "We lived in a huge mansion and now we have to live in a smaller house. That would be a disaster in some people's lives, but from our point of view it wasn't really," Mansouri insists. "I guess deep down we always hoped that we would get back to where we were financially, so we said, 'Okay, if we have to suffer some temporary differences. That will change in the future.' "

Now as ardently Canadian as a veteran like Hakim, who made it here from the ground lenses up, the Mansouris no longer talk of returning to the golden olden days (though they kept the house in Europe they've owned for years—part of their jet set past). If the Iranian political and economic situation stabilizes, they would like to go back, but only as Canadian business people. Sirus makes a point of adding, "We're very happy at having chosen Canada. We've been treated as better than equals in every sense. . . . We think we owe something to Canada for giving us that first opportunity. And we think other people feel the same way. It's an emotional thing."

The Khayamis had also considered the West Coast ("Too much rain. It was like England," Saeed Khayami says) and Montreal ("Too risky, unstable. We went through that once [in Iran]. I even got into a fight with a separatist," chimes in his brother, Hamid), before settling on southern Ontario as the sanctuary of a family that built a huge industrial conglomerate in Iran. Their empire now consists of a low-profile property development business and a couple of lucrative car dealerships in Kitchener and Toronto.

Saeed and Hamid Khayami are sitting in their plain grey office behind identical black vinyl-topped desks which face the door, on the second floor of their surprisingly utilitarian Mercedes dealership on the western fringe of Toronto. Downstairs, a shiny selection of every wealthy immigrant's favourite brand name awaits eager buyers from fancier districts. Upstairs, it's strictly used-Chevy country.

The engaging pair speak openly, good-naturedly,

sometimes simultaneously and almost always on the record (a rarity among wealthy Iranians living here) about what it was like being caught up in a flood of events that swept away their billion-dollar family fortune and a lifetime of dreams. "We were involved inside Iran so much that we never thought that anything would happen. Probably that was our mistake. We believed in what we were doing. Suddenly, it went up in smoke," says Saeed, fixing another Vantage cigarette into a gold-and-black holder. "We didn't come out penniless. It's the difference between one dollar and one million dollars. My father had a house in Europe. We had to liquidate it to be able to live and then do some business. We bought and we sold real estate in London. And then we immigrated."

Asked if they'd agree with some of their fellow expatriates, who've tagged them the richest Iranians to set up house in Canada, Hamid says drily, "We certainly weren't running a contest down there. We were always involved in active businesses, producing things, creating things, and we had a lot of people on our payroll. There were a lot of others who were probably richer than us, but these people mostly were in property. They had a lot more liquid assets and got away a lot better. That's why we got burned, because we could not sell the things we had."

Picture Chrysler merging with the McCain frozen french-fry family, toss in Eaton's, stir lightly for fifteen years and you come up with something approaching the recipe for success devised by the Khayamis' ambitious father under the supportive gaze of the Shah, who had embarked in the early sixties on his doomed dream—the so-called "White Revolution"—to bring in enough Western technology to turn his backward country into an industrial power in a hurry, regardless of the huge social costs.

Khayami was a risk-taker after the Shah's heart, turning a single Mercedes distributorship into the Middle East's only major indigenous auto, truck and bus manufacturer by the mid-sixties, at a time when the Koreans were still figuring out how to make cars and the Japanese were working on a way to get Americans to buy theirs. Everybody said he was nuts, that Iran couldn't possibly make its own vehicles from the wheels up. But by the time Khayami's company was snatched from the family's grasp after the Shah's overthrow, it was turning out some 150,000 a year.*

The innovative Khayami threw his energy into a string of other enterprises as well, such as department stores and climate-controlled warehouses for storage and preservation of locally grown food. Now in his seventies and retired from the wars, he lives quietly with his wife in an affluent north Toronto suburb, leaving what's left of the deal-making to his eldest sons.

Saeed and Hamid went back to their father's business roots when, in 1981, they took over a nearly moribund Mercedes dealership in Kitchener, relying on the old family ties to the German car maker to secure the franchise. "We forgot about what we had in Iran," Saeed says. "That's why we came and started a very small dealership. We knew what our possibilities were. We knew where we wanted to go."

Hamid, two years younger than his brother at forty-two, arrived from London first, while Saeed set sail for sunny Hawaii. "The weather's great every day. It was beautiful. I hated it," Saeed chuckles. It's a deep, tobacco-stained laugh, broken by a thick cough. "Everything was so slow. You have an appointment, and the guy comes three hours late. I was too young to go to a place like that. But I wish I had bought some properties there."

Two other brothers and a sister in their thirties live in the States. "Their actual growing-up process started

---

* Khayami started assembling cars with the inner works provided by Chrysler UK. By the time of the revolution, the family had its own engine and metal-stamping plants, and a thriving parts manufacturing industry had grown up around them. Their buses and trucks were built under licence from Mercedes. Today, under the state mullahpoly, the company produces about a tenth of what it once did, according to Saeed.

with the revolution, which was really hard for them,"
Saeed says of his younger siblings, who spent their teens
at school in Switzerland. "At least Hamid and me, we had
some fun in Iran."

When the fun came to an abrupt end, Saeed was
in Europe buying machinery for their expanding
woodworking factory (they were into furniture, too).
His wife and children were with him on a holiday.
They would never see their homeland again. "We had
to flee because we would have been shot if we had stayed.
Our family was very close to the Shah." He shrugs. The
words come slowly, deliberately. He sometimes stops in
mid-sentence to search for just the right phrase. That he
usually finds it reflects his years of schooling in England,
where he obtained an engineering degree.

Saeed didn't have to tell me he was still a Shahman.
The walls of their Spartan office hold but one bit of deco-
ration, directly behind and above his desk: a gold-framed
black-and-white photo of the tyrant, taken during one of
his tours of a Khayami plant. (Dedicated supporters of
His Majesty brook no criticism, even at this late date, of
their former leader. The Shah and his cronies may have
taken a cut of the action, but he left enough on the table to
make some of his subjects enormously rich as he pursued
his grandiose schemes of modernization.)

Those who had even more tenuous royal links than
those of the Khayamis qualified instantly for the firing
squad or a lengthy jail term,* which explains why Hamid
might have been more than a little nervous about being
left behind. Before boarding one of the final flights out of
Tehran—after several close calls, without his real passport
and with unspecified help from friends still clinging to high
places—just three days ahead of Khomeini's triumphant
return from exile in Paris, Hamid was sleeping with a
loaded gun under his pillow and wondering when the
mob would come bursting into his fashionable residence.

---

* Manoucher Etminan, for example, says his troubles stemmed from the
fact he'd bought his house from the Shah's sister.

With his family already safely out of the country, his only companions were two private armed guards.

Hamid uses the flat of his hand as a comb to push his dark curly hair back off his forehead. He's got more of it than his heavier-set brother. He's also more casual in dress, manner and defence of the old regime, perhaps the residue of his years as an economics student at laid-back schools in Colorado and Southern California. He wears a black-and-white-check sports jacket to Saeed's expensively tailored dark grey suit. While Saeed puffs on his filtered Vantages, doodling impatiently on the package, Hamid keeps his hands busy with the ritual of cleaning and refilling his well-used pipe.

"Nobody was safe. By nine each evening, the power would be off. The city would be dark. People were shouting in the streets. It was terrifying. All these voices in the dark. That's how bad it was. We just had to get our own lives and get the hell out of there."

Today, their two Ontario dealerships employ about fifty people and bring in a combined annual revenue of about $30-million, a fly-speck on the windscreen to a family that once dreamed of selling its own Iran National cars in North America. ("We were ahead of the South Koreans. Hyundai started after my father. And now look at what they're doing," Saeed observes.) They won't say what their office and retail development business brings in. "I guess we're contributing a little bit," Hamid grins.

The talk turns to the hefty sales tax bill on their luxury products. "The federal government is like our mullahs [in Iran]. They have long pockets," Saeed sighs. They may have lost hundreds of millions of dollars, but not their ability to laugh at life's vicissitudes. Maybe that's why Saeed's round, smiling face remains singularly unlined despite the pain of what he's been through.

"You can always make the money. But this, you can never make," he says, pointing in the direction of his heart. "It's the pride which really hurts more than the money. You don't really need that much, because you never can use it. But the pride of what you have achieved and what your country was going through suddenly goes down the drain. It's with you for the rest of your life."

Like most wealthy refugees with plenty they'd rather forget, fearful of reopening old wounds or putting friends and relatives in peril, the Iranians rank with the Greta Garbos of the new money here. Though they face a readily apparent image problem among members of the old money establishment, who make no allowances for cultural differences and—completely ignoring our own glass house—figure that anyone with fat billfolds from their part of the world must be as corrupt and dishonest as the governments they supported, most of the powerful Iranian families here would prefer to leave the past buried. Even some of those who speak openly do so only with the greatest reluctance. But beside the Vietnamese, they act like film stars panting for publicity.

After trying for months to find a wealthy Vietnamese family willing to describe what they've been through and where they're going, I finally located one Tan Doi Nguyen, once a prominent private banker in South Vietnam who ended up jailed for political reasons by his own government before its final collapse.

In one of those supreme ironies that are threaded through the lives of so many escape artists, the ultimate capitalist was released, along with other prisoners in 1975, by the victorious Vietnamese Communists. He then made his way to Montreal. (Nguyen Van Thieu, the head of the government that imprisoned him, has sought refuge in the same city, where a sister lives.)

Tan Doi Nguyen seemed the perfect candidate to relate the great truths of his hard life and times. After all, he'd already written his memoirs, baring his soul to all who can read Vietnamese. No doubt he'd be eager to tell me what it was like to go from running a large credit bank, with some seventy branches, to cleaning floors in Montreal office buildings, and then to his resurrection in the property game, the great elixir for so many former movers and shakers who find themselves in Canada. (In real estate, an Iranian explains, "people do not need to fight too hard or compete. Their culture and education, what they did, do not matter. If they have the money or they can find some, they will make money. That's why you see so many of us.")

A young woman answers the phone in a suburban Montreal home. Her French is halting, but she seems to know exactly who I'm seeking. Yes, she says, this is the home of Tan Doi Nguyen. Yes, he is a real estate agent. And yes, he's written a book about his life. Success at long last! Just leave a polite message and wait for the interview that's sure to follow.

There's no interview. Or even a return call. More messages are left for him. Then, one day, another voice is at the end of the line, speaking better French. Yes, this is the home of Tan Doi Nguyen, but no, he isn't in.

One last try, and, oh joy! It's actually the old Doi himself. Or is it? The voice is tired, hesitant. The very mention of his life story ends the conversation abruptly. "This is the wrong person," he says.

"Aren't you Tan Doi Nguyen, the real estate man?"

"Yes, but you have the wrong person," he repeats just before the line goes dead.

Other once-influential Southeast Asian refugees have found peace and quiet here. They don't want to be discovered either. "The bottom line is, what do they have to gain by talking," says a Montreal journalist who's poked around the community in that city. The answer: Nothing at all. "They don't have businesses that could benefit from the publicity. They made their money in Vietnam or Cambodia, probably illegally, maybe from running a little heroin.* Now they just want to hand the money to the next generation. They don't want people pointing at their kids and saying things about them. These guys are not living high. They've got their money and they're sitting on it. They've gone clean and have nothing to say."

He adds something ominous about overzealous and unwanted overtures. "There's a danger factor here that you should be aware of."

Danger? Perhaps that explains my decision to spend more time in the warm, life-embracing ambit of Navin Chandaria, where the only real risk might be to an overly sensitive digestive system. Chandaria's family has been called the Procter & Gamble of East Africa, one of the half-dozen wealthiest clans in the region. When you spend any time around this tall, perpetually sunny promoter with the cigarette-husky voice and booming laugh, an entrepreneur who decided Canada was just the place to manufacture items even the Americans were importing from slave-wage states, the incongruous starts looking perfectly natural.

That's why I find myself not thinking twice about the Japanese tempura (soggy), French white wine (medium-dry) and German chocolate cake (both) being consumed late one afternoon at an American-run hotel in the middle of Toronto's suburban flatlands. We've come here to continue an interview

---

* The most notorious is probably Lt.-Gen. Dang Van Quang, formerly South Vietnam's chief intelligence officer and reputed heroin trafficker, now in his sixties. The last I heard he was an accountant in a Montreal restaurant. He wouldn't talk to the *Globe and Mail* when approached a couple of years ago through the local Vietnamese community, and I had no better luck the second time around.

that started nearby at his large, single-storey glue factory, which doubles as the low-key headquarters of Conros Corporation,* the Chandarias' Canadian incarnation.

Before the *maître d'* can lead us to our table, though, Chandaria spots an old friend (a classification that seems to include just about anybody he's ever met), the head of a rich family from Bangladesh who's into office furniture here. The next thing I know I'm sitting with a group of friendly East Asian strangers, among them a visiting artist from Karachi who's trying unsuccessfully to draw a sample of his work on one of the hotel's heavy linen napkins. Between the impromptu art lesson and a lunch conversation that ranges over such topics as the role of the bootlegger in modern-day Pakistan, the questions for Chandaria have to stay in their notebook, to be answered another day.

I'd come to the Kenyan native to find out more about the "Idi Amin factor," which had sent a wave of rich East Asian refugees from Africa across the ocean as fast as they could pack up their belongings. An entire self-contained upper caste, many of whom were leading lives of ease and luxury—in what one rich immigrant from Nairobi bluntly describes as a "fool's paradise"—were abruptly forced to reassess their futures after the Ugandan dictator expelled thousands of their fellow Asians in 1972. Some of them were third-generation descendants of railway workers and traders who'd never seen their ancestral lands, but were still treated as interlopers, relics of British colonialism.

"I felt like a guest in my own country," says Amin

---

* The company was formerly known as Consumer Chemical Corporation. But Chandaria didn't care for the name. "Chemical is a dirty name. And we weren't even in the chemical business. Our concentration is in environmentally safer convenience products." Conros is a combination of the old name and Ross Adhesive, a big Detroit manufacturer bought by the Chandarias from its German multinational owner and transferred lock, stock and gluepot to Toronto.

Jivraj who, like his father before him, was born and raised in Dar es Salaam but saw no prospects for himself in the Tanzanian capital after training in England as a chartered accountant. "When I came over here [as a twenty-five-year-old in 1975], that feeling was never there. It gave me the freedom to explore ... mentally and otherwise." As a result, the Ismaili Muslim* says he felt confident enough to set up his own business, now a chain of about seventy-five franchised clothing and accessory shops that stretch across the country under his Signor Angelo and Madame Angelo trade names. (With only one store, he talked his way into a tiny spot in Toronto's tourist-trapping Eaton Centre by convincing the management he was part of a large Italian company looking to open in Canada, showing photos he'd taken in Italy of elegant boutiques, their names carefully out of camera range. "Given all the obstacles I was confronted with, I had to be creative.")

Idi Amin was often portrayed as an utter buffoon, but in 1972, when he expelled the lawyers, shopkeepers, traders and industrialists who controlled as much as 90 percent of the Ugandan economy, he was a demagogic crowd-pleaser who spread fear beyond his country's borders. A lot of East Asians throughout the region began re-evaluating their futures.

"I was just married. After this Uganda thing, we were looking at all of our fortunes in those countries," confirms

---

* The tightly knit Ismaili community, a branch of the Shia Muslims, perhaps numbers some 45,000 in Canada, about two-thirds of them with links to former British colonies in Africa. Many have gone into business with assistance from their fabulously wealthy spiritual leader, the Aga Khan, or other Ismailis. While they say they don't worship the man, best known to outsiders for his racehorses, wine collection and philanthropy, he is certainly venerated. Beside the usual prominent framed picture of him, one Ismaili proudly displays, beneath the glass top of his desk, quotes of his clipped from various newspapers.

Chandaria, who packed up for Canada in 1975, when he was twenty-six. "We thought, if this ever happens again, we would be in a very bad situation overnight. We were young and said, 'Hey, guys, do we want to see something like Uganda when we are in our fifties?' "

Chandaria hastens to add that his family, whose fortune is based on industrial chemicals and consumer items like soaps, pharmaceuticals and packaged food, is still pouring money into Kenya's future; in 1989, for instance, they put up a massive detergent plant to supply seventeen African countries. And he's careful not to reveal how much money has been moved out of Kenya (the legal limit is $40,000 a person). His father and oldest brother remain behind, operating at full tilt. But Amin reminded them all how shallow their roots really were in the fragile African soil, and how easily they could be dug up. It was time for a transplant to more welcoming ground. Affluent Asians, after all, had felt secure in Uganda too.

"I had never expected that I would leave. I was very well-respected," says Kewal Khosla, who crept out of Uganda just before the expulsion deadline in October 1972, with his family and little else but a memory of his $6-million worth of prosperous enterprises. "I was a director of the Uganda Development Corporation and many other government bodies. Wherever I used to go they used to salute me." He started over from scratch in Canada at the age of forty-seven, first selling insurance in Vancouver and then rebuilding his public profile and his business world, with the backing of overseas partners who helped him acquire Columbia Concrete Products, a manufacturer of roof tiles and ornamental brick in Surrey.

Among other Ugandans of means who followed the same path were the far wealthier, much more publicity-shy Laljis who, since fleeing here, have carved out a real estate empire in Vancouver and Toronto under their Larco

Enterprises umbrella*—with apartments alone worth more than a half-billion dollars.

At the next meeting with Chandaria, he is holding court again, this time as host of a family barbecue in the manicured backyard of his large suburban home. The impressive four-storey house, previously owned by the architect who built it, is big enough to hold the requisite indoor swimming pool (balanced by the outdoor hot tub and sauna), separate guest quarters and other mandatory trappings of the good life; but it's far removed from the new money monsters that darken this and other expensive neighbourhoods. Navin and his stylish wife, Sarla, wear their deep pockets well.

Even dressed in casual brown cords and a colourful T-shirt, fittingly labelled HAKUNA MATATA (Swahili for NO PROBLEM), he is a striking figure, with his handsome features, longish hair and Perrier personality. He never stops selling, forever pitching the environmental merits of his wax-and-sawdust fire logs ("they burn five times cleaner than wood, and we save the trees") and amazing purple-coloured gluesticks ("this is where the future of the glue business is going. It's totally non-toxic. The traditional school glue, which we also manufacture, has been found to cause cancer in laboratory animals.").

---

* There were once five brothers, all Ismailis. One was shot in Uganda and another died here of a heart attack. Their first unwelcome media exposure occurred in 1986 when they made a belated $430-million bid—rejected by the courts—to buy most of the 10,931 Toronto apartments that had been flipped in the now infamous Cadillac Fairview-Leonard Rosenberg deal back in 1982. They fared better in 1981, picking up three large Toronto apartment buildings for $43.5-million and again a couple of years ago when they outgunned some high-profile national developers to buy the $160-million Park Royal shopping centre in Vancouver from the British Guinness family interests. "Once I went for a helicopter ride with somebody in Vancouver," says a property master who has a long list of ex-East African clients. "It was just amazing what they had picked up very quietly. They're very much in the background doing their own thing, while all the publicity's going to the Hong Kong Chinese or Japanese or Singapore investors."

His youngest brother Dhiren is there, a thirty-two-year-old bachelor who keeps one soft-leather loafer in Africa and the other in North America, searching for packaging ideas that can be adapted back in Kenya. Later another brother, Kapoor, and a friend from London looking over his family's expanding North American steel holdings drop by as part of the evening ritual. Later still there will probably be a call to Chandaria, Sr. in Nairobi, as there usually is morning and night. This is one close-knit clan, by any standard.

"I guess we've seen a lot of families through the stages and we realize our strength is in being together," says Dhiren. He and Kapoor, who lives with his wife, Nimi,* in a trendy downtown condo and suits up in dark pin-stripes for his role as the family financial brains, are as affable as Navin the marketing maven; though Navin seems to have cornered all the flamboyant genes in the family pool. A sister who is a food chemist and two other brothers—an engineer and a chemist—complete the remarkable group portrait, all adding their separate colours to the corporate canvas deliberately left blank by their father, who'd come to Nairobi from India as a fourteen-year-old in the early 1940s.

Together with his three brothers, Chandaria, Sr. began making polishes and other household items "at a time when Africa was still wild. We are doing what he did. Moving West," Navin says, laughing.

When he decided his eldest sons had come of business age (ironically, it was 1972—the year of the Ugandan calamity), he announced that it was time for them all to have some fun and promptly sold his interests to a brother. "He gave us 40,000 shillings [about $5,000,

---

* Nimi is the daughter of a late industrial kingpin who settled in London after being forced out of Uganda. The still loaded family once had an optical frames business in Canada and owns a shopping centre in Fredericton, along with property and enterprises in India, Africa and Europe. Her mother returned to Uganda a couple of years ago to try to restore some of the industries seized from the family and run into the ground. But Kapoor makes it clear his future is right here.

combined] and said, 'That's all I have for you to start, but I give you my credit. Now, build something.' He didn't want to have anything on the plate for us," recalls Navin, who intends to do the same thing when his unsuspecting eleven-year-old son's time comes. "We weren't starting with empty pockets. Our father's credit was excellent everywhere in Africa, in Europe. But it taught us to be innovative." The brothers opted to go into trading first. "Our forte was chemicals. Forty thousand shillings was a laugh. It was mainly our father's credit, his word that got us started."

The brothers stop to ask if I've heard of anyone who wants to dispose of a manufacturing company. I've become part of the extended family, if only for a few hours, an outsider-turned-confidant expected to hold up my end, to trade news and gossip and share in their easy camaraderie and banter.

I do my best to contribute to their expansion plans. "Not really, but I know a person who inherited a food company and—"

"Does he want to sell?" Navin and Dhiren pounce. "We'll give you a finder's fee."

"Are you looking for a food-processing business?"

"Any established business," the Greek chorus answers.

"Anything with brand recognition," says Navin, the quintessential marketer.

"Any business," concludes Sarla, no wilting violet living in her husband's shadow. Equipped with a needle-sharp wit wrapped in enough charm to make it painless, she genuinely seems to enjoy turning her home into the clan's nightly gathering ground on this side of the world, cooking platefuls of spicy East Indian vegetarian specialties (with milder versions for guests with untutored palates). She smiles at the good-natured jokes tossed about at her expense, giving as good as she gets, as Navin helps his impeccably behaved son and two daughters clear the table.

The daughter of a Nairobi tire merchant, she admits she has found life in her suburban Canadian cocoon a bit dull, having given up a job with the United Nations when they immigrated, and with her children off at an exclusive private school all day. So she's doing what her neighbours do, learning how to play golf in the company of bored Japanese housewives equally busy trying to kill time.

Sarla says she has finally adjusted to the drastic change in lifestyle (servantless) and climate (twelve degrees Celsius is a cold day in Nairobi), though it took a few years. It didn't help that she lost what would have been their first child just before their arrival. "When I first came, I would not even shop here. I went to London frequently and did all my shopping there, even for my children's clothing."

Fashion and weather aside, Navin agrees it isn't easy leaving behind friends, culture, traditions, a challenging job. But they know their decision to pack up, to get away "from an area where there is a question mark over the next day," was the right one. They're also certain they've come to the right spot. Like the Iranians and so many other rich refugees from the Third World who've rebuilt their lives here, the Chandarias found the thought of the United States too unsettling. They simply refused to take any more risks with their future. "Every time I looked into the major cities, I never felt comfortable. The environment wasn't right to bring up kids," Navin says. Bespectacled, smooth-featured Kapoor the number-cruncher prefers his language more black-and-white: "I'd rather not live in the armpit of the world."

They also rejected other possible safety zones, including Australia and England, where they'd all gone to university, following the usual East Asian path through elite British private schools such as Harrow. "Opportunities-wise, England is very much set in its own tradition and clubs, whatever you like to call the old schoolboys' network," Navin notes, leaving the issue of racism hanging in the night air. "North America is wide open."

They started here in fire logs, the most logical step in the world for an African manufacturer suddenly plunked down in a cold-winter country. "For a guy coming from an equatorial climate, I couldn't think of any better product. We saw all these houses with fireplaces everywhere," Navin chortles—a rumbling, earth-moving sound, accompanied by a glint in his dark eyes as he contemplates his coup in grabbing 90 percent of the Canadian market, some $50-million in annual sales, soaring exports and no ceiling in sight for a product that's made cheaply from little more than sawmill by-products held together by wax.

Navin lights one of his logs in the East African-style open barbecue, to take the chill out of the air. He talks of ambience and lifestyle and the best thing of all about his product: "It's consumable. Once you put one match to it, it's gone. They have to come back for more and more."

Shortly after immigrating, the family purchased a small New Brunswick plant owned by the company that makes Johnson's Wax and moved it to Toronto to cut down shipping costs to the big city markets. Once they decided they liked the business, they swiftly bought out the leading Canadian log maker (under the Northland brand name) and went international, erecting a huge plant in Mexico, inking a licencing deal with Colgate-Palmolive in the States and sending their waxed sawdust as far afield as Israel and Japan. (The family had never been into logs before, but knew plenty about burning sticks, having manufactured the first domestic matchbooks in Kenya.) Today, they employ more than 200 people in North America, making and peddling logs, glue sticks, mosquito coils and adhesives.

Chandaria is a job creator, unlike some of the other rich newcomers, says Paul Curley, a well-connected Tory lobbyist and consultant who knows the family well and has been a useful bridge between the new money and the old guard. "Most of them bring money and I'm not sure what they do with it. The Chandarias are different. They have an opportunity to build a significant mid-size Canadian corporation."

Puffing on another of the many low-tar cigarettes he's lit up, Navin remarks, "We haven't targeted any goals, but we enjoy what we are doing now. The financial rewards are the result of how well we are enjoying it. To hit a few hundred million in this country in terms of building an empire is not very difficult."

The family had stakes in a few high-rise apartment buildings, but discarded them. They still own 150 acres north of Toronto, as well as their own factories and warehouses; but they retain the manufacturer's contempt for the property business. To create something of lasting value, "you have to establish brand names, with quality products. You have to establish market share. That's where we're fighting with the big multinationals. And we find it very easy. They are not that innovative."

Though utterly without airs, Navin and his wife are working hard to fit into the local establishment; schmoozing at charity fund-raisers; attending premières at Stratford; partying at Peter Mansbridge's house (they were introduced by Curley); even going into part-ownership of an expensive racehorse as a lark. They would never say so, but like most wealthy immigrants they miss the perks of power and prestige that came with their previous lives. Blending into the background is fine for some; but as one member of the Hong Kong elite once told me, it's a heck of a lot more fun when everyone else knows how important you are.

A keen observer of people and situations, Chandaria the marketer also knows it's good business to make himself more visible at the troughs where money and power congregate. The right word in a well-placed ear could help down the road, especially in his frustrating efforts to crack the lucrative school glue market, where the traditional supply lines are protected by the "old boys' net." Then too, he and his brothers may just luck on to some rich third-generation ne'er-do-well who's dying to be rid of the musty old family business, secure in the belief there's no further profit to be drained from manufacturing anything in Canada. The Chandarias couldn't agree less.

Ali Ahmed is never going to invite a journalist to his hide-away for a free-wheeling family dinner, or even lunch in a bad hotel dining room. I should be thankful, as Ahmed reminds me, that he's agreed to see me at all, breaking a personal rule about keeping family business in the family. Still, the refugee from Pakistan won't allow his real name to be used and doesn't intend to say much. "I don't need people to know who I am," the reserved, formal fifty-year-old engineer says softly from behind his spotless desk. "I just want to go about my business."

I once asked an equally reticent Hong Kong investor why he'd bother telling me his life story if he didn't want anyone to know who he was. Surely, I pressed in the hope he'd let me use his name, people will be able to identify you from your own detailed description. "Only the people who already know who I am will know who I am," he replied with unassailable Yogi Berra-like logic. Ahmed, the Pakistani entrepreneur, is a graduate of the same class.

The story he tells would strike familiar chords in any entrepreneurial dynasty that's weathered the vicissitudes of Asian, African or Latin American politics. Sharp governmental shifts in any country can make big money downright nervous—as the separatist Parti Québécois discovered in 1976 when, soon after René Lévesque's stunning election victory, the moving vans started rolling down Highway 401 toward Toronto. But apart from some painful new tax or migraine-inducing regulation, the gold bloods can count on life and profits continuing in Canada.

Ahmed's family has been done in by politics, civil strife, even war. When their hard-won fortune was threatened yet again in 1974, the iron-willed Ahmed, Sr. finally said enough was enough and shipped two of his sons off to Canada in search of a more serene future.

Ahmed the Elder, together with enough brothers and cousins to get up a decent cricket squad, had built a profitable manufacturing and distribution business in

India in the forties; but the family was caught on the wrong
side of the partition line in 1947 when Muslim Pakistan
was carved out of the subcontinent. Fleeing to Karachi
and picking up the pieces of their lives, they eventually
forged an impressive corporate machine, branching into
insurance, textiles, fertilizer (the family's biggest joint
industrial venture, and Ali's personal baby—he grows
misty-eyed talking about it), and with huge investments
in pulp, paper and jute mills and a gasoline distribution
business that made them the Irvings of Pakistan.

The trouble was that a big chunk of their holdings,
including the string of gasoline stations, were in East
Pakistan. And it was no New Brunswick. There were
demands for secession, backed by the arrival of the Indian
army in 1971. The family lost everything it owned in what
became independent Bangladesh. "We've been through a
few of these times," Ali Ahmed says drily.

The inept military rulers suddenly decided civilian
government might not be so bad for Pakistan after all, and
that's when life really became miserable for the Ahmeds.
They started hearing *non sequiturs* like "the rich have too
much" from the people around Zulfikar Ali Bhutto, the
populist leader with upper-crust roots. It was enough to
drive any right-thinking capitalist to the nearest airline's
first-class ticket counter. "The whole basis of Bhutto's
coming to power was 'I'll get the rich,' even though he
was a rich man himself," Ahmed contends. "He made a
speech saying he was going to keep my family to ransom.
He named twenty-one others of wealth. After that, we were
called the twenty-two families."

The Ahmeds lost their passports for several months. "If
family members had to leave the country for business,
they [the government] made sure the women and children
stayed behind. There was that sort of atmosphere. They
nationalized a number of our companies, so we decided
to look for a safer haven."

They would have been welcomed just about anywhere,
Ahmed assures. He'd spend most of his youth in private
boarding schools in England and stayed long enough to

obtain a doctorate in chemical engineering; but like so many others here he had no desire to live in the land of the old colonialists. "We are a well-known family internationally. Various countries' ambassadors said, 'Well, why don't you come?' So we had a choice. But on the basis of language and the large size of the North American market, I preferred Canada. It was a nicer place to live than the United States."

When Ahmed was sketching these events for me, the government of Pakistan was, after years of military dictatorship, in civilian hands again—under Bhutto's daughter, Benazir. His still important family was on better terms with her than with her late father; and he was again daydreaming about bigger and better fertilizer plants. All that, of course, may change now that Benazir has been bounced from power. And even though Ahmed the engineer would dearly love to put his expertise back to work in his native land, he insists he's here to stay, no matter what happens there. He lives among the old Toronto money, and made sure his son and daughter went to the proper private schools (Upper Canada College and Bishop Strachan, respectively).

After a rocky start, he now presides over a handful of manufacturing companies that turn out textiles and chemicals. He's also "dabbled" in high-tech and has large land holdings. Like Chandaria, though, he doesn't regard real estate as the way serious people make their mark. "We have not done, and I do not see us doing, any property for the sake of property. We are productive-oriented," he says. "Because the family has been in textiles for such a long time, we felt that it was there that we should go in Canada." He twirls a pencil, pausing for dramatic effect. "We were wrong. We got into the wrong ends and we lost a lot of money. We got into weaving and the costs were too high. We also got into the fashion business and did not know much about it. But that's part of the learning curve, isn't it?"

The brothers ate their losses, dipped further into the security chest they'd brought with them and tried another tack. They're nothing if not pragmatic, the result of surviving under conditions far worse than any the family ever expects to face in Canada. "We've had some terrible times, but you're going to get terrible times in business anyway," Ali says, leaning back in his custom-made black leather chair.

Shifting gears to the lower end of the cloth business, they bought a family-owned company that had been operating since 1910, turning out material for industrial use as well as sturdy products like newspaper carrier bags. They then added a firm that literally makes rags. "It's in old clothing, so we're really in the schmata business," Ahmed says, a broad smile creasing his stern schoolmaster's features for the first time. He's fully aware that the rag trade has spawned more than one immigrant Jewish fortune in North America. And like many East Asians (and other outsiders like the Chinese) he sees lots of similarities between the two groups. (Navin Chandaria says rather proudly that his family and other Asians in his part of the world were known as the "Jews of Africa.")

Ahmed ventured into the world of weapons with the acquisition of a company that makes propellants for explosives. He's a big supplier to the U.S. military, as well as to the Canadian war machine. I ask if that's another reason he'd rather keep a low profile, but he just smiles again. "I visited the ARMX [military hardware] show in Ottawa. I went through the demonstrators, who called me a death merchant and all the rest of it." But a few peacefully chanting protestors weren't going to bother a man who's seen the havoc wreaked by serious mobs armed with more than slogans. Canadians, says Ahmed and other refugees, are among the most agreeable, patient people on earth, even on picket lines. ("You can do whatever you want to Canadians. If half of the things that happen here happened anywhere else in the world, they would be marching in the streets," says one Iranian.)

Ahmed's mood abruptly turns sombre, as if trying to keep pace with the rapidly fading daylight outside his window. He talks of the bitter quarrel that has driven apart his father and uncles back home, another good reason to stay here. And he observes sourly that the parent usually gets the credit for creating and building the dynasty, while the next generation supposedly sits around figuring out ways to spend the money. "Hopefully, I will establish something bigger than this," he says, gesturing in a sweeping motion around his factory. There's a clear note of 'I'll show the old man and maybe the uncles too' in his tone. "Being in a different country, it's my business."

In his desire to leave behind a much grander legacy than one of cloth and chemicals, he's looking to diversify, the way his father did. "Possibly, we will go into packaging or financial services. That's the sort of achievement that you can say: 'I have done this on my own.' As you grow your manufacturing base, those things [financial services, merchant banking] have to come."

But what of his own children, now at university? Will they have the same drive to continue what he's building here? Or will they become the flaunt-it-while-we've-got-it generation Ahmed's seen in other families? "I hope my children and grandchildren will not reach that point," he shrugs. "Beyond my grandchildren, I don't know and I don't care."

The government that had so frightened the Ahmeds into seeking sanctuary here in 1974 gave Narin Khan rare hope that his country might finally pull itself out of its vicious cycle of poverty and despair. When it was swept away by the new regime, he too hopped aboard the refugee airlift to these shores. The reason was simple: Khan knew the hard-line generals wouldn't be particularly sympathetic to a student activist—and a Maoist, no less—who was far more interested in bringing down the clubby elite of Ahmed and his ilk than in joining it.

He seems an unlikely radical, this heavy-set, reserved man in a conservative blue suit, white shirt and plain tie, as he sits in a familiar restaurant near his former residence in Old Montreal, trying a *pêche mousseux* to be sociable. He holds up the glass of sparkling wine and peach juice like a worried scientist about to test an unknown formula. Next time, he'll probably stick to his dry white wine.

Khan would rather not dwell on the awkward past. He wants to talk about the starry future, about the telecommunications empire he's setting out to build here, about his plans and dreams and hopes in his adopted homeland. And from the look of utterly confident determination in the dark eyes flashing from under those thick brows, it wouldn't be wise to bet against his achieving them. Not when he's got so much to prove to other Canadians—and to himself.

Narin grew up comfortably in a well-to-do Karachi household, but dreamed as a youth of joining in a great revolution, destroying feudalism, bringing literacy to the illiterate, turning Pakistan's largest city into a great modern metropolis that would have urban planners throughout the world gaping in admiration.

By 1974, in the final months of the ill-fated Ali Bhutto regime, he was an architecture student in his early twenties, busily researching how to build better housing for the poorest of Pakistan's poor. He was also a committed activist, a dangerous pursuit at a time when a tough army general named Zia al Haq was bulldozing his way to power. The police started interrogating and arresting Narin's more political friends. They were able to pass on one message to the young idealist that would irrevocably change his life: "Get out of the country. Finish school and make money to send back to our families."

He intended to do just that, arriving in Montreal with twenty-one dollars in his pocket and a total inability to speak French—which, he swiftly surmised, would rule out any attempt to study there. Making his mark in this vibrant, European-flavoured city that so attracted him would become yet another obsession.

Moving on to the University of Waterloo, Khan worked his way through school by washing floors and doing a stint as a hotel doorman. Life in a southern Ontario town was a far cry from the happy times he'd known growing up in the midst of a large family. "I was lonely. There was no one to help me. I never could like that place. I would go into a bar alone, sit alone, knowing everyone was looking at me, wondering about me, treating me as though I didn't belong."

With impeccably bad timing, he came out of school at the height of the worst economic conditions since the Great Depression, knowing he had to find work fast. That, after all, was his assignment in the first place. But what few jobs could be had seemed reserved for "real Canadians." Khan, dejected, fearing failure, slumped in the school cafeteria, wondering what to do next, how to face his friends back home.

"I heard two guys, white Canadians, talking at a table nearby. One was saying, 'If Pakistanis can get a job in Saudi Arabia, we can.' " He still smiles at the memory. There was a place he might be wanted after all.

The Saudis were an architect's dream, erecting whole cities out of the sand. Best of all, a close friend was already working there. When Khan finally raised the cash to join him, he found his classmates had been right. The two Pakistanis, starting on a frayed shoestring, were soon operating the second-largest architectural firm in the country. "I was making thousands of dollars a month, with all living expenses paid."

But five years and 250 buildings later (and with Saudis holding 51 percent of the company by law), Khan felt he'd gone as far as he could. Somewhere along the way, in the desert kingdom where enormous oil wealth had lured some of capitalism's ugliest practitioners from the far corners of the globe, the idealist gave way to the hard-nosed businessman. He sputters when he tries to explain the transformation: "I was very disappointed when I left Pakistan. I couldn't do anything for my people. I think I decided that at least I could do something for myself."

An older brother, Abdul, who'd studied electronics, was working in Guelph, Ontario, and the two went into business providing some of the new technology for telephone links in Saudi Arabia. The business flourished until oil prices plummeted. Canada again beckoned, and by the end of 1983, Khan had set up Khantel Distribution, a telecommunications equipment wholesaler, in Mississauga, Ontario. But, still smarting from his school memories, he never could warm to frigid southern Ontario, especially Toronto, a city the architect genuinely dislikes.

By 1985, he was back in Montreal, settling into a two-storey apartment in the old city and slowly adding manufacturing (cabling systems, modems) in nearby Lachine to his distribution business, now left in the hands of a younger brother in Toronto.

Then, in 1988, at the age of forty, he did something he hadn't thought of before. He got married, in the most traditional way imaginable, without ever having laid eyes on his bride—a doctor ten years younger than him but from the same privileged background. The wedding, which took place in Pakistan, was arranged by his parents. "I went straight from the airport [in Karachi] to the marriage hall. And I met her there," Khan says earnestly.

Although fully aware of how strange it must seem that a one-time reformer desperate to break the old feudal bonds would take the most feudal of paths to a family life, he's resolutely unapologetic. The untutored Western reporter will simply have to accept that tradition exerts a strong hold, perhaps even more so on those who rail against it most, who find themselves drifting in the New World without the comforting anchor it provides. His bride didn't join him in Montreal until early 1990, two years after the ceremony, when the standard lengthy immigration process was completed.

His friends in Karachi have long since been forgiven their youthful exuberance and taken up their rightful places in the club. Khan, who doesn't enjoy his visits home, has no desire ever to join them. "The problem is that I'm an idealistic person. And nothing has changed in Pakistan. It is still so backward. I'm a stranger in my own country. When I was young all my projects were politically oriented. I wanted universal education—there are twenty million kids not going to school there. As far as I'm concerned they can never be a dynamic society."

So the middle-aged dreamer concentrates all of his boundless energy on building his company up from its current level of $7-million in annual sales. He's opened an office in Vancouver and is planning a move into Texas, in a joint venture to produce a modular cabling system that makes it easier and cheaper to hook up computer terminals. It could catapult him into the lucrative billion-dollar European market.

And although his French hasn't improved much, Montreal will remain home. "I feel that Montreal belongs to me. It's on a human scale. People are warm here, and in Ontario I never had that kind of feeling."

His voice still carries the residue of pain from his time as a struggling student, a pain he desperately wants other Canadians to understand. He speaks with resigned weariness, but also a clear note of defiance. "I was well-educated when I came here, and you forced me to do the mopping," he says. "I did all the work you wouldn't do, and then no one would give me a real job." His is the plaintive voice of a refugee who didn't arrive here with millions, but has ended up with them, not because of any help he got from us but because he'd come through a crucible most of us can scarcely imagine.

An Iranian multimillionaire does his best to explain it. Tracing a straight line on a piece of paper with his gold Dunhill pen, he says, "Your life in Canada is like this." Then, scribbling up and down in a reasonable facsimile of a politician's lie detector test: "Our life is like this. It gives you special experience when you don't know what is going to happen to your life tomorrow."

CHAPTER 9

The Inheritors

JONATHAN WAITED UNTIL the housekeeper was asleep. Even with his parents far away in Hong Kong, it was impossible to sneak off at any other time; not while the loyal family retainer had her hawk-like gaze on him. She'd just stand there, short, chubby arms folded across her chest, a sentinel guarding her teenage charge from the dangers of the scary new world outside.

But once the early-to-bed gatekeeper was asleep, he could slip out the back door to explore this oddly quiet place where his rich parents had parked him and his sisters a few years earlier without so much as asking them first. If they had to move—as his father had insisted they did—why not Taipei, where some cousins lived? Or San Francisco? He liked that city. Why not London, where Mom went shopping? No one ever explained.

Jonathan (his identity and a few details of his life have been disguised, so his parents won't find out what he was up to, and because his anonymity was the only way to get friends, teachers and family advisers to talk freely about him and his lifestyle) had been like a tropical fish out of water his first couple of years in Canada. Shy and

awkward, his English too poor and manner too lacka-
daisical to get him into the private schools his father
coveted, he kept mostly to himself, watching cartoons
on TV, sleeping much of his free time away or thinking
up ways to avoid all but the ridiculously easy math homework handed out by his public school teachers.

He seemed a perfect match for the stereotypical teen
profiled by some of the people who make house calls on
the new money. "They all have this languid air. It's usual,
not just with these Hong Kong kids but anybody, when
they never have to work. You're lucky if they have enough
energy to answer the door," says an air-conditioning technician who spends much of his working life in the vast
basements of the super-rich (and sometimes upstairs too,
"just for the hell of it. I like to see how they live. I tell
them I have to check something. They don't know what
I'm doing anyway").

Jonathan's tutor won't listen to such nonsense. Maybe
some kids are like that, but not her favourite student. His
lassitude, she insists, had more to do with him having
been wrenched from the world he'd always known and
plunged into this strange, cold sea, where all his father's
millions weren't going to make it any easier for him to
learn to swim.

Whenever his parents weren't around, which was most
of the time, he'd try every trick in the textbook to avoid
the water. But ever patient, on call at crazy hours (mid-
night queries about the mysteries of the English language
were routine), his faithful coach refused to let him retire
to his isolated little island. She was constantly cajoling,
scolding, pushing, comforting, guiding him through the
educational maze that's intimidating enough for adults
who can handle the language, let alone kids who can't,
and standing in for his parents at meetings with teachers
and administrators from hell.

Gradually, inevitably, he emerged from his protective
shell, gaining confidence, even a touch of cockiness, as
he began finding his bearings. It wasn't long before he
was his old pranksterish self, plotting ways to outwit his

strict father—who never seemed to leave their enormous home or his lounging pyjamas when he was visiting, doing all of his business by phone or fax (unlike his mother, a retailer's dream who thought nothing of carting home a $7,000 mirror or a $10,000 pair of earrings from her daily shopping excursions).

And once his parents were safely back in the Orient, Jonathan could sneak past the snoozing watchdog's guardpost for an illicit night of unchaperoned frivolity. Climbing into a friend's car or the used American luxury number left for his use, he could almost taste the heady freedom in the night air of his adopted home. He wasted no time in letting down his short hair, rushing off to the nearest luxury hotel for wanton evenings of coffee and pastries, almost always paying with quarters.

Cakes? Quarters? Well, what else can you do when you've got this sweet tooth for Western goodies you can't find in your own fridge? The coins were his only source of mad money. While still in his teens, Jonathan was left in charge of collecting the rents on the family's local properties—as part of his careful grooming for a future as an international tycoon, and no doubt because his father would just as soon have avoided outsiders when it came to his very private business (he kept a set of books in the bedroom). Jonathan had to account for every nickel; but his father didn't think of the quarters in the washers and dryers of his apartment buildings, providing his enterprising son with all the laundering money he could stuff into his bulging pockets. "That's how he paid for everything," a former cakemate laughs, "no matter how much it cost."

The school chum recalls some of their adventures together with an equal mixture of awe and amusement. "One day he called me to go to a stockholders' meeting. It was some huge company, and he wanted me to vote his sister's proxies. We were eighteen years old and we only wanted to go for the free food. There's always a good lunch at those things. I thought the proxy was for, like, $1,000. But then I looked at it. His sister had $300,000 worth of shares in her name, and he had double that.

So there we were, two kids and we were controlling $1-million worth of proxies. I couldn't believe it. My knees were shaking. To him, it was the most normal thing in the world. It was just a playful investment that they got for a birthday present or something."

Later, when Jonathan had completed his business degree at a Canadian university and become a young globe-trotting deal-maker under his father's firm hand, he was describing to his friend a celebrated house he'd acquired in California. "I asked him how much he paid, and he said, 'Oh, $3-million US or so.' I said, 'What? $3-million?' He thought I meant that wasn't very much money. He almost apologized. He was assuring me that the house wasn't meant to be lived in full-time, that he had this great flat in Hong Kong. [He said] the real estate agent was going on and on about the estate's illustrious history. And he finally said, 'I'm not interested in any of that. I just need a place to live.' "

The size of the fortunes behind the kids like Jonathan is indeed knee-buckling. Some of the richest offspring in the world have been adding Canadian ties to their chic monochromatic outfits (black Claude Montana preferred). And it's these kids, far more than their conservative parents, who will ultimately determine what direction, if any, their families and their money will be taking in this country.

Jonathan is typical of the many flown over by nervous families seeking the safety and comfort of a Canadian identity. For all their millions, his parents continue to cloak themselves in ill-fitting refugee garb. They remain cut off from their roots, steeped in the bitter memories of their flight, more than four decades earlier, from the murderous excesses of war and revolution in their broken piece of China. They are determined to keep the children—and hard-won material success—away from their recurring nightmare that it's all about to fall on their heads again when the boys from Beijing march into the British colony in 1997.

Fear of the Red Menace lurks in the luggage of every rich Hong Kong immigrant, but that doesn't explain why the first-class compartments of jets bound for Canada are being booked up by, among others, the kids of the Japanese construction magnate; the Pakistani shipbuilder; the Korean politician; the Malaysian hotelier; the German retailer.

Some are playing designated roles in scripts carefully crafted by regionally powerful families who are spreading their wings globally like any multinational corporation, establishing beachheads in previously uncharted territory. Others are merely looking to put as much distance as possible between themselves and the stifling hothouses in which they've grown up. Many are out to accomplish both at the same time.

One way or another, the family remains the driving force behind most such moves, according to an Asian banker. "There is a powerful linkage. A few years ago, people were more passive. They would just put money here and then go back. Now we see more of them establishing their children here. They are educated abroad, and then—we're not talking about teenagers, but children in their twenties and thirties—they are running the family businesses at this end."

That's certainly why German businessman and equestrian Timur Leckebusch has been here full-time since 1986, running the Canadian arm of his family's $100-million construction business, Normbau 2000. His father, Hermann, had been looking to expand outside Europe for some years, turning thumbs down on the States before finally settling on, and in, Canada.

"He asked us children if we could live here, and we were all pretty excited about the idea. So he said, 'Okay, let's start a business,' " Timur says in his million-dollar penthouse in midtown Toronto, which is filled with furniture and music that are much more Old World than New.

His father opened the Canadian operation in Brampton, Ontario, in 1983, but Timur wasn't quite ready to take over; he was still attending the University of Munich and competing in equestrian events. (He's a member of the horsey set here too, but doesn't have as much time as he once did. He keeps only five horses, compared with a string of about twenty-five in Germany.) By 1986, the tall, slim, broad-shouldered twenty-five-year-old was in command here.

"When I deal with people in Canada, I say the same things as I would say to clients in Europe. But in Europe, they would probably ask me if I should go back to my father and ask him if I'm really allowed to deal on these matters," he says just before taking a call from his father in Germany. They're in almost daily contact, and the elder Leckebusch makes five or six trips here each year. "People in Europe wouldn't believe that a young guy would have the authority to run a business. You have to be older before they'll really accept and recognize you. Canada is a fantastic place for young and aggressive business people."

Others with even more dollar power are on a similar tack. Many of their kids, waiting to take their rightful places among the world's billionaires, are busy acclimatizing themselves to North American ways and expanding family networks, all in preparation for a world different from the one their parents have so effectively dominated.

"The old generation made their mark. They started up the foundations," says a confidant of some of the wealthier families from the Far East. "Now suddenly you're talking to an MBA from [the University of] Western Ontario, a Cambridge lawyer, a U of T accountant, a Stanford engineer. This generation will have a different, more global focus. Who is doing this and that in Canada? It's the sons [and sometimes the daughters] who are expanding the horizons."

Beverage baron David Ho fits the family pattern to a tee on his University Golf Club course in Vancouver.

"I will say honestly that the reason [for immigrating] was not because of 1997," says the engaging, fairly high-profile thirty-eight-year-old chairman of both the golf club and Gray Beverage Company, a major West Coast bottler and distributor of such household names as

Pepsi, Seven-Up, Orange Crush, Dr. Pepper, Schweppes and Perrier, which he picked up in 1989 for a figure in excess of $100-million.

Ho, who was schooled in Virginia, made three visits with wife Rita before deciding that British Columbia was the right place to settle down. Rita obviously influenced the decision; she'd lived in Canada for six years before returning to Hong Kong after her graduation from the University of Toronto.

"The reason for me leaving Hong Kong [in 1984] is quite simple; mainly for the children. There's lots of places that I can go. We have investments down in the States [where his brother and sister have lived for more than a decade] and other places. There's a lot of business opportunities everywhere, but you put the whole thing together and you decide which is the best place you want to be," Ho explains in his modern, white office at the golf course. Two sets of new-looking clubs huddle in a corner behind a large, black-leather-topped desk outfitted with enough phone lines to qualify him for his own area code. The golfing gear doesn't look as though it gets outdoors much. "I never have time [to golf], but one of these days I hope to learn,"* Ho cheerfully admits, lighting up another in a long chain of cigarettes. It would be a real act of defiance if this affable, hale-looking entrepreneur weren't puffing away; his grandfather and father built their considerable fortune on tobacco, first in Shanghai and then Hong Kong, where they'd fled in 1949. They manufacture such popular cigarette brands as Good Companion and, under licence, Marlboro and Rothmans.

Ho doubts either his father or grandfather will hit the

---

* This makes Ho unusual among wealthy Asians. The golf-mad Japanese have been buying Canadian courses because it's usually cheaper to fly over here to play than to try to take a golfing vacation at home. A group of Taiwanese families sought to acquire their own course near Toronto, so they could play every day without worrying about tee-off times. The $14-million cash deal apparently fell through when it turned out there weren't enough lots available for each family to build a house right on the property.

trail again, even after the British flag comes down. "The lifestyle is different for them. They are very happy there. It suits them." It also probably hasn't escaped their notice that there's nothing like a little high anxiety to sell a few extra cartons of cigarettes. But no matter what happens, the children will all be safely out of harm's way, busily broadening the family's operations beyond a relatively narrow product and geographic focus.

Not all sons or daughters are so eager to advance their families' interests. Some are only too happy to escape the fearsomely long reach of their autocratic parents, which sometimes extends from beyond the grave. All have plenty to prove on their own, as eager as any black sheep of an old English fortune in bygone days to carve their name and reputation out of the Canadian Shield.

"That's one of the reasons why I'm here and not there," agrees the son of a rich Hong Kong-based investor. He's lived in Canada since he was brought over as a fifteen-year-old by his parents in 1967, when the first wave of wealthy kids were moved out in the aftermath of the bloody riots that shook the colony to its bank vaults during the Cultural Revolution. "There will always be people like you who sort of look at me and say, 'Well, it's not his money. It's his father's.' You should know that there are sons of wealthy fathers who are doing serious things in Canada."

The Canadian member of an even wealthier Hong Kong clan offers another reason for being here instead of there. "Being Christian, I find sometimes I'm not competitive enough to do business in Hong Kong," he says in an unusually frank moment. "I cannot do the things that the other guys are doing, because I have ethical problems."

So has Canada gained one rich immigrant seeking not only a quieter path but a straighter one? "I shouldn't comment on that. In general, I feel that if you have a very high standard of ethics, you will be handicapped in some places. Period. The rules they play by are quite different. My father is comfortable with that. His standards are slightly different from mine. I keep telling my former partners and employees, 'You don't know how lucky you are that you're dealing with me.' " He lets out a sudden, unexpected cackle, a large smile creasing his round features.

"It so happens that with my lifestyle, Canada suits me better. I like the seasons. I don't mind the cold. I play winter sports. My family is very comfortable here. Life is too short."

He hurriedly follows his paean to the good life with a description of how hard he works. "I pride myself on being an entrepreneur. I forget how many jobs I've created in my lifetime, something like 3,000. And everything's from scratch. I built it from the ground up."

In contrast, a few spoiled heirs are far too busy spending the family money to worry about creating or expanding anything. Like the young Chinese show-off who can be seen tearing around Toronto in his Ferrari Testarossa ($300,000), flashing his careless affluence at every opportunity.

"He makes money in spite of himself," sniffs another rich man's son. A traditionalist, he has little use for the expensive toys of the young and the restless, whose conspicuous consumption gladdens the hearts of local merchants, but makes Canadians think they've been acquiring an entire generation of undisciplined millionaire bums. "These devices are symbols for status-seekers," the buttoned-down émigré pooh-poohs. The truly wealthy older generation wouldn't touch such things: "Only pimps, undesirable characters, brokers of stock, real estate, movie stars and contractors."

There's no need to ask what he would say about the attractive teenager from his old stomping grounds who desperately wanted a Porsche for her sixteenth birthday, no doubt to help her make the tough transition to a chauffeur-less life in Canada. Her parents declined, on the perfectly reasonable grounds that she didn't have her driver's licence yet. She glumly settled for a full-length mink coat; but not for long. She had her Porsche before reaching seventeen.

Far more ostentatious than his conservative father could ever imagine being, Jonathan adores his luxury baubles as much as the next have-it-all; but he's no Ferrari jockey out to turn family gold into pyrite in three generations. A fiercely loyal only son, imbued with the proper respect for heritage and the family's approximately $200-million (a trifling amount barely worth mentioning in Hong Kong dispatches), he has no intention of frittering away what his grandfather begat. "Business and the famiy interest quickly became very important to him," a university classmate remembers. Presumably, he started handing in the quarters and cancelled the *Playboy* magazine subscription that he'd had mailed to a friend's house so his father wouldn't find out (not because the content might have offended, but because he would have had to explain how he got the money for such an extravagance).

"They appreciate the value of money very early," says a banker who knows many of the adult children of the wealthy from Asia and Europe. "In some families, they have succeeded one generation after the other, but others have not because of reasons of upbringing. Not necessarily because of education—they all went to the same best schools. But their learning experience was a different one."

Listen to the banker's description of how a typically old-world billionaire kept the kids in line. "He would not allow his children to drive a brand new car. He would hold them on a very tight allowance. He told me, 'They have to learn from an early age how to appreciate money and how difficult it is to make money.' " The stern parent could double for Jonathan's father, except that he's the somewhat richer Li Ka-shing, mightiest of the empire-builders to ship his children to a Canadian port.

"He could have given his sons $100-million each and said, 'Well, enjoy your life.' But [he] won't do that; and you have to understand why," the banker says. "Because they are family enterprises, it is very important that their children succeed in business and take over from them. They want them to learn the hard way too, so they will have some of the tough experiences that their fathers went through. They don't want the family business to pass into the hands of other people, and they don't want it to fail either."

Li Ka-shing's sons, Victor and Richard, both in their twenties, have both taken Canadian citizenship although they spend the bulk of their time outside the country.

The family had a long discussion about which country the boys should immigrate to, the Hong Kong money king told *Globe and Mail* reporter Jacquie McNish in one of the few full-length interviews he's granted a Western journalist in recent years. Knowing Li's autocratic reputation, the discussion may have been somewhat one-way. Li hints as much when he says, "They agreed with me that they wanted to become Canadian citizens and they really want to develop their future in Canada. . . . I always remind them that they should be first-class citizens and I strongly believe they will be."

The decision to come to Canada was really an easy one to make, Richard Li tells me. "The family has holdings in the U.S., Australia, Europe—everywhere but Africa. We could live anywhere. Why not Argentina?" He swiftly answers his own question, observing that most countries just can't guarantee that the family and its investments will stay safe and sound. "There are not too many choices. North America, mainly. And that leaves Canada and the U.S. Canada seems to be bigger than any other part [of the Li foreign holdings], which has a lot to do with the direction of the family. It's a modern country with a proper British law foundation to protect property ownership. Canada is going to be my home and my brother's home."

This will happen, he insists, regardless of what the future holds for Hong Kong after 1997, when, incidentally, Li Ka-shing will be sixty-nine and retired ("I don't want to work until 1997. I started to work too early"). Quite apart from his father's continuing optimism about the colony's future (what else can he be if not publicly confident, especially with billions of dollars at stake and everybody else in the place following his lead?), he believes that Hong Kong's future after 1997 "would not affect us in a positive way or in a negative way. We ourselves are Canadian citizens and will remain here."

The United States, where the family's been boosting its investments lately after recovering from a disastrous run-in with Texas property in the late seventies, doesn't seem to appeal as a permanent future headquarters.* And Victor Li told a Canadian magazine writer that the family had yanked most of its money out of Australia, where foreign real estate purchases haven't been viewed with the same equanimity as they are here, and where more than one Oriental immigrant has felt less than welcome. "If I cannot live there, my money cannot live there either," Victor said matter-of-factly.

As befits someone whose father's status in Hong Kong, a place that worships money, property and street smarts, is close to god-like, Victor has the highest profile by far of any of the offspring of the colony's new money in Canada—whether he likes it or not.

He must wish sometimes that he could trade places with Walter Kwok, a son of another mighty colonial magnate, Kwok Tak-seng, who can slip in and out of North America without so much as a ripple; or Henry Cheng, who manages to stay out of the spotlight even when he's engineering huge deals like the takeover of the Ramada hotel chain; or Kin Yeung, a son of the late property, jewelry and commodities tycoon Yeung Chi-won. Or perhaps Peter Lee, one of billionaire Lee Shau-kee's five children, who occasionally spends time in a borrowed office in Toronto. This deal-making bunch of heirs would sooner sell property at a loss than consort with time-

---

* "If Li wants a hedge to Hong Kong, he has little option but to develop his Canadian interests," a veteran correspondent once observed in the *Far Eastern Economic Review.* "Li should also find Canada a more congenial environment than the tempestuous U.S. market. Disclosure laws are more lax and business is more closely ingrained with politics, relationships at which Li excels."

and money-wasting Western journalists or the rest of the hoi polloi.

Victor can't even enjoy an afternoon on the slippery slopes without being recognized. "At Whistler, I'd be in heavy ski gear with only my nose exposed, but someone from business would yell my name from another chairlift," he told the *Vancouver Sun* in 1989. "People are beginning to notice me."

The reason may have something to do with a lot of publicity that saw his lean, ascetic-looking features plastered all over a parade of periodicals, accompanied by suitably thoughtful quotes.

Victor Li, who handles many of his father's North American interests, was caught in the middle of a public outcry over the questionable way in which the B.C. government had handled the sale of the huge Expo lands (covering what amounts to about one-sixth of downtown Vancouver) in the spring of 1988. Critics have called it practically a giveaway to his father and the other investors in the deal, including the Cheng and Lee families.

Victor, who says he has a sentimental attachment to this, his first major Canadian project, told the *Globe and Mail* his family could have handled the entire project itself. "No problem from a money standpoint, but if you got a successful project and if you want a celebration party, you better bring in enough shareholders to have a party. It's no fun celebrating by yourself."

That's not unique to Hong Kong, nor is flipping property for a quick, juicy profit, which is exactly what Li, Jr. did with Vancouver condos in late 1988, shortly after purchasing them with a partner. Eager Hong Kong speculators snapped up the 216 units in three hours, on the strength of the Li name and a full-page colour ad in the *South China Morning Post*. Unfortunately, Victor hadn't bothered offering any of them to the locals first; a strict taboo in a community already sensitive about the size and scope of the Asian investments in its midst.

"If I came into a new country with that kind of money, power and expertise and such a major undertaking to change, really, the skyline of Vancouver, I would pay special attention to my public relations," huffed a prominent Hong Kong immigrant. "I would say, 'We're so thankful to be given this opportunity. We want to show that we are good corporate citizens. We're not just coming in here to make a few dollars.' "

The same man rhymed off examples of some Japanese companies, like Toyota, which carefully cultivated the locals when setting up shop in North America. The Li family, on the other hand, preferred to play it low-key. "When people asked them questions, they didn't answer. They said, 'Talk to my PR man. We haven't made any money here yet.'

"When people don't know, they ask, 'What are you trying to hide from us?' The rumour mill will start saying those guys are coming in to take us to the cleaners. . . . They have no time for anything but the project. Then they look around and wonder, 'What goes on? Why am I painted black?' "

Victor made amends for his actions in the condo deal as soon as he realized how damaging the fallout was going to be. He assured one and all that he'd made his biggest investment when he became a Canadian and a British Columbian. "It is always our intention to be a good, blue-chip Canadian corporate citizen." *

Admirers wrote the whole thing off to a lack of experience, and Victor's father subsequently told the *Globe* that residences on the Expo site would definitely be sold to local buyers before anyone in Hong Kong had even heard of them. "If the general public is happy, then I am happy," he intoned. "I always tell Victor it is very important that the society be number one."

---

* "My reputation," Victor's father has said on more than one occasion, "is my most important asset." The embodiment of free-wheeling capitalism Hong Kong-style advised the 1989 graduating class at the University of Calgary to work hard, learn patience and "always remember that your greatest asset is your reputation."

The Chinese-language press in Hong Kong reported virtually nothing about any of this, partly because bad news about the Li family is rarely reported unless it might affect the colony's well-being. But it was probably also because the local papers would have had a tough time explaining what could possibly be wrong with making a quick return on a land deal to people who've been known to sell, for $1,500 a crack, places in line for new residential developments.*

In his bid to alter perceptions that he was bringing that sort of free-wheeling style to Canada (some worried Chinese immigrants say it's too late, forgetting what short memories most people have), Victor began spilling his innermost thoughts, with considerable aplomb. "It's not nice being photographed and having exposure, but we're making an extra effort in Vancouver," he told the *Vancouver Sun* in the same interview that dealt with his unwanted celebrity status on the ski slopes. The paper presented the earnest, dark-suited, conservative, multibillionaire's kid as a laid-back Lotusland businessman who watched his pennies and rode around town in an old, brown Jeep Wagoneer. (In fact, he spends most of his time at family headquarters, which occupy the top three floors of his father's institutional-looking China Building, located right in the centre of the anything-but-relaxed financial district of Hong Kong.)

At twenty-four, Richard, two years younger than Victor, has escaped the public eye, but when given the chance he too comes across as a down-to-earth kind of guy whose greatest joy is a long, hard day at the office. "I live by myself downtown in a small condominium, 700 square feet or maybe less," he said in a rare interview during a two-and-a-half-year stint with Gordon Capital, a Toronto brokerage house with a penchant for absolute secrecy

---

* And the Hong Kong buyers of Victor Li's condos certainly weren't complaining. In early 1989, just a few months after their purchase, four units were put up for sale in the colony at twice the estimated original price of $170,000 each.

that would fill a Hong Kong tycoon's eyes with tears of joy. "The primary concern is that I can come to work very early."

He even took public transit to get there, just one of the regular Bay Street novices working his way up the ladder—except that he was starting on the top rung, with a name that could open just about any boardroom door in the world. He probably would have got the same red-carpet treatment even if Li, Sr. didn't have a small but important stake in Gordon's merchant banking arm and in the Canadian Imperial Bank of Commerce, another key Li ally in Canada, which is a 50 percent partner in the Gordon venture.

I first attempted to talk to Richard Li at one of those blowhard sessions about Hong Kong that have become *de rigueur* in the West since the first cry went up in the early eighties that the British were going; the kind of seminar where self-satisfied bankers, brokers and bureaucrats, whose jobs depend on keeping the money flowing, drone on about the marvels of doing business in the capitalist paradise on earth. But too many pinstriped schmoozers were ahead in the line. It would be weeks before I could track the precocious investment banker to his lair at Gordon, where he had been steered by his father and had acquired a partnership.

Not bad for a then twenty-two-year-old fresh out of Stanford University with a degree in electrical engineering. Brother Victor, with masters degrees in civil engineering and construction management, is also an alumnus of Stanford—a school carefully selected by a father who leaves nothing to whim or chance.

Li Ka-shing made the decision in his own inimitable fashion. He first toured several American schools, top-notch name brands like M.I.T. and Harvard, as well as Stanford—or at least their parking lots. "I looked at the cars the students were driving," he told an astounded business connection. "From an educational point of view, two or three of the universities were relatively the same.

But I chose the one that had more used cars and older cars than Porsches and Mercedes."

What could this billionaire learn in the parking lots of the higher institutions of American learning? "It indicated to me that these children were that much more interested in the education than in the prestige; and therefore they would try much harder and the competition would be that much harder."

While Victor bounces off the property development ropes, Richard has been soaking up the corporate finance side of things (and today helps manage the family's corporate billions out of the Li-controlled Hutchison Whampoa conglomerate in Hong Kong, which has global interests in property, telecommunications and retailing). This complementary allocation of tasks has worked well in other powerful families. Each member acquires expertise in a different aspect of the business, which is then combined under the baton of the no-nonsense parental orchestrator and conductor.*

Richard Li surprised me by picking up the phone himself in his Gordon office, and positively floored me by agreeing to a lengthy interview there and then. He spoke freely about some things, not at all about others. And he set certain conditions. There would be no face-to-face meeting and positively no questions about his work for Gordon.

Like his older brother, Richard comes across as pleasant, courteous, reflective, just another humble chip off the old block, the product of a careful upbringing. When

---

* The super-rich Kwok family of Hong Kong's Sun Hung Kai Properties is a typical example. Walter, who has a masters in science from London University, tends to handle the hotel side of things. Raymond, who attended Cambridge and has an MBA from Harvard, looks after the finances. And Thomas, armed with a masters from the London Business School, takes care of project management and construction. The trio comes together when it's time to talk corporate strategy.

the *Sun* asked Victor about life as a billionaire's kid, he replied, "I don't believe in fancy parties or surroundings. I believe in good friends, good company, good food and maybe good skiing. My living standard has not changed at all in any sense since I was born."

When shopping, "I still look to see whether something is $1.25 or $1.50." That shouldn't be surprising. The stories of money-conscious billionaires are legion: H. L. Hunt and his paper-bag lunches; J. Paul Getty and his pay phone booth at home; Ken Thomson, who is said to have once told a food purveyor that while the farm-made strawberry jam he sold was good, it was too darn expensive.

Richard didn't say if he squeezes his pennies, but the lifestyle he described wouldn't leave much time for spending. Work, work, work and maybe the occasional concert. His hobby? Business. Not a mention of some of the more interesting things I've heard about the youngest Li: that he's the fun-loving member of the family, with a taste for fast cars and racing (which he occasionally indulged near Toronto in the company of a diligent banker of similar interests) and night life. But maybe that was all in his youth. After all, he is hitting his mid-twenties.

At the time we spoke, Richard was shopping around for a nice merchant bank that would be his first major investment in Canada. It's important for Canadians to understand, he said, that such an investment would be made not by some powerful Hong Kong corporation but by a Canadian businessman. "We are no longer foreigners. We would like to become genuinely Canadian, to sink deep roots. The primary interest of Victor and me is any type of venture that is profitable and beneficial to society. I am open to all possibilities."

This is subject, as Richard freely admits, to his father's stamp of approval. A veteran banker puts it all into perspective: "If Li can make more money here than in Hong Kong, then his money will come here. It all depends on the brains of the second generation." Both sons will have to prove themselves on the field of battle.

"We have a good team of management," Li Ka-shing

told the *Globe.* "They [my sons] need to show me that they are better than other people. Right now I don't see that the both of them will run my Hong Kong business. . . . At this hour, I don't plan for them to take my position in the company in the future. Maybe one day when everything is right. It is not easy to let them have this house because we already have a good team."

The billionaire baron's son sifts through the photo album slowly, lost in thought about what never was but might have been. He stops at simple, long-ago snapshots of a boy and his elderly father. They've obviously been fishing, sharing a good time together. The shy, gangly youth, who looks no older than about twelve, is holding a fish that must be as big as him. He's smiling. The casually dressed adult sitting on the expensive cream-coloured sofa isn't.

Gerhard von Finck stares off into the middle distance of his memories before abruptly ending the photo session. "Would you like to see the race?" he asks suddenly, the dark clouds consigned to the attic for the time being. "I have a tape." He plunks in the video, clicks his remote, and transports himself instantly to a considerably more romantic location, the Hippodrome de la Côte d'Azure, a racetrack in southern France, a few furlongs from Nice.

As the deep tones of the French announcer envelope the large, airy living room of his luxury penthouse in midtown Toronto, von Finck's calm blue eyes light up. For the umpteenth time he's watching his prize filly cop first prize in the mile-and-a-quarter Prix Policeman, a big race for the vacationing French provincial horsey crowd; but he's as delighted as if the outcome's a complete surprise. The shadows vanish from his dark, coarsely handsome features anchored by a strong, square jaw. The child in the photos is suddenly back in the room.

Von Finck, understandably, would much rather be running colour videos of his life's highlights than dredging up black-and-white memories of his pain and insecurity. He carries a legendary name, belonging to one of the mighty business families of Europe, but unlike many rich kids here, he's not out to stretch its vast tentacles into Canada. If anything, he seems determined to avoid them.

Life isn't necessarily a crystal bowl of cherries for the rich kids of famous parents. Just ask any British royal, or their equivalent in places where money is king.

Pansy Ho, outspoken daughter of Macau gambling czar Stanley Ho, once accurately opined to an interviewer that the only reason she'd become a favourite target of the local paparazzi (which tracks her jet-setting social life with film stars and other entertainment types as if she were a Monegasque blue blood) "is because I am my father's daughter."

She went on to explain, after insisting at length (again correctly) that she'd done nothing on her own to merit such attention, that "any other twenty-seven-year-old girl can do certain things, and they won't be looked at twice because they are considered a normal, expected part of life. But I will not be pardoned. Even silly, trivial things like not wearing makeup. I hate having to wear cosmetics, but if I attend a big cocktail party and don't look 'made up' people will comment because they always expect me to look perfect."

She moved to Canada with her mother, Lucina, stayed long enough to pick up a Canadian passport and then headed back to Hong Kong. Like Victor and Richard Li, she describes herself as down-to-earth, but she can recall the days when she wasn't. "I went through that phase when I was in my college days. I thought I should be treated like an adult, but I acted more and more like a spoiled child. I guess I got greedy and behaved like a typical spoiled brat, wasting my money at posh restaurants and staying out all night. But it didn't last long. Soon I realized that I was fed up with the fast life."

Pansy, now twenty-nine, considered the most independent of Stanley Ho's eight children and often touted as the likely successor to her father, told the interviewer she still knows how "to appreciate a luxurious lifestyle, but it is not a lifestyle I would fight to maintain. I have to be prepared for the future and not to simply assume that I can always have anything I want."

The wine-loving, Montecristo-puffing von Finck knows how to enjoy the good life too. Besides the horse-racing at French resort tracks, there are the yearly sojourns at some of Europe's finest hotels (the Lido in Venice is a particular favourite for the lover of things Italian, especially the food and drink); a 750-acre horse-breeding farm in Virginia; the night life in the company of old friends in Munich. But it was at least partly to escape that sort of existence, to prove himself in a place far removed from the long shadow cast by his late father and older half-brothers, and far from the party brats of the old establishment in Europe, that he's opted to spend a good chunk of his time working quietly in Canada.

"He's better off here," one of his friends says. "The rich people in Munich, they don't do anything, just sit around and say, 'Should we go skiing? Let's go to St. Moritz.' Here at least he has to work. It's hard for someone from such a rich family."

By all accounts, including Gerhard's, his father was an unusual man. When Baron August von Finck died in April 1980 at the age of eighty-one, in his beloved country home outside Munich, he left behind one of the larger fortunes in Europe. Estimated at well in excess of $1-billion (US), it's impossible to pin down because so much of it consisted of enormous landholdings that are unlikely ever to be sold. The bare-bones obituaries carried over here tell us only that the baron was a banker who had big investments in insurance and beer, owned forests and estates around Munich and was a faithful patron of the arts.

They don't tell of a man who spent much of his life avoiding risks, concerned mainly, according to his son, with preserving the remarkable empire carved out of then backward Bavaria by his own father in the latter part of the last century and the early part of this one;

especially after watching part of it go up in flames with the German defeat in the Second World War. A tyrannical parent—Gerhard declines to go beyond calling him "a very, very stong personality"—he sought to run his children's lives as if they were growing up in the eighteenth instead of the twentieth century.

A genuine eccentric, in the habit of travelling in a chauffeured Volkswagen Beetle with the front passenger seat removed so he could stretch his legs, he refused to invest a dime in North America, even at the height of the sixties' Red Scare in Europe, because the Americans had jailed him briefly and seized his holdings after the war for suspected Nazi links. He got everything back when he was cleared six months later. "It's a very mixed-up family, even by European standards," understates a handler of European money.

The patriarch was fifty-four and long set in his old-fashioned ways by the time Gerhard was born in 1954, the first of two sons with wife number two. His younger brother Helmut, of whom he is obviously fond, had similar problems coping with an autocratic parent. For a while, he turned to Indian guru Bhagwan Shree Rajneesh, but now seems to be putting most of his energy into developing the top racing stable in Germany. The brothers are partners in a couple of horses.

The sons by the baron's first marriage, stern-looking Wilhelm, sixty-three, and August, sixty-two, aren't into horse-racing. They've been too busy running the vast family holdings they inherited, including such corporate monoliths as the Löwenbräu brewery, the private Merck Finck & Company bank (it was sold to Barclays Bank in September, 1990, partly because August's own children had no inclination to get into the banking business), and lucrative stakes in insurance companies, an electrical utility and thousands of acres of forest and farmland. *Forbes* ranks their known investment portfolio at more than $3-billion (US).

Their considerably younger half-brother is not exactly

a male Cinderella waiting to be liberated from a life of penury and drudgery. He manages to eke out a jetset existence on $20-million or so and various investments of his own, as well as through his work as a stockbroker.

The horse-race over, a favourite *vin rosé* almost finished, von Finck returns to his family ties. He skips quickly over his domineering father, and his powerful brothers—with whom he insists he's on friendly terms, though his expressive eyes hint otherwise (he sold his Löwenbräu shares after disagreeing with their decision to sell off the company's pubs and other real estate in exchange for more stock in the brewery). It's his brilliant grandfather he'd most like to talk about and the person he'd most like to emulate.

That would be quite an achievement. Grandfather Wilhelm von Finck started in Frankfurt as a bank clerk before moving to Munich, then an unimportant provincial backwater, in about 1870 to take another banking job. He eventually gained control of the bank, while launching one of the more remarkable industrial careers of the day. Among his numerous business ventures, he electrified Bavaria, after visiting Thomas Edison in his New Jersey lab to see how the newfangled invention worked. "Edison showed him how and he founded the first major utility in Germany," says his proud grandson, sipping more wine.

The taste for great wine may well have come down from his father, another oenophile. On the old man's seventieth birthday, Baron Rothschild sent along a case of Château Lafitte from 1898, the year of his birth. "Each of us had a glass, and we didn't like it. The mess that night! He was not pleased," he laughs. Gerhard himself has a cellar of 1,800 bottles back in Munich, but can't find anyone who will ship it to his Virginia farm. (The wine-hating province of Ontario was already out of the question because of the costs. Besides, there isn't enough room in the condo, where he's already got a selection that would put some good restaurants to shame.)

He doesn't mention his revered grandfather's taste in alcohol, but he did build a big brewing company by amalgamating, à la E. P. Taylor many decades later in Canada, three small breweries to form one Munich giant, Löwenbräu. The family still owns most of the stock, worth several hundred million dollars today. "He was a real founder," von Finck says between puffs of his ever-present cigar. "It's more my kind of thinking of my own life than continuing to preserve what has been done already. It's too boring. He did new things. I don't want to sit behind a desk and grow old. My father always said, 'I want to stay in the backyard. That's where I have my expertise. That's where I know what I'm doing.' He had sugar refineries in Yugoslavia before the war. He lost them all, and I think that was the reason for his attitude."

His father was also acting true to his arch-conservative nature, aware, like most wealthy survivors of his generation, how fragile the whole comfortable structure could be. It's easy to see why the expansive young son would clash again and again with the cautious, aging patriarch. "My father did not really approve of me coming to Canada, but I wanted to keep my independence," von Finck says, lighting another Monte Cristo. "I didn't want to sit in an office living off the family money."

Others in and around investment circles and the new money warn that young von Finck isn't exactly the best example of an immigrant success story. "Gerhard doesn't work too hard," one acquaintance says. "But I think there's a nice guy under all that. . . ."

Von Finck says he invests in ventures he finds interesting and, preferably, innovative—somebody's dream, even if it's not his own: a private radio station and car leasing company in Germany; a small Bay Street brokerage house, where he first took his business and now hangs his hat when he's in town; an upscale French restaurant in his Toronto neighbourhood; the large horse-breeding operation in Virginia; James Ting's attempt to build a Canadian-based international electronics and trading conglomerate (at one point, von Finck was the largest individual shareholder not connected to the company, with about 7 percent of Ting's International Semi-Tech Microelectronics); a gold-mining venture in Greenland; oil and gas in Utah, California, Colorado and Texas. "I like to help people fulfil their dreams," he says.

He even briefly held a chunk of Maple Leaf Gardens shares, until he realized other stock market players were busy betting that owner Harold Ballard would die any moment. "I don't like such things. It was a stock for ghouls, so I sold it. Of course, I made a profit." He smiles.

Apparently, that is not always the case. "Gerhard has an interesting investment style," says a business associate. "He buys high and sells low . . . usually on the same day. He gets nervous."

Von Finck grows animated talking of his business plans, of exciting ventures never attempted before, of perhaps sinking money into Eastern Europe—he's off to Prague to check out some property with a friend from Munich—and of his plans to leave the brokerage industry soon to try something new.

Eventually, though, he comes back to those old photos, to the obvious sore spots in his past that have so shaped the present. His father, Gerhard says calmly, didn't speak to him, except on formal occasions or on those fishing holidays, from about the time Gerhard was an impressionable boy of six until a reconciliation of sorts not long before the old baron died.

"He liked what I was doing here. [Had he lived] a month or two months more, things would have changed," he says. "When he saw I was doing all right, that I had a steady job and a degree and did my exams [to become a stockbroker], he approved of that, you know."

By then, von Finck was already living in Canada, where he'd moved in 1978 to work on Bay Street while studying business at night at York University. "I tried to see if there was a spot in the world where I could feel comfortable and live my life and try to accomplish something." He returned to Germany shortly after his father's death, but soon realized he was better off here.

"It was a time when I got no help from home. I didn't really know what to do. I was basically on my own. I never found what I would really like to do. On one side, there was pressure from everybody. On the other side, they never helped you. So I was stuck. I said, 'What the hell am I supposed to do?' So one day I decided: 'Enough!' and I ended up here."

He became a citizen in 1981. "I still remember it," he chuckles, his natural good humour briefly brushing aside the dark clouds. "There were sixty of us in a room, maybe forty-five Chinese, ten or so from India or a place like that, and five I guess you would call European. They played 'O Canada' in English and in French. In English, only the judge sang. In French, no one sang. They played a record, an old, scratched one."

Of his relationship with his father, von Finck says, "I had a lot of personal problems with him.* I don't know," he says, his voice dropping almost to a whisper. "He just decided I wasn't the perfect son that he wanted."

The baron, who kept up a punishing work schedule into his seventies, didn't want young Gerhard out playing with

---

* This is a common thread that runs through the yarns of more than one immigrant son. Carlos Ott, without doubt the best-known Uruguayan ever to settle in Canada, an architect vaulted to instant international fame and wealth after winning the competition to design the new opera house in Paris, left home to prove himself far from his father, Uruguay's richest and best-known architect.

"My father was very tough," says his son, who was born to privilege and comfort. "He was very good at everything. I started working for him and he had me sharpening pencils. I said, 'Screw you' and started working for his competitors." Ott, who ended up here on a coin toss, says, "I always had an inferiority complex. He was always ten times better and ten times faster."

other children—he still remembers having to climb out of windows and down rope ladders to visit friends, even as a teen—or attending a normal school. He insisted on bringing in private tutors, just as the great moneyed families had always done. His mother, who still lives in Munich, stood up to her husband then, insisting that their son lead a normal childhood. He went to a regular school in Munich, switching to a boarding school near St. Moritz when he was twelve.

"He was extremely strong, but he gave up and just let my mother do everything. Then when it didn't work out the way he wanted, she got the shit. My mother said no [to private teachers]. That's how he grew up at the beginning of the century in Bavaria. He just expected that the children would go exactly the same way he went."

Gerhard wasn't singled out for special treatment. His father, he says, was just as hard on his brothers. "What he couldn't understand was a son just taking off and wanting his own life. My father never had his own."

He remembers the photo album, now closed beside him. "The best time was when we were fishing. He was always okay there. That was a long time ago," he says wistfully. His mood grows sombre again, but not for long. "Shall we go to the restaurant?" he says, smiling. He wants to introduce his visitor to the new chef.

CONCLUSION

THE LANKY, LOW-KEY banker has been shepherding some of Asia's mighty fortunes here for years, and has watched European money even longer. The huge investment numbers hold no surprises for him. But when he gazes into the bottom of his china cup to divine the future, he grows visibly excited, almost breaking into a full smile. "The real action is yet to come," he exclaims, unable to mask the glee in his voice.

The Europeans are much more interested in their own lucrative backyards these days. Canadian political stability—our most valuable and underrated export—has significantly less appeal to people who no longer wake up in cold sweats wondering if Communist tanks are about to roll through the streets. The Hong Kong crowd certainly does worry about such things, but there's still plenty of time to make a killing or two in the high-stakes colonial casino and a good deal of the serious money that was heading here has already landed. So, what is it that gives the banker the look of a kid who's discovered where the cookie jar is hidden? It's the prospect of Mercedes full of fresh money coming in from Asia for years to come—

particularly from booming Taiwan. "The immigration and investment flows from Taiwan in the years ahead will truly overshadow Hong Kong. That's saying something. But I think the money's there. And the will to invest in North America is there."

Like many developing countries trying to hang on to the cash of their capitalists, Taiwan once had strict limits on how many dollars its citizens could take out of the country. Now a regional economic powerhouse with huge foreign exchange reserves (second only to Japan in the world), the country removed forty years of currency controls in 1987, allowing individuals to cart out as much as $5-million (US) annually; but they can only bring back $50,000 of it.

Taiwan wants the money out there doing something useful. "Those funds are not of great value unless you can deploy them around the world. And you want to make sure that your population is global in its capability," another banker says. "It really enables an enormous capital shift, because the typical Chinese family is quite large—eight, nine, ten in a family. Sixty million or seventy million dollars is not a problem for them."

Real estate professionals tell of cautious Taiwanese investments in Canadian stores, hotels, small office buildings, golf courses, plastics factories. Their preferred location still seems to be southern California, but they have also been making their presence felt in Toronto, where they have become major investors in and around the downtown Chinatown district. "Believe it or not, Taiwanese own almost 60 percent of the property from University Avenue to Spadina on Queen Street," says a lawyer who shows them the ropes here. "They are investors, not property speculators."

One middleman is helping a powerful family weigh more than $100-million worth of property deals in Toronto alone. "They are talking about big-scale stuff. The head of the family's in his seventies and wants to make his mark on the world stage before he steps down. Ten million dollars from Taiwanese people [the size of some of the largest personal investments so far] is absolutely nothing."

As if to prove the point, Taiwanese tycoon Tan Yu went public late last year with plans to pump $1-billion into property in Canada and California. His daughter, Emilia Roxas, handed over $14.5-million in September 1990 for the family's new Canadian headquarters, Fantasy Gardens in Richmond, British Columbia, owned by the province's Premier, William Vander Zalm. Just another day at the land office in the West Coast province.

Like Hong Kongers, but with somewhat less urgency, Taiwanese will be looking for their escape hatches—just in case. "People are saying, 'I want to get some of my funds out of Taiwan,' " the middleman says. " 'I am not prepared to take the risk. I want a second passport.' "

Korea, like Taiwan, under intense pressure from Washington to trim its huge trade and foreign exchange surplus, has also eased stringent rules on the export of private capital. As of January 1989, up to $2-million (US) per person could be shipped out each year. As a result, Canadian bankers may end up drooling no matter what happens in the new Europe or in Hong Kong after 1997. A lot will depend on how secure the new money feels here. If wealthy foreigners decide that tax or other disadvantages start to outweigh the country's attractions, if Canada looks as though it is about to become an economic or political basket-case—the Uruguay of North America, in the words of one émigré—and other areas show more promise, they will look elsewhere.

As Richard Li and others have noted, there aren't many safe places in the world for them to go, but international capital is nothing if not flexible and fluid. The flood of new money could slow suddenly. Instead of tens of billions that could breathe life into the domestic economy, we could be looking at smaller sums biding time in easily liquidated bonds or treasury bills, or jumping in and out of speculative ventures that offer little long-term benefit. If the currency crumbles, interest-rate spreads narrow or land prices collapse, even these would lose their appeal overnight. Some large investments are already on hold, awaiting better conditions.

Meanwhile, though, the capital that's already here will be weaving its way inevitably into the Canadian fabric, if not in this generation, then in the one to come.

Some of the children of the rich and foreign are edging into middle age, set in their ways, ill at ease outside their tight circle of family and business intimates, separated from the older Canadian establishment by large social and cultural gaps and unwilling—or unable—to use their millions as a bridge. As much outsiders here as any previous wave of poorer immigrants, it wouldn't occur to them to reach for a seat at the old guard's table.

A Hong Kong-born investor, from an industrial family worth several hundred million dollars, explains why he still keeps an incredibly low profile after nine years here. "I didn't go to UCC [Upper Canada College]. I don't have the school ties. I'm not one of the boys, so to speak. So it's an uphill battle."

But like most wealthy immigrants, he's made sure his own kids are wearing the right uniforms, as ready as money can make them to take their rightful places among the country's elite. It's these children who will decide just how much a part of the Canadian establishment they and their far-flung fortunes should become. They could stay in their own growing ethnic circles, networking among other rich arrivistes, just as their parents have usually done. But that would be as unthinkable for most of them as doing business solely within the confines of a country that is still only a small player on the international stage.

The new money is different from the fortunes that built or were built by this country—less conscious of national boundaries, more volatile. It glows with enthusiasm and vitality, unlike some of the passive remnants of the old money, who can only wave helplessly at the faster, smarter competition.

With plenty to prove to themselves and to us, the members of the hidden establishment may, in fact, be our last best hope of turning into an economic force for the next century, instead of the neglected backwater we seem doomed to become on our present course, a farm team for the major-league players elsewhere.

At the same time, even staunch supporters of the new money aren't convinced it will be enough to counter the utter dominance of Corporate America in our lives. As one astute observer notes, "A lot of people are guessing they [rich immigrants] will bring their aggressive qualities to Canada. The jury is still out. It depends on how they perceive their investments. Are they more of a safety valve or are they going to come here in earnest and actually create businesses which require risk capital? It's still hard to say."

It's certainly true that many newcomers are looking more to what's behind them than what's ahead; many still have more back home than here. But their children, often with their encouragement, are shedding the garb, the mannerisms, the language, even the religion and culture that have held them to another world. "We've got to face the fact that we're Canadian, we live in Canada, and we have to work for Canada, whatever that is," says a wealthy developer from the Middle East. "I sympathize with my original country, but I cheer for Canada more." Thus begins the steady process of assimilation and diffusion that has defined the immigrant experience here from the beginning, when the aboriginal people boldly crossed the land bridge from Asia into unknown country.

INDEX